THE ROUGH GUIDE TO

THE
DA VINCI
CODE

ODDEST MAN

AN UNAUTHORISED GUIDE
TO THE BOOK AND MOVIE

ODDEST HAND

ROUGH GUIDE CREDITS

Text Editor: Mark Ellingham
Design/layout: Dan May and Link Hall
Picture research: Suzanne Bosman
Cover design: Dan May
Production: Julia Bovis
Cartography: Miles Irving and Katie Lloyd-Jones

PUBLISHING INFORMATION

This revised edition published March 2006;
first edition published November 2004
by Rough Guides Ltd,
80 Strand, London WC2R 0RL

Distributed by the Penguin Group:
Penguin Books Ltd, 80 Strand, London WC2R 0RL.
Penguin Putnam, Inc. 375 Hudson Street, New York 10014, USA
Penguin Books Australia Ltd, 487 Maroondah Highway,
PO Box 257, Ringwood, Victoria 3134, Australia
Penguin Books Canada Ltd, 10 Alcorn Avenue,
Toronto, Ontario, Canada M4V 1E4
Penguin Books (NZ) Ltd,
182–190 Wairau Road, Auckland 10, New Zealand

Typeset in Optima, Metaplus and Garamond to an original design by Dan May.
Printed in Italy by Legoprint S.p.A.

ISBN 10: 1-84353-713-3

ISBN 13: 978-1-84353-713-7

THE ROUGH GUIDE TO

THE
DA VINCI
CODE

Written and researched by

Michael Haag and Veronica Haag

with

James McConnachie

Dedicated to

This Refined Menace

CONTENTS

Part I

THE DA VINCI CODE **Basics**

Part II

THE DA VINCI CODE **Context**

Part III

THE DA VINCI CODE **Book and Movie Locations**

Part IV

THE DA VINCI CODE **Author**

Part V

THE DA VINCI CODE **Movie**

Part VI

THE DA VINCI CODE **Glossary & Index**

'Everyone loves a conspiracy'

Dan Brown's novel *The Da Vinci Code* is a modern quest for the Holy Grail that in medieval legend was the chalice from which Jesus drank at the Last Supper. But in *The Da Vinci Code* the Holy Grail is not a physical object, rather it is a two-thousand-year-old secret that goes to the very heart of Christian belief. The novel argues that our modern understanding of history is based upon the deliberate suppression of an ancient truth – a truth that challenges the assumptions underlying Western civilisation.

The Da Vinci Code is a thriller – and a phenomenon with more than 50 million copies in print – and is written as a fictional entertainment. But Dan Brown asserts that it has a basis in fact, and the backdrop to his novel touches upon matters of serious debate among scholars at leading universities and in books issuing from the presses of Cambridge, Oxford, Yale, Harvard, Princeton and others. Indeed, his book returns us to matters that were the subject of impassioned controversy in early Christian times.

Now that *The Da Vinci Code* has been made into a film, many millions more people are being introduced to the controversies it has inspired. Both readers and cinema audiences alike want to know how much is fiction and how much is really true. They also want to know if the filmmakers have given in to complaints and pressure from such quarters as the Vatican, Opus Dei and Evangelicals who protest that *The Da Vinci Code* is offensive and even blasphemous. *The Rough Guide to The Da Vinci Code* examines Dan Brown's arguments and his sources, and provides the historical, cultural and religious background material to enable you to make up your mind, or take your own research further.

THE
DA VINCI
CODE
Basics

What THE DA VINCI CODE says

AND DOES IT CLAIM TO BE MORE THAN A NOVEL?

'The days of the goddess were over. The pendulum had swung. Mother Earth had become a man's world...'

THE DA VINCI CODE [CHAPTER 28]

D an Brown's *The Da Vinci Code* combines startling twists of plot with a menacing atmosphere of invisible intrigue, right from its opening scene where, late one night in Paris, Jacques Saunière, curator at the Louvre, is shot in the Grand Gallery of the museum by Silas, a crazed albino monk of Opus Dei. In his dying moments Saunière removes his clothes and arranges his naked body on the parquet floor, his arms and legs akimbo so that he looks like Leonardo da Vinci's famous drawing of the *Vitruvian Man* – in effect a five-pointed star, the ancient pentacle representing the sacred feminine.

This bizarre scene contains the first of numerous coded clues that transform a murder mystery into a quest for a modern-day version of the Holy Grail, a profound but long-suppressed truth that challenges the foundations of Western beliefs and culture. Brown's argument is that there was once a time when people worshipped Nature's divine order, which involved a balance between the male and the female spiritual principles. This brought about harmony and peace. But the Christian Church, by asserting the male principle and denying the female, has brought us two thousand years of chaos and violence. Furthermore, this was in contradiction of Jesus's real teachings and the role of Mary Magdalene in his life, matters that the Church took care to write out of the New Testament and the history books in order to justify its institutional power.

Dan Brown's plot

According to Dan Brown's novel, the truth about **Jesus and Mary Magdalene** was known to the brotherhood of the **Priory of Sion**, who through their offshoot the **Knights Templar** had obtained their evidence at the **Temple Mount** in Jerusalem, following the conquest of the city during the First Crusade (1099). The brotherhood has kept the secret, ready to reveal it at a propitious moment. But a secret figure known as **The Teacher**, apparently working through the conservative Catholic organisation **Opus Dei**, whose cult of asceticism and self-mortification represents the worst aspects of Christian imbalance, is determined to seize the evidence and destroy it.

Four figures in the brotherhood of the Priory of Sion are the sole keepers of the secret, but as the novel opens we learn that they have just been murdered by **Silas**, a crazed albino numerary of Opus Dei; and the secret, it would seem, has died with them. Except that one of the brotherhood, the **Grand Master Jacques Saunière**, who is also curator at the **Louvre museum**, spent his dying moments leaving clues for his cryptologist granddaughter **Sophie Neveu** and for **Robert Langdon**, a Harvard symbologist.

In what amounts to a thriller on a cosmic scale, it is desperately important that Sophie and Langdon decode the clues (which are largely contained in works by **Leonardo da Vinci**, himself a supposed past Grand Master of the Priory of Sion) in order to preserve one of the greatest and most important truths in history. But Langdon, who is suspected of Saunière's murder, is on the run from the French police, abetted by Sophie, who is convinced of his innocence. The detecting duo seek refuge with **Sir Leigh Teabing**, an expatriate Englishman who inhabits the grand **Château Villette**, outside Paris, and is a leading expert on the Holy Grail, only to discover that they are also being pursued by Silas – under the control of the Teacher, who seems to possess the uncanny ability to anticipate their moves.

It is while Langdon and Sophie are at Teabing's château that Dan Brown reveals his controversial big idea. **The Holy Grail** is not literally the chalice used by Jesus at the Last Supper; rather it is a coded reference for a secret collection of documents which prove that **Mary Magdalene** was married to Jesus and gave birth to his daughter, called **Sarah**, whose descendants are alive today. Mary Magdalene, and not Peter, was the rock on whom Jesus had intended to build his Church, its purpose not to promote his own worship, for he made no claim to divinity, but to foster the worship of the sacred feminine.

The tension of the plot drives the reader forwards through a succession of **riddles**, **codes**, **anagrams** and interlinking associations of all kinds in an effort to decode the clues to the **sacred feminine** and its suppression by the Church. But this mix of thriller, history and theology understandably leaves many readers wondering where to draw the line between fiction and reality and how far to trust in the truth of Dan Brown's claims.

The Louvre's glass Pyramid, a synergy of ancient structure and modern method, signals
the museum's ambition to be a cathedral of light and colour in the new millennium.

Hidden History Revealed

It is the **winners who write history**, says Dan Brown in *The Da Vinci Code*, and Christian history is no exception. As he tells it, the original story of Jesus – the meaning of his life and teaching – was suppressed and perverted by the Church in collaboration with the Roman emperor Constantine in the fourth century, so that as one of Dan Brown's characters says, 'Almost everything our fathers taught us about Christ is *false*'.

The Da Vinci Code, says Dan Brown on his website, is, as well as a novel, a means of airing ideas. 'While it is my belief that the theories discussed by these characters have merit, each individual reader must explore these characters' viewpoints and come to his or her own interpretations. My hope in writing this novel was that the story would serve as a catalyst and a springboard for people to discuss the important topics of faith, religion and history.'

But in an ABC television interview in New York, Dan Brown went much further. 'This is a novel', the interviewer said, but then he asked: 'If you were writing it as a non-fiction book, how would it have been different?' To which Dan Brown answered: 'I don't think it would have. I began the research for *The Da Vinci Code* as a sceptic. I entirely expected as I researched the book to disprove this theory [about Mary Magdalene being the wife of Jesus and the mother of his child]. And after numerous trips to Europe and about two years of research I really became a believer. I decided this theory makes more sense to me than what I learnt as a child.'

In other words, Dan Brown is telling his readers that *The Da Vinci Code* is more than just a discussion piece and certainly more than an entertainment; he is asserting that the integrity of his research has led him to believe in the historical truth of the events he relates. Referring to actual statements in the novel, **the truth of history according to Dan Brown** is set out below.

THE MARRIAGE: JESUS AND MARY MAGDALENE

According to *The Da Vinci Code*, chapter 58, **Jesus and Mary Magdalene were married**, and both were of **royal blood**. She was of the tribe of **Benjamin**, which had given rise to Saul, the first king of Israel. He was descended from **King David**, who had carved out an empire unmatched in Israel's history, and from David's son, **Solomon**, who built the great Temple in Jerusalem. Together, Jesus and Mary Magdalene made a potent political combination; their marriage fused the bloodlines of two great royal houses and gave Jesus a legitimate claim to the throne of Israel.

Jesus *must* have been married, says *The Da Vinci Code*, as according to Jewish custom celibacy was condemned. The silence of the Bible supposedly confirms the point; had Jesus *not* been married, at least one of the gospels would have offered some explanation for his unnatural bachelor state. Mary Magdalene was his wife, but though the Bible is silent on this matter too, there are 'countless references' elsewhere to their union, and these have been 'explored ad nauseam' by modern historians. In particular there are the Gnostic gospels, long lost but rediscovered in 1945, which along with the Dead Sea scrolls are described in *The Da Vinci Code* as 'the earliest Christian records'.

One of these references is found in the **Gnostic Gospel of Philip**: 'The companion of the Saviour is Mary Magdalene. Christ loved her more than all the disciples and used to kiss her often on her mouth. The rest of the disciples were offended by it. They said to him, "Why do you love her more than all of us?"'

Sir Leigh Teabing, who as one of Dan Brown's characters is an Oxford-educated historian, helpfully explains: 'As any Aramaic scholar will tell you, the word *companion,* in those days, literally meant *spouse*'.

Moreover **Peter** was *not* the rock on whom Jesus intended to build his Church. In another Gnostic text, the *Gospel of Mary Magdalene*,

Peter is angry that Jesus has confided in Mary Magdalene rather than in his male apostles. 'Did the Saviour really speak with a woman without our knowledge? Are we to turn about and all listen to her? Did he prefer her to us?' To which Levi (another name for Matthew) answers: 'Peter, you have always been hot-tempered. Now I see you contending against the woman like an adversary. If the Saviour made her worthy, who are you indeed to reject her? Surely the Saviour knows her very well. That is why he loved her more than us.' In other

This study for a head of Mary Magdalene by Leonardo da Vinci presents her as the reformed prostitute, submissive and repentant, an image that was central to her cult.

words, according to *The Da Vinci Code*, 'Jesus was the original feminist. He intended for the future of His Church to be in the hands of Mary Magdalene'.

The story is continued in chapter 60 of *The Da Vinci Code*. Mary Magdalene was made pregnant by Jesus, and after his crucifixion – which was followed by no resurrection, as he was only mortal – she secretly fled with the help of **Joseph of Arimathea** to France, where she was given refuge among its Jewish communities and gave birth to her daughter **Sarah**. Purportedly a genealogy of the early descendants of Jesus has been preserved, along with the **Q-document**, which may be an account of Jesus's life and ministry written in his own hand, as well as Mary Magdalene's own diaries, telling the story of her relationship with Jesus, of his crucifixion and her life in France.

Among these papers, too, are thought to be the **Purist Documents**, tens of thousands more pages of information written by the early followers of Jesus. These papers show that until the early fourth century, when the Church entered into its alliance with the Roman emperor **Constantine the Great**, Jesus was revered as a wholly human figure and prophet, not as God, and that the real object of worship was the sacred feminine.

CONSTANTINE TURNS JESUS INTO GOD

According to *The Da Vinci Code*, chapter 55, **Constantine the Great**, who was a pagan and a worshipper of Sol Invictus, the Unconquered Sun, saw an opportunity to unify and strengthen the Roman Empire by co-opting the growing Jesus movement. In this he had the support of the Church hierarchy, which stands accused of stealing Jesus from his original followers, hijacking his human message and turning him into God, all for the purpose of expanding their own power.

The matter was accomplished in 325 AD at the **Council of Nicaea**, where many aspects of Christianity were debated and voted upon, including the date of Easter, the administration of the sacraments, the role of bishops, and the divinity of Jesus. Until that moment, the novel contends, Jesus was viewed by his followers as a great and powerful prophet but nevertheless only a mortal man.

But the churchmen whom Constantine had summoned to the council from all over the Christian world voted to endorse his view that **Jesus was the Son of God**. 'Now the followers of Christ were able to redeem themselves *only* via the established sacred channel – the Roman Catholic Church.' At a stroke, Constantine had succeeded in turning Jesus into a deity whose power was unchallengeable, which meant that Church and empire were beyond challenge too.

To ensure the hegemony of his new religion, Constantine ensured that Christianity took on the **trappings of its pagan rivals**, so that **Egyptian sun discs** became the **halos** of Catholic saints, while **Isis suckling Horus** became an iconic image of **Mary and Jesus**. Virtually all elements of Catholic ritual, says *The Da Vinci Code*, were taken from earlier pagan mystery religions. **Mithras** also had been called the Son of God and the Light of the World; he too was buried in a rock tomb and then resurrected in three days; and Mithras was born on **25 December**, a birthday he shared with Osiris, Adonis and Dionysus. 'Nothing in Christianity is original', says the novel.

CHRISTIANITY DEMONISES THE SACRED FEMININE

In the process, says *The Da Vinci Code* chapter 28, Constantine converted the world from **matriarchal paganism** to **patriarchal Christianity**, which then began to demonise the sacred feminine. The Church – or as Dan Brown more often calls it, **the Vatican**

– launched a crusade against pagan and feminine-worshipping religions. In particular, the pagan ritual of **Hieros Gamos** – in which spiritual wholeness was achieved by sexual union – was forbidden, while **sexuality** itself became shameful, especially in the case of women, in whom sexual urges were identified with the devil.

The **Catholic Inquisition** published the **Malleus Maleficarum**, that is *The Witches' Hammer*, which indoctrinated the laity on the dangers of free-thinking women and instructed the clergy on how to torture and destroy such '**witches**' – who were deemed to include all female scholars, all priestesses and mystics, all gypsies, all nature lovers, all herb gatherers and any woman regarded as suspiciously attuned to the natural world. Midwives were also killed for their skill and knowledge in easing the pain of childbirth, a suffering says *The Da Vinci Code* that the Church claimed was God's punishment for Eve's partaking of the Apple of Knowledge, a transgression that gave rise to Original Sin.

During three hundred years of witch hunts, Dan Brown writes in his novel, 'the Church burnt at the stake an astounding five million women'. Earth became a man's world, out of balance and at war.

EDITING THE BIBLE AND REWRITING HISTORY

Because Constantine raised Jesus to divinity centuries after his crucifixion, says *The Da Vinci Code* chapter 55, there were already many thousands of documents in circulation chronicling Jesus's life as a mortal man. The emperor therefore decided on a bold stroke, nothing less than the eradication of the past and the rewriting of history. He commissioned and financed a **revised version of the Bible** for which **eighty versions of the gospels** were considered for inclusion. Those that dwelt on Jesus's human traits were omitted, while those which spoke of him as godlike were embellished and included.

From now on the banished gospels were deemed heretical; they were gathered up and destroyed. But fortunately for historians some early gospels survive, and according to Dan Brown they speak of Jesus's ministry in very human terms. Among these he counts the **Dead Sea scrolls**, which were discovered in Israel in a cave near **Qumran** in the 1950s, and what he calls the '**Coptic Scrolls**' – that is the **Gnostic gospels**, which were found in Egypt at **Nag Hammadi** in 1945. These scrolls clearly confirm that 'the modern Bible was compiled and edited by men who possessed a political agenda – to promote the divinity of the man Jesus Christ and use His influence to solidify their own power base'.

THE SECRET OF THE HOLY GRAIL

Mary Magdalene was chief among the victims of the Church's assault on the sacred feminine. According to *The Da Vinci Code*, chapter 58, the Church launched a smear campaign against her, calling her a prostitute, in order to cover up her dangerous secret, that she had been the wife of the mortal Jesus, and that the couple had produced a **child**. A child would undermine the divinity of Jesus and so destroy the Church.

But the truth about Mary Magdalene was preserved in the ingeniously conceived allegory of the **Holy Grail**. Some have naively believed that the Holy Grail was the cup from which Jesus drank at the Last Supper. In fact the Holy Grail was a metaphor for **Mary Magdalene** herself, whose womb was the chalice for Jesus's child. It was a metaphor as well for the **bloodline of Jesus**, and for the generations of his descendants, and it also referred to the secret documents that prove the entire story. In French the Holy Grail is known as *Sangrael*, derived from *San Grael*, but more anciently the phrase was **Sang Real**, meaning royal blood.

THE TEMPLARS AND THE PRIORY OF SION

The protector of the Holy Grail is the **Priory of Sion** – a *real organisation* says Dan Brown on a preliminary page of his novel – which was founded in 1099, the year the First Crusade conquered Jerusalem. In chapter 37 we learn that the leader of the crusade and Priory's founder was **Godefroi de Bouillon**, whose family possessed the secret of the bloodline of Jesus, a secret he wanted to corroborate and protect by finding certain documents buried beneath the ruins of the **Temple of Solomon in Jerusalem**. To pursue this aim, he founded the priory, which in turn created a military arm, the **Knights Templar**. The Templars eventually found something, something they would not reveal, but soon they achieved great power, wealth and influence. According to the argument in *The Da Vinci Code*, they were receiving money and privileges from the Vatican in exchange for not revealing the truth about Jesus and Mary Magdalene.

For two hundred years the Templars flourished as soldiers, church-builders, bankers and financiers in Europe and the Holy Land, until suddenly on **Friday October 13, 1307**, on orders from the Vatican, their leaders were arrested and charged with heresy, sodomy and other crimes, and were burnt at the stake, and their **order suppressed**. Before the blow fell, the Templars passed their secret to the Priory of Sion, which still guards the treasure – presumably documents which form part of that long hidden history known as the Holy Grail. Since then, suggests *The Da Vinci Code,* the priory lived a shadowy underground existence, safeguarding their secret and protecting the bloodline of Jesus and Mary Magdalene, and offering reverence to the sacred feminine. Its intention is to release its secret to the world at some propitious moment, but meanwhile it is avoiding the attentions of the **Vatican**, which would like to seize and destroy the Holy Grail, eradicating its evidence forever.

LEONARDO DA VINCI'S CLUES

Also on the preliminary page of his novel, Dan Brown states *as a fact* that parchments known as **les Dossiers Secrets**, found in 1975 at the Bibliothèque Nationale in Paris, identify numerous members of the priory, among them **Sir Isaac Newton**, **Victor Hugo**, **Sandro Botticelli** and **Leonardo da Vinci**. Indeed, in chapter 48 of *The Da Vinci Code*, he states that each of these men, as well as the film-maker, writer and artist **Jean Cocteau**, have been 'incontrovertibly confirmed' as Grand Masters of the priory by historians who have examined *les Dossiers Secrets*.

This is crucial material for the novel. For if the Priory and *les Dossiers Secret* are real, then as Grand Master, **Leonardo da Vinci** (1452–1519) would have known the whereabouts of the Holy Grail – and throughout the book his paintings, drawings and notebooks are closely examined for clues. Most illuminating, according to *The Da Vinci Code*, both for appreciating Leonardo's reverence for the sacred feminine and learning the location of the Holy Grail, are his drawing known as *Vitruvian Man* (chapter 8) and his paintings the *Mona Lisa* (chapter 26), the two versions of the *Madonna of the Rocks* (chapters 30 and 32), and, most especially **The Last Supper** (chapters 55, 56 and 58), which is reproduced in colour on the back cover – and in sections, the inner covers – of this book.

'Da Vinci sets it all out in the open in *The Last Supper*', says one of Dan Brown's characters. 'This fresco, in fact, is the entire key to the Holy Grail mystery.' Jesus sits at the table with his disciples on either side, but though the gospels of Matthew, Mark and Luke all relate that Jesus passed round a cup of wine, saying 'Drink of my blood', there is no such cup or chalice in the fresco. But the Holy Grail is there if you know where to look and understand the true meaning of the Grail legend – that really it represents the union between Jesus and Mary Magdalene. And indeed Mary Magdalene is in the fresco,

This red chalk drawing of Leonardo da Vinci was long thought to be a self-portrait and has largely determined our idea of his appearance. Nowadays it is thought to be a fake, or at best a copy of a lost original.

according to Dan Brown's characters, who see the figure to the left of Jesus not as the disciple John, but instead a woman – her appearance not clearly evident until the once grimy and damaged fresco was cleaned and restored in 1999.

Moreover, if you follow *The Da Vinci Code*, Leonardo incorporated a number of clues into the picture which point to a marriage between Mary Magdalene and Jesus. For example, though they lean away from one another, we are told that they appear to be joined at the hip, and the space between them forms a **V** – the feminine symbol of the sacred which resembles a chalice and suggests fertility and a woman's womb. The blue and red of their robes and garments mirror one another, and this introduces another way of looking at their two figures – their torsos the uprights on either side of the linking V-space between them, so that altogether they form the letter **M**, standing for *Matrimonio* perhaps, or *Mary Magdalene*. A further clue, according to *The Da Vinci Code*, is the threatening gesture made by Peter, who thrusts the edge of his hand across the throat of Mary Magdalene, recalling his jealous anger described in the long-hidden Gnostic gospel found at Nag Hammadi in 1945, the *Gospel of Mary Magdalene*.

THE VATICAN AND OPUS DEI

'Sophie, the historical evidence supporting this is substantial', says Robert Langdon in chapter 60. 'This was the secret the Vatican had tried to bury in the fourth century. That's part of what the Crusades were about. Gathering and destroying information.'

From first to last in *The Da Vinci Code* it is the Church, often described as the Roman Catholic Church, or simply as the **Vatican**, that has distorted and suppressed the truth about the life and teachings of Jesus and his embracing of the sacred feminine. Its brand of Christianity has warped the whole of Western culture and has

When Father Josemaría Escrivá, the founder of Opus Dei, died in 1975, no time was wasted in elevating him to sainthood. Miraculous cures were soon attributed to him and he was canonised by Pope John Paul II in the Vatican's St Peter's Square in 2002.

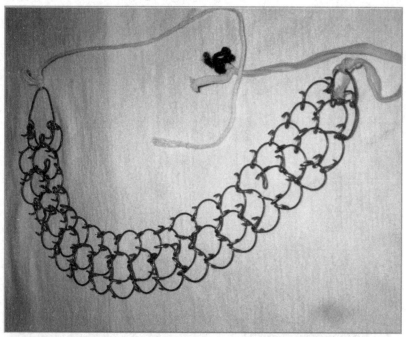

Self-mortification is one of Opus Dei's more controversial traits, inherited from medieval monasticism. The picture above shows a *cilice*, which some members – like Silas in *The Da Vinci Code* – wear for up to two hours a day around their thigh.

ensured chaos where there should be harmony, aggression where there should be peace, and guilt where there should be joy. However, a small band of people belonging to the Priory of Sion keep alive the old rituals, including the *Hieros Gamos*, and offer reverence to Mary Magdalene. Until the time is right to reveal the truth of the Holy Grail to the world, they safeguard it against those who would destroy it – which in the pages of *The Da Vinci Code* is the Vatican and its ultra-conservative ally **Opus Dei**.

Silas, the albino monk who murders Jacques Saunière, Grand Master of the Priory of Sion, and his three *senechaux*, is described as a **numerary** (a full time member) of Opus Dei. He is the epitome of the repressive, joyless and self-lacerating aspects of Christianity. For at least two hours every day he wears around his thigh a **cilice** – a leather strap studded with sharp metal barbs that cut into the flesh as a reminder of Jesus's sufferings on the cross – and for good measure he whips himself with a knotted rope until the blood runs down his back. 'Pain is good', Silas says; he tells it to Saunière after he shoots him in the stomach and leaves him to die a slow and terrible death, and he tells it to himself.

'**Pain is good**', we are told in chapter 2 of *The Da Vinci Code,* is the sacred mantra of **Father Josemaría Escrivá**, who founded Opus Dei – literally 'God's work' – in Spain in 1928. The words are uttered daily round the world by thousands of true followers of Escrivá's book *The Way* as they kneel on the floor and perform the sacred ritual called corporal mortification. Dan Brown adds as fact on his novel's preliminary page that Opus Dei, a Vatican prelature, is a deeply devout Catholic sect that has been the subject of recent controversy due to reports of brain-washing, coercion and its ritual of corporal mortification. Opus Dei, he adds, has just built a $47 million National Headquarters at 243 Lexington Avenue in New York City.

Opus Dei has grown hugely powerful in recent years, we are told in chapter 7 of *The Da Vinci Code*, after Pope John Paul II elevated it to a personal prelature of the pope in 1982, officially sanctioning its practices, which are even more severe for women. As it happens, its ascension occurred in the same year that Opus Dei allegedly transferred nearly a billion dollars into the **Vatican Bank**, saving it from bankruptcy. Nor in some quarters did it come as a great surprise when Father Josemaría Escrivá was put on a fast-track to sainthood, so that a process normally taking at least a century was accomplished in twenty years, his canonisation announced by Pope John Paul II in 2002.

Just as the Knights Templar and the Priory of Sion are portrayed in *The Da Vinci Code* as the champions and defenders of the true meaning of the Holy Grail, so Opus Dei is the militant wing of Catholicism which is determined to suppress and destroy that truth, just as Constantine and the Church attempted to do at Nicaea one thousand and seven hundred years ago. The battles fought then shaped the world we live in now, and the battles still continue.

This is the message of *The Da Vinci Code*, but how much of it is true?

DA VINCI
CODE

Context

Early Christianity

THE WORD MADE FLESH, MAYBE

'Many historians now believe (as I do) that in gauging the historical accuracy of a given concept, we should first ask ourselves a far deeper question: How historically accurate is history itself?'

DAN BROWN, INTERVIEW

In *The Da Vinci Code*, Dan Brown says that for nearly two thousand years we have been led astray from an earlier, gentler, more balanced and humane way of life by the Christian Church, which has betrayed the life and teachings of Jesus of Nazareth and his consort Mary Magdalene. Those who have known the truth and have tried to abide by the original ways have been branded heretics, great numbers have been killed, and their writings have been destroyed. In place of these lost histories, the Church imposed its own canon of scriptural writings which are nothing more than propaganda and lies. The Church's motive, in league with the Roman Empire, was to garner authority and power. By cynically declaring Jesus to be divine and making itself the sole means to salvation and the afterlife, the Church has succeeded in dominating the lives of countless millions, has distorted the roots of our culture, and has suppressed the sacred feminine.

In opposition to what he argues are the falsehoods of the Church, Dan Brown has presented a very different version of history, one that he says makes more sense to him than what he had been taught, and which he would confidently repeat again if he were writing *The Da Vinci Code* not as a novel but as a work of non-fiction based on his years of research.

To inform ourselves of the argument we will look at the historical contexts and examine the sources on both sides.

MAN OR GOD: WHAT DID THE EARLY CHRISTIANS THINK ABOUT JESUS?

A central claim made by Dan Brown is that throughout the lifetime of Jesus (c4 BC–c30 AD) and for nearly three centuries after, his followers revered him as a teacher and a prophet, but that he was always wholly human and certainly not divine. The doctrine that **Jesus was one and the same as God** was imposed, says Brown, by the Roman emperor **Constantine** in collaboration with the Church hierarchy at the **Council of Nicaea in 325** to consolidate their political power.

The simplest answer to that claim can be found in the **Gospel of John**, the fourth book of the New Testament, which is uncompromising in presenting Jesus in divine terms — a deity dressed in human flesh but a deity nonetheless. John makes this clear right at the start of his Gospel, when he writes: 'In the beginning was the Word, and the Word was with God, and the Word was God. … And the Word was made flesh, and dwelt among us' (John 1: 1, 14) – a straightforward equation amounting to Jesus equals God.

Relying on internal evidence, scholars date the composition of John's Gospel to between 85 and 100 AD. But a papyrus fragment of the Gospel was found in Egypt early in the twentieth century,

This Byzantine mosaic shows Mary Magdalene and the Virgin Mary visiting the tomb of Jesus after his crucifixion, only to discover that it is empty. The resurrection became the central doctrine of Christianity, though it was a matter of indifference or even of frank disbelief for many early Christians.

and this has been dated to 125 AD, plus or minus 25 years, making it the earliest surviving manuscript of the New Testament. After 150 AD we have references to John's Gospel in the surviving works of other writers. So even if we discount the earliest date of 85 AD, preferring more solid evidence, it nevertheless seems fairly safe to say that the **doctrine of the divinity of Jesus** was in place and being circulated among Christians by about 100 AD and certainly no later than 150 AD. This is two centuries before Dan Brown's version of history.

But what do the other Gospels say? In character the **gospels of Matthew, Mark and Luke** stand apart from the Gospel of John which was probably written later and reads like a treatise on the divinity of Jesus, whereas the first three gospels of the New Testament have something of the qualities of history or biography – you feel that you are learning something about Jesus the man. Those portions which underscore Jesus's divine aspect can seem more like afterthoughts – as sometimes in fact they were.

Matthew, Mark and Luke are known as the **Synoptic Gospels.** Synoptic means 'seen together' because when you set them out in parallel for comparison it is immediately apparent that they all tell roughly the same story. Scholars are in agreement that the Synoptic Gospels were written in the closing decades of the first century AD – that is within fifty years or so after the death of Jesus. The first gospel to have been written, and the briefest, is thought to have been Mark, which is dated to about 70 AD. Matthew and Luke are thought to have been written a bit later, but not later than 100 AD, and they contain much material, sometimes almost identical material, to that found in Mark, from which they clearly borrowed.

Mark's version is the simplest: it opens with accounts of **John the Baptist, Jesus's baptism** and his **temptation in the wilderness** (John the Baptist incidentally is a **cousin**; Jesus also had **four brothers** and unnumbered **sisters**, suggesting that Mary did not remain a virgin for long – see Mark 6:3), and continues with Jesus's **ministry in Galilee**, his **journey to Judaea** and the climax in Jerusalem, culminating with the **crucifixion** and the **discovery by Mary Magdalene of the empty tomb.**

And there Mark's Gospel originally came to an end. However, further verses (Mark 16:9-20) were added during the fourth century, in which after the resurection Jesus appears before his disciples and then **ascends to heaven** to sit on the right hand of God.

Matthew and Luke both begin with prologues narrating the **virgin birth**, something entirely missing in Mark, and both conclude with epilogues that give much fuller accounts than Mark of appearances by the **risen Jesus** to his disciples. Otherwise Matthew and Luke have borrowed their basic structure from Mark's Gospel.

But Matthew and Luke also draw on some other source or sources which existed as oral tradition or as one or more written documents, a body of lost material which scholars call **Q** from the German *Quelle*, meaning source.

THE Q DOCUMENT AND ITS SECRETS

This is what Dan Brown calls the **'legendary "Q" Document'**, which he describes as a book of Jesus's teachings, perhaps even written in Jesus's hand, which is among the secret papers comprising the Holy Grail, that treasury containing the long-suppressed truth that Jesus had been wholly human and had never been divine.

Here Dan Brown is touching on a point of potentially enormous significance which since the **Q hypothesis** was raised in the nineteenth century has unsettled churchmen and scholars alike. Jesus's central message, according to the Church, lies in his **death for the sins of the world** and his **resurrection with its promise of man's salvation**. But it turned out that when Q was reconstructed (using those passages found in Matthew and Luke but not in Mark), it consisted almost exclusively of Jesus's teachings and made no reference whatsoever to the crucifixion or the resurrection. Was it possible that the very first Christians, those who belonged to the generation before Matthew, Mark and Luke and may have met Jesus face to face, believed that the significance of Jesus lay not in any supposed divinity and resurrection? That instead they revered him as a teacher and believed that salvation lay in correctly understanding what Jesus had to say?

But Q was hypothetical and the questions that it raised were hypothetical too – until a cache of long-lost gospels were discovered in 1945 at **Nag Hammadi** in Upper Egypt, gospels that never found their way into the New Testament but bore a resemblance to Q. We will look at those **Gnostic gospels** later, but meanwhile we will pursue the implications of Q, that the earliest Christians were of more than one view on the nature of Jesus and that some or even most did not accept the idea of salvation through his crucifixion and ressurrection.

ORGASM AS PRAYER

Dan Brown in *The Da Vinci Code* paints a picture of Christians in the first three centuries AD following the lessons of their teacher Jesus while at the same time preserving a **reverence for the feminine** which went back to pagan times. A man was spiritually incomplete without carnal knowledge of the **sacred feminine**, and so he accessed the divine by practicing **Hieros Gamos**, sacred union. At the moment of climax, explains Brown's character, the Harvard professor Robert Langdon, a man could see God: or 'orgasm as prayer', as the lovely auburn-haired police cryptologist Sophie Neveu so elegantly puts it.

Sometimes reading the New Testament **letters of Paul**, you think this might be true. The letters date to the 50s AD and are even earlier than the gospels of Matthew, Mark, Luke and John. In fact they are the oldest Christian documents we possess and are contemporary with Q. The letters show that Paul was having a running battle with the **Christians of Corinth** who believed that they already had been saved – and were joyfully indulging the sensation (see 1 Corinthians). They did not believe in some future resurrection of the physical body. Instead they saw resurrection as a spiritual event that came at the moment of baptism. At their communal meals, an institution common in the infant church, where **agape** – spiritual love – was shared among the congregation, the faithful feasted themselves on generous supplies of food and wine, compared their sexual exploits and explored new varieties of cohabitation, one member unabashedly announcing that he was sleeping with his father's wife. They no longer needed to obey the laws and conventions of this world; salvation was already theirs, and they were free to do as they pleased.

THE RESURRECTION AND THE VIRGIN BIRTH: WHAT CHRISTIANS BELIEVE TODAY

According to surveys conducted within the last five years, 95% of Christians in the United States believe in the resurrection, but only 67% of American church leaders do. In Britain only 47% of Christians believe in the resurrection, but among Church of England clergy 66% believe. Women clergy in the Church of England are more sceptical than men: only half believe in the resurrection, and while half of all Church of England clergy believe in the Virgin Birth, only a third of female clergy do.

PAUL PREACHES SALVATION THROUGH THE CRUCIFIXION

The events at Corinth (perhaps misunderstood and distorted by Paul) illustrate something of the variety of **ways to salvation** in the early Church. If there was a general conviction that salvation was owed to Jesus's death on the cross and to his resurrection, it certainly was not a universal conviction. That eventually it became the fixed doctrine of the Church is owed to the efforts of **Paul**, who has been called a daring doctrinal innovator and virtually the **inventor of Christian theology**.

Paul (or Saul as he was first known) was a Jew from Tarsus, in present-day Turkey, and was descended of a family of Pharisees. As well as speaking Aramaic and Hebrew, he also spoke Greek, for the inhabitants of Tarsus were thoroughly Hellenised, and Paul would have been familiar with **Stoic philosophy**, of which the city was a great centre, the 'Athens of Asia Minor'. Additionally, Paul came from a wealthy family that had been granted Roman citizenship. By background, therefore, he was a man of several worlds.

Yet at first Paul chose to be narrowly sectarian. Jesus had already been crucified when Paul came to **Jerusalem** to study at the rabbinical school, where in about 35 AD he approvingly witnessed the stoning of **Stephen, the first Christian martyr**. Stephen belonged to a small circle of Jesus's followers who were endeavouring to keep his teachings alive: a circle that was perhaps no more than a Jewish sect, without rituals or holy places or a priesthood of their own, and which, with the death of their teacher might in time be reabsorbed into the mainstream of Judaism. If they asserted the divinity of Jesus, then that was heresy and there was no going back. But for the followers of Jesus there was no going forward unless they could succeed where Jesus himself had already failed – to **reform or transcend Judaism** by finding salvation beyond the fulfillment of the law, those 613 conflicting injunctions and prohibitions that no man could hope completely to honour, and so casting all men as sinners.

Yet legalism was the stock and trade of the Pharisees, and by background Paul was one of their number. Nor was the role of complicit bystander at the stoning of Stephen enough for Paul, who now 'made havoc of the church, entering into every house, and haling men and women committed them to prison' (Acts 8:3). Yet the way the story is told, the impression is given of a man driving himself towards fanaticism lest something within himself gives way: Paul 'breathing out threatenings and slaughter against the disciples of the Lord, went unto the high priest, and desired of him letters to Damascus to

Istoure du saint vaissel quon appelle
grial. le precieulx sanc au sauueur fu
receu au iour quil fu crucifies pour
le peuple rachater deuser. ioseph le
mist en ramambrance pour la men
aon de la tois auecques un angle po
ce que la ueite fult scene par son escript & par son telmo
iguage des cheuailliers & des preudomes comment il
vouldrent souffrir panine & triuail pour lonneur ihu

In this fourteenth century French illumination, Joseph of Arimathea kneels at the foot
of the cross, collecting the blood of Jesus in a cup or grail.

the synagogues, that if he found any of this way, whether they were men or women, he might bring them bound unto Jerusalem' (this and the following from Acts 9:1-25).

'And as he journeyed, he came near Damascus: and suddenly there shined round about him a light from heaven: and he fell to the earth, and heard a voice saying unto him, Saul, Saul, why persecutest thou me? And he said, Who art thou, Lord? And the Lord said, I am Jesus whom thou persecutest.' Paul rose from the ground blinded by the vision and had to be led to a house in town, where for three days he neither saw nor ate nor drank. But on the third day a Jewish convert to Christianity called **Ananias** put his hands upon Paul, 'And immediately there fell from his eyes as it had been scales: and he received sight forthwith, and arose, and was baptised.'

At once Paul rushed round the synagogues preaching the very **heresy** that Jesus's followers in Jerusalem had hesitated to embrace, that **Jesus was the living Son of God.**

BREAK WITH THE JERUSALEM JESUS CULT

In the instantaneousness of Paul's conversion, he dispensed with the doubts, the hesitations, the halfway houses that accompany argument and reflection, and became free to find radical solutions to the predicament of the Jesus cult. The very divinity of Jesus, the idea that a man could be a god, while utterly alien to Judaism, was in keeping with **Hellenistic culture**, even if the more sophisticated looked at it askance. As Paul himself said when he preached the divinity of Jesus: 'For the Jews require a sign, and the Greeks seek after wisdom: But we preach Christ crucified, unto the Jews a stumbling block, and unto the Greeks foolishness' (1 Corinthians, 1:22-23).

Nevertheless, to that Hellenistic culture, shared by the gentiles and the Jews of the diaspora, he directed his mission, bypassing the Jerusalem brethren. They had known Jesus in his lifetime, as a Galilean, as a Jew, as a teacher who had tried to work within the particularity of his environment. But **Paul's authority** was to have known Jesus through that vision on the **road to Damascus**, to have known him as divine, as boundless and universal. Abandoning such Jewish shibboleths as circumcision, objectionable to the gentiles, while presenting his doctrines in the concepts and terms of Greek language and thought he had known at Tarsus, Paul embarked on a series of proselytising journeys that took him from the Middle East to Asia Minor, Cyprus, Greece and ultimately to Rome itself, where he is thought to have been martyred in about 65 AD.

WAITING AND WAITING FOR THE SECOND COMING

The faith preached by Paul was founded absolutely on the **resurrection**. 'And if Christ be not risen', he wrote to the Corinthians, 'then is our preaching vain, and your faith is also vain' (1 Corinthians 15:14). Also Paul expected that **Jesus would return to Earth** within the lifetime of those still living: 'For the Lord himself shall descend from heaven with a shout … and the dead in Christ shall rise first: Then we which are alive and remain shall be caught up together with them in the clouds, to meet the Lord in the air: and so shall we ever be with the Lord' (1 Thessalonians 4:16-17).

This image of a triumphant messiah appearing amidst the clouds of heaven can be traced back to the **Book of Daniel**, a late addition to the Old Testament and written about a hundred and fifty years before the birth of Jesus: 'Behold, one like the Son of man came with the clouds of heaven … and there was given him dominion, and glory, and a kingdom, that all people, nations, and languages, should serve him: his dominion is an everlasting dominion, which shall not pass away' (Daniel 8:13-14).

Nowhere do the Gospel authors have Jesus say that he is divine (with one possible and ambiguous exception: Mark 14:61-62). He never calls himself the **Son of God**. But he frequently calls himself the **Son of Man**, a turn of phrase referring to oneself, rather like 'my mother's son', so that Jesus by saying the 'son of man' need have meant no more than 'me'. But there are times when Jesus is clearly alluding to the Book of Daniel, and there the 'Son of Man' is an allegorical figure standing for God's faithful people in Israel and their supernatural deliverance from centuries of occupation by Romans, Greeks, Persians, Assyrians and Babylonians. Jesus probably saw himself as a **deliverer**, not in any political or military sense, but as one who came to release the Jews from their history, over which they had lost control, in order to enter another dimension, a living dimension filled with the presence of God.

This sensation of **divine immanence**, called *parousia* in Greek, was taken over by Paul to describe the return of Jesus to Earth, the **Second Coming**, when men would be judged and those who had professed themselves believers in his divinity would be saved – that is, washed of their sins and given eternal life. But even Paul, towards the end of his life, began to think that he would die before Jesus would appear to him again in the sky, and others thought the same. As long as the Second Coming had seemed imminent, there had been no time, and no need, to write anything longer than an urgent letter. But now, as the *parousia* slipped away, and with it the generations who could remember Jesus, or who had known someone who had known Jesus, the new urgency was to establish something lasting: the time had come to **organise and write**.

The Sacred Feminine

In Search of the Lost Goddess

'The ancients envisioned their world in two halves – masculine and feminine. Their gods and goddesses worked to keep a balance of power. Yin and yang. When male and female were balanced, there was harmony in the world. When they were unbalanced, there was chaos. This pentacle is representative of the female half of all things – a concept religious historians call the "sacred feminine".'

THE DA VINCI CODE [CHAPTER 6]

Arguably the most important and interesting discussions in *The Da Vinci Code* concern the 'sacred feminine'. As the novel's characters point out, seeing God in solely masculine terms misrepresents and limits the divine – which is precisely what happens in Christianity with its vocabulary of **Jesus the Son of God the Father**. That is the starting point of those who argue for recognition of the **sacred feminine** and what they see as the restoration of spiritual balance to the world. True, the **Virgin Mary as Mother of God** brings something of the feminine to the Christian godhead, but it is not a full partnership and entirely lacks that element of **Eros** in which the feminine and the masculine most intimately meet.

Here a Greek version of Isis shows her as a fertility goddess. She lifts up her skirts to reveal her bounty.

The argument for recovering the sacred feminine finds a tradition of sacred union in ancient cultures in which the feminine and masculine were celebrated as intimate and equal partners; examples include **Isis and Osiris**, **Astarte and Tammuz**, **Cybele and Attis**, and **Aphrodite and Adonis**. In these sacred pairings there is the theme of **death and new life**, with the female playing an active and restoring role, raising her dead lover or bringing forth new life by bearing his child.

Yet this role of the sacred feminine is missing from Christianity, and there are those who in searching for **Christianity's 'lost bride'** find her in the figure of **Mary Magdalene**, and who say the time has come to listen to her story.

The Greek Gods

The **ancient Greeks** worshipped their gods, including innumerable local deities, at sanctuaries great and small, in market places and by roadsides, in cities and on islands, on mountaintops and headlands – everywhere, in fact, because the gods themselves were everywhere. But the **great gods** known to all were the twelve who lived on Mount Olympus. Ten (four of them women) were already recognised by Homer in the eighth century BC: **Zeus**, the lord of the heavens and supreme power on Olympus; **Hera**, his wife and sister, and goddess of fertility; **Athena** the goddess of wisdom, patron of crafts and fearless warrior; **Apollo** the god of music, of prophecy and the arts; his sister **Artemis** the virgin huntress and goddess of childbirth; **Poseidon** the god of the sea and the forces of nature; the beautiful **Aphrodite**, goddess of love and desire; **Hermes** the messenger who leads the souls of the dead to the underworld, but also the protector of the home and of the market; **Hephaestus**, the lame god of craftsmen and for a while the husband of Aphrodite; and **Ares**, the god of war, who in cuckolding Hephaestus was subdued by the goddess of love. In the fifth century BC these were joined by two deities who embodied the mystical quality of rebirth: **Demeter**, the goddess of crops and female fertility; and **Dionysus**, the god of wine and intoxication. They answered a growing need among the ancient Greeks for a doctrine of the soul otherwise lacking in the Olympian religion.

THE ELEUSINIAN MYSTERIES

Every September a great torchlit procession made its way from Athens to Eleusis on the Saronic Gulf in the west of Attica, the scene of the **Greater Eleusinia** held at the temple of **Demeter**, literally **Earth Mother**, goddess of agriculture in the Olympian scheme. A statue of **Dionysus** was carried at the head of the procession; then came the priests with the sacred objects of the cult hidden from sight in baskets; and finally there was the huge crowd of *mystai* or initiates. No other festival in Greece was of more consequence or surrounded with greater secrecy. We can only guess at the nature of the **Eleusinian Mysteries**, as throughout their entire history no one ever revealed what transpired.

But it was here, according to the myth, that Demeter came, searching by torchlight for her daughter **Persephone**, who had been abducted to the Underworld by Hades. Threatening perpetual winter, so that crops would no longer grow and mankind would be extinguished, Demeter forced Zeus to order Persephone's release for nine months of the year, when the world once more enjoyed the fruits of spring, summer and autumn. And so the mysteries in some way celebrated death and rebirth, and certainly the response could be profound. The poet Pindar wrote that 'he who has seen the holy things and goes in death beneath the earth is happy, for he knows life's end and he knows too the new divine beginning', while the Roman statesman Cicero, who came four hundred years later, said 'the greatest gift of Athens to mankind and the holiest is the Eleusinian Mysteries'.

Artemis as she was worshipped at Ephesus was covered in potent symbols, including bees and bulls' testicles.

WILD AND EXCITABLE WOMEN

The **theme of rebirth** is a very ancient one, and not surprisingly women played a central role. But when viewed as part of a cycle, rebirth is preceded by death, so that women played the role of killers as much as nurturing mothers. The Greeks who lived on the eastern shores of the Aegean in Asia Minor worshipped **Artemis**, their goddess of the hunt, at her temple in **Ephesus**, which was one of the

EX DONO DVCIS SFORTIAE SFORTIAE

The goddess Cybele is shown on this relief with objects of her cult. Her priests castrated themselves, and her priestesses offered sacred sex to male devotees.

Seven Wonders of the World. But this was not the chaste huntress, the sister of Apollo, who had asked Zeus her father for the gift of eternal virginity. Instead this was an oriental version of Artemis, a woman with a past, whose cult statue was adorned with bees and the testicles of bulls.

From this peculiar fact it is possible to trace her ancestry back many hundreds of years to **Cybele**, an earth goddess of Asia Minor whose son and lover was **Attis**. There were stories of mountain-top affairs during which Cybele, like a queen bee, would tear out her lover's sexual organs. Cybele combined within her death and life, nature, man and the divine. Her temple rites were often ecstatic acts of self-sacrifice or self-abandonment: her priests castrated themselves in an ecstasy of identification with Attis, while the high-born women who were Cybele's priestesses also served as temple prostitutes; known as *melissai*, or bees, they offered up their bodies to the act of **Hieros Gamos**, sacred sexual union.

The story has a strange sequel, for according to a strand of Christian tradition, Jesus confided his mother to the care of his apostle John, who brought **Mary to Ephesus** where she lived out her days. At a site said to be the remains of Mary's house, local Christians long celebrated mass on **August 15**, the date set by the Church as her **assumption into heaven** – though the date has a far older resonance than that, for August 15 was also the annual feast day of Artemis at Ephesus. Nor is it likely to have been a coincidence that in the Christian Church the virginity of Mary is symbolised by a bee.

MONTANISM

The ancient power of the goddess also found an outlet in the form of **Montanism**, a Christian heresy that arose in the second century AD in **Phrygia**, the region of Asia Minor that was once home to Cybele. The descent of the Holy Spirit was imminent, said Montanus its founder, declaring that as a sign it spoke from the mouths of prophets like himself and two prophetesses close to him, one of whom was said to have seen Jesus Christ dressed as a woman.

Montanus was accused of having been one of Cybele's eunuch priests; that he gave such a prominent role to women, those 'gateways of the Devil', was unforgivable; he even admired Eve as the source of knowledge, not of sin. But Montanus's real offence was to assert that men and women could achieve a **direct apprehension of God**, and that by being filled with the Holy Spirit prophets could be trusted as well as bishops. Instead the Montanists' ecstatic pro-physying was deemed demonic, and one modern Christian writer has pointed to the danger that 'had Montanus triumphed, Christian doctrine would have been developed not under the superintendence of the Christian teachers most esteemed for wisdom, but of wild and excitable women'.

GODDESSES AND THEIR LOVERS

All over the ancient world you find versions of the goddess who is at the centre of the drama of life and death. For example in the mountains of **Lebanon**, which were the setting for the love affair between **Adonis and Aphrodite** as related by the Greeks. Adonis was a mortal born of an incestuous relationship between the king of Byblos and his daughter. Aphrodite hid the infant in a chest, which she placed in the care of Persephone, queen of the underworld. But when Persephone opened the chest and saw the child's beauty, she wanted to keep him for her own. Zeus was called in to mediate in this dispute between death and love and decreed that Adonis must live part of each year in the dismal underworld but during the other part could return to the shining world above. There in the mountains above Byblos Adonis and Aphrodite became lovers, exchanging their first kisses and also their last at the spring of Afqa, for near the gorge Adonis was gored by a wild boar, and though Aphrodite tried to heal his wounds, Adonis bled to death, bright spring anemones growing where his blood touched the ground.

It is an eternal story, the alternation of seasons expressed in the death and rebirth of men and gods, the theme resonating through the stories of **Osiris, Attis and Jesus**. Aphrodite is, of course, the Roman **Venus**, and in her earlier Semitic form she was **Astarte**, and in Babylonia **Ishtar**, the great mother goddess who was the embodiment of the reproductive energies of nature. Her lover was **Tammuz**, addressed by his devotees as **Adon**, that is 'Lord', his title mistakenly taken by the Greeks to be his name. Tammuz was a vegetation god who every year was believed to die, his divine mistress journeying into the underworld in quest of him. In her absence the passion of love ceased to operate in the upper world: men and animals forgot to procreate, and all life itself was threatened with extinction.

At **Byblos**, the principle centre of the Adonis cult, these were days of lamentation: 'He is dead, Adonis the beautiful, he is dead!' Women would beat their breasts and shave their heads, or they could offer themselves for sacred prostitution. Then, on the eighth day, the sorrow turned to rejoicing: 'He is risen, Adonis, he is risen!' And today still the old fertility rites are recalled, though not in carnal form. Christians are numerous in this part of Lebanon, and in the days before Christmas and Easter the mountain villagers place 'Adonis gardens' on their window sills or by their doors, earthenware pots planted with quick-growing seeds that spring to life in commemoration of the birth and resurrection of Jesus Christ.

ANTI-SOCIAL CHRISTIAN VIRGINS

Artemis, Aphrodite, Astarte and Cybele: these were formidable women who took what they wanted from a man. And then there was the no less formidable **St Thecla of Iconium**, now Turkish Konya, who wanted no man at all. Supposedly she lived in the first century AD, but she may never have existed at all, as elements in her tale suggest that an ancient pagan cult was perverted to Christian ends.

The legend goes that she was converted to Christianity in her native city by the apostle Paul, whereupon she broke off an engagement to marry and devoted her maidenhood to God. She was young and beautiful and her loss to the world of men seems to have been too great to bear. Her fiancé had her flogged, but failing to win her in this way he obtained a sentence of death by fire, only to see Thecla saved by a thunderstorm and make her escape. Another frustrated admirer tried to prise her from chastity by the threat of wild beasts, but again she got away, finally withdrawing to a mountain cave. When her persecution was yet again renewed at the age of 90, this time by local medical men jealous of her healing powers, the rocks opened up and swallowed her.

The story of St Thecla is reminiscent of other tales of mountain passion like those of Adonis and Aphrodite, Attis and Cybele – indeed the mountain outside Konya to which Thecla withdrew had once been named for Cybele. But the life of Thecla perverts the ancient dramas of fertility, death and resurrection, and their concern for the **seasons of cultivation and of man**. With its other-worldly fixation on the Second Coming, the story of Thecla's life illustrates one of the most fundamental threats that early Christianity posed to human society.

The ancient world was 'grazed thin by death', as St John Chrysostom put it. Average life expectancy was 25 years, and only four men (and fewer women) in every hundred lived beyond the age of 50. For the population of the Roman Empire not to decrease, every woman needed to bear five children. Paul preached resurrection, yet an excess of Theclas could mean the extinction of the human species. **True resurrection**, said Paul's opponents, is 'that which takes place through the nature of the human body itself, and which, through human means, is accomplished every day'.

But for Christians awaiting the Second Coming, and meanwhile eager to avoid any worldly temptation and sin, the collapse of human society was irrelevant. **Chastity** was venerated for the sake of gaining access to the next world, while Thecla and Christians generally, perceived as anti-social in the most fundamental sense, were persecuted for the sake of the world of the living.

ALLAH AND ALLAT

The rejection of the sacred feminine was not only an early Christian phenomenon. According to pre-Muslim Arab belief, **Allat** (properly al-Lat, meaning goddess in Arabic) was a sun goddess and daughter of Allah. The centre of Allat's worship was a rich temple at Taif in Arabia, but there were many others, including the one erected in the first century BC at the great trading city of **Palmyra** which stood at the crossroads of the desert caravan routes, making it a place where many influences met. An inscription to Allat at her temple in Palmyra described her as 'Allat who is also Artemis', tying her to the great cycle of stories about the sacred feminine found throughout the ancient world. But when **Mohammed** conquered Mecca in 630, Allat's worship at Taif survived for only another year, her overthrow marking the final **victory of Islam over paganism,** the Koran stating (Sura 53:22) that the old pagan deities 'are but names which you and your fathers have invented: Allah has invested no authority in them'.

ANCIENT EGYPT'S CONTRIBUTION TO CHRISTIANITY

Christianity came early to **Egypt** and spread rapidly from the Greek and Jewish environment of the cities to the native Egyptian countryside, where it took strong root despite ferocious persecution – the worst anywhere in the Roman Empire. Egyptians were already familiar with the doctrine of the **resurrection and personal immortality** which had been central features of their **Osiris cult** for three thousand years, and indeed it is possible that

In life a pharoah was identified with the god Horus, in death with his father Osiris, god of the underworld, who promised eternal existence for the soul. Here the pharaoh Sesostris I (c1950 BC) is shown with his arms crossed in the Osiris position, each hand holding an ankh, the cross-like symbol for life. It was a small step for Christians to see the cross of Jesus' crucifixion as a symbol of life.

Christianity borrowed these and other ideas from the ancient religion that lingered in Egypt well into the sixth century. What is more certain is that Christianity borrowed much of its symbolism and popular art from the Egyptians, so that from **Isis and Horus** came the **Virgin and Child**, and from the **ankh**, the ancient Egyptian sign for life, came the paradox of the **Cross** as representing rebirth.

'Nothing in Christianity is original', asserts Sir Leigh Teabing in *The Da Vinci Code*, as he and Robert Langdon launch into an impromptu lecture on Christianity's pagan roots. ('Sophie was surprised'.) The **halos** hovering over the heads of saints were derived from ancient **Egyptian sun discs**, and images of the **Virgin Mary** holding the infant Jesus in her lap come from yet more ancient images of **Isis suckling her son Horus**. But, the Teabing-Langdon lecture continues, although pagan rituals, festivals, symbols and themes were absorbed into the growing Christian tradition, behind it was a deliberate plan to convert the world 'from matriarchal paganism to patriarchal Christianity', to **demonise the sacred feminine** and to assert the dominance of men. ('Sophie's head was spinning'.) If that indeed was the intention, then Christianity found its most formidable opponent in the Egyptian goddess Isis.

ISIS: THE LAST GREAT GODDESS

The divine triad of **Isis, Osiris and Horus** goes back at least to 3000 BC, by which time Horus was already identified with the reigning pharaoh. His father Osiris was a king who ruled and was greatly loved in distant times. Isis was his sister and wife, Seth his brother. When Seth killed Osiris and dismembered his body, Isis searched out the pieces and put them together again, wondrously restoring Osiris to life in the underworld, where he reigned as judge and king. Moreover, Isis was sufficiently able to arouse her dead husband to have intercourse with him (a scene illustrated on the walls of Egyptian tombs) and conceive their son Horus. Isis therefore played the vital role in transmitting the kingship from the dead Osiris-king to the living Horus-king, a role repeated endlessly throughout the generations of pharaonic rule in Egypt.

Through her **suffering over the death of Osiris** and her **joy at the birth of Horus**, Isis offered an emotive identification so powerful and satisfying that she became identified too with all other goddesses of the Mediterranean, whom she finally absorbed. Isis was the Goddess of Ten Thousand Names, Shelter and Heaven to All Mankind, the House of Life, the Great Mother of All Gods and Nature, Victorious over Fate, the Promise of Immortality, Sexuality and Purity, and the Glory of Women who alone could save. She was passionately worshipped by men and women alike. **Cleopatra** deliberately identified herself with Isis, and called herself the New Isis, casting Antony as Dionysus, the Greek equivalent of Osiris, so that on earth they re-enacted the already existing cosmological bond.

Christianity, with its male-orientated antecedents in Judaism and to a lesser extent the Zeus-centred worship of the Greeks, may never have given the prominence it did to the **Virgin Mary** had not a figure been needed to absorb in turn the great popularity and success of the rival Isis cult. It was a rivalry that continued well into the Christian era.

A temple was founded in Isis's honour in Rome by the emperor Domitian himself during the 80s AD. And in spite of the edicts of the emperor Theodosius I, which succeeded in terminating the Olympic Games after a thousand years in the fourth century AD, **pagan Philae** continued as a centre of Isis worship until the sixth century, when the emperor Justinian closed the temple of Isis at Philae, imprisoned its priests and had its cult statues carried off to Constantinople. In 553 part of Isis's temple at Philae was turned into a church, the occasion commemorated by a

The Egyptian goddess Isis was often depicted suckling her infant son Horus, an image that found its way in Christian iconography.

contemporary inscription in Greek: 'This good work was done by the well-beloved of God, the Abbot-Bishop Theodore. The Cross has conquered and will ever conquer'.

MARY MAGDALENE: FROM APOSTLE TO WHORE

There are only twelve mentions of **Mary Magdalene** in the four gospels of the New Testament, and eleven of them relate directly to her presence at the **crucifixion of Jesus** and his **resurrection**. The twelfth reference is in Luke (8:2-3) where we are told that Jesus freed several women from evil spirits and infirmities, among them Mary Magdalene, from whom he drove out seven devils, and that these women then provided for the itinerant Jesus and his twelve disciples out of their own resources. And that is all the Bible tells us about Mary Magdalene, though she does appear in some Gnostic Gospels, and we will look at those in the following chapter.

Nevertheless, two striking things stand out from these New Testament accounts. First, Mary Magdalene seems to be an entirely independent woman. Magdalene is not her surname; it is the place is she from, a town on the Sea of Galilee. This makes her the only woman in the Gospels who is not defined in terms of a man; that is, she is not described as the wife or sister or daughter of a man. She has her own resources, enough to keep herself in the company of Jesus and his followers, and she also contributes to their **mission** in the field. Second, Mary Magdalene is present at the most important moments of the Jesus story, his **death and resurrection**.

At the crucifixion of Jesus his disciples have gone into fearful hiding. However, Mary Magdalene is at both the cross and the tomb, and it is she who carries the news to the disbelieving disciples that Jesus has arisen. Her appearances in the Gospels may be brief but they are telling. It is as if she fulfills the role of those ancient goddesses whose lives embraced the deaths and rebirths of their men.

This Coptic icon shows Mary Magdalene washing the feet of Jesus.

Nonetheless in the year 591 **Pope Gregory I**, 'the Great', pronounced **Mary Magdalene a whore**. Pope Gregory had been reading the Gospel of Luke 7:37-38, where a woman described as 'a sinner' came to Jesus and 'brought an alabaster box of ointment, and stood at his feet behind him weeping, and began to wash his feet with tears, and did wipe them with the hairs of her head, and kissed his feet, and anointed them with the ointment'. The ointment, said the pope, must previously have been used by her 'to perfume her flesh in forbidden acts'.

This woman is nameless in the Gospel of Luke, but her anointing of Jesus occurs just a page before that scene where he drives the devils out of Mary Magdalene. Though the connection between these two episodes is tenuous at best, the Pope felt free to say, 'We believe that this woman Mary Magdalene is Luke's female sinner'. Only fourteen centuries later, in 1969, did the **Vatican** admit that Gregory had made a mistake.

DEMONISE OR LIBERATE?

According to Dan Brown, who wrongly gives the impression that it was Constantine and the Council of Nicaea in 325 who were responsible for portraying Mary Magdalene as a whore, this charge of harlotry marked the beginning of the Church's campaign to **demonise the sacred feminine**. In reality Christianity was a largely **liberating influence** on women's lives, for the everyday truth about women in pagan societies was that their worth was judged almost exclusively on their success as sexual and reproductive beings. This gave women importance and authority within the domestic sphere, but it was Christianity, especially once it had been legitimised by Constantine, which opened up horizons of new promise, and women were not behind in seeking out established roles.

In this they were building on their already considerable contribution, for it was very much through the agency of women that

Christianity had spread throughout the Roman Empire and into every level of society. The evidence in the New Testament, from the Gospels, the letters of Paul and the Acts of the Apostles, shows that **Jesus treated women equally with men**, that women were functioning as **disciples and missionaries**, and that they were **conducting church services** in their homes (eg Acts 12:12). In fact, at the beginning women were probably more important than men in nurturing and spreading Christian belief.

But an aspect of that belief was a tendency among both men and women to choose a life of **celibacy**. In men that was not considered problematic, but the independence of women, when it emulated the life of St Thecla, was perceived by the post-Constantine Church as a threat as much to itself as formerly it had seemed to society – for now the Church and society were one.

Consequently there was an assertion of the old paternalistic attitudes of the pagan world. Men kept for themselves the more important and powerful **roles in the Church**, such as that of bishop, though they made somewhat slower headway in **monopolising the priesthood**, for there are records of women priests officiating at Mass right through the fifth century. Women were encouraged to be passive and submissive and to breed, and so it was that towards this end Mary Magdalene, that model of independence, that apostle to the apostles, was transformed into the very model of a humble and repentant sinner, the ideal for every woman seeking identification with the Church.

MARY MAGDALENE IN FRANCE

After the crucifixion, Mary Magdalene had no choice but to flee the Holy Land, according to *The Da Vinci Code*, and so she travelled secretly to France, where she sought refuge with the Jewish community. The origin of this story, whether Dan Brown troubled to look into it himself or simply picked up a garbled version from a book like *Holy Blood, Holy Grail*, is found in a legend still alive today at the fishing village of **Les Saintes-Maries-de-la-Mer** in the Camargue. Here, says the legend, Mary Magdalene along with **Mary, the sister of the Virgin**, and **Mary, the mother of the**

A sixteenth-century altarpiece shows Mary Magdalene and her companions setting sail from the Holy Land for France.

apostles James and John, landed in about 40 AD, together with their servant **Sarah**, and **Martha, Lazarus, Maximinus** and **Sidonius** – all having fled from persecution in the Holy Land. The event is celebrated by a gipsy pilgrimage every year on May 24-25, as the gipsies identify with Sarah, who is said to have been an Ethiopian and dark-skinned like themselves.

From there Mary Magdalene struck inland to the **Ste-Baume massif** where she lived as a **hermit** in a cave, only venturing down into the plain as she felt her approaching death in order to receive communion from Maximinus. There in the abbey church **St-Maximin-la-Ste-Baume**, they say, lie the bones of Mary Magdalene.

THE BONES OF VEZELAY

Yet the earliest trace of a legend placing Mary Magdalene in France says nothing about Provence at all; nor does it go back before the eleventh century. Rather it is a claim made in the 1050s by the great abbey church of **Vezelay in Burgundy** that it possessed her relics, an assertion supported by a papal document dated April 27, 1058.

The Muslim Arabs, who had invaded and occupied the entire Middle East during the seventh century, had recently been making it difficult for Europeans to undertake pilgrimages to the Holy Land, a factor which encouraged the development of pilgrimage sites within Europe itself. Various well-known New Testament figures were suddenly discovered to have travelled to the West and died there, their bones unearthed by enterprising churches. Glastonbury had already laid claim to Joseph of Arimathea in this way; in Paris was announced the discovery of the bones of St Denis, a convert and student of St Paul; while St James had turned up in Spain at Compostela, and St Mark had arrived at Venice.

Unfortunately the great ninth century Romanesque church at Vezelay had been dedicated to the Virgin Mary, but as she had bodily risen to heaven at her assumption, there was no question of finding her relics. But Vezelay lay along the profitable pilgrimage route from Germany to Compostela, and the profits to be gleaned from the passing trade, not to mention the prestige and the protection to be had, made the happy discovery of some suitable remains all but unavoidable. And who better than Mary Magdalene, the very essence of the redemptive power of the Church, both as witness to the crucifixion and the resurrection, and as a fallen woman saved by her submission to Jesus.

The shrine of **Mary Magdalene at Vezelay** became immensely popular, but how, the faithful wondered, had her bones come to Burgundy? A pious fiction was circulated saying that her relics had first been in Provence but were threatened by Saracen raiders, and so they were removed and brought to Vezelay for safekeeping. But how had the bones come to Provence in the first place? Another legend was invented to conveniently explain that Mary Magdalene and her companions had escaped from the Holy Land by sea and landed at Marseilles, or in an alternative version at Les Saintes-Maries-de-la-Mer, from where she made her way inland and died at St-Maximin-la-Ste-Baume. It was from there that a monk from Vezelay had dug up her bones and taken them back to Burgundy.

Mary Magdalene's bones were soon performing **miracles**; she was associated with the liberation of prisoners, assistance with fertility and childbirth, spectacular cures and even the raising of the dead. Such wonderful stories demanded yet wider circulation, a challenge taken up in the thirteenth century by the Dominican writer **Jacobus de Voragine**, the Dan Brown of his age. To his account of Mary Magdalene in his compendium of saints' lives called the **Legenda Aurea** (Golden Legend), he added the plethora of new miracles put about by Vezelay and produced what very quickly became a medieval bestseller that was soon translated from Latin into nearly every European language, including Dutch and Czech.

Meanwhile **King Charles of Anjou** (1226-85) was establishing a Mediterranean empire based on Naples, Sicily and his newly-acquired territory of Provence. Learning from the *Legenda Aurea* that Mary Magdalene's bones had originally been associated with **St-Maximin-la-Ste-Baume**, he went to have a look for himself. And what did he find? The bones of Mary Magdalene. Clearly the church at Vezelay had been mistaken. Charles installed the Dominican Order as caretakers of Mary's shrine, and they in turn proudly broadcast the importance of their mission by fabricating the **Book of Miracles of Saint Mary Magdalene**, documenting all the miraculous intercessions and cures the saint had wrought at her provençal sanctuary, a publication whose success was measured by the fact that Vezelay as a centre for the miraculous soon went into decline.

Indeed, still the pilgrims come to Les Saintes-Maries-de-la-Mer to see where Mary Magdalene came ashore and visit St-Maximin-la-Ste-Baume to kneel before her bones.

The Lost Goddess

But there are further stories still. To the claims of Vezelay and St-Maximin must be added those of Senigallia, near Ancona, which also possessed a body of Mary Magdalene, as did the church of St John Lateran in Rome and the church of St Lazarus in Constantinople. Abbeville in France claimed to have her skull and Aix-en-Provence her jaw. Cologne had two arms, Sicily another, Hainault yet one more, as well as Venice and Marseilles. Mary Magdalene's fingers were also widely distributed; the cathedral at Exeter possessed one until it was thrown away during the Reformation. There are many more examples, but also there may be some double-counting, as some say that the body in Rome was that which had previously been in Constantinople, which in turn had been brought from Ephesus at the end of the ninth century. But at **Ephesus** they disagree, for in addition to the tradition saying John the Evangelist settled there accompanied by the Virgin Mary, there is another saying that with them was Mary Magdalene, returning as you might expect to familiar company with Artemis and Cybele.

Gnosticism

EVIL AND COSMIC REDEMPTION

'"These are photocopies of the Nag Hammadi and Dead Sea scrolls, which I mentioned earlier", Teabing said. "The earliest Christian records. Troublingly, they do not match up with the gospels in the Bible."'

THE DA VINCI CODE [CHAPTER 58]

Teabing, rather oddly, shares a popular confusion over the Nag Hammadi finds (the Gnostic Gospels) and the Dead Sea scrolls. The **Dead Sea scrolls** are not Christian; they are the documents written in Hebrew and Aramaic of an ascetic sect of Jewish monastics known as the Essenes who lived at about the same time as John the Baptist and Jesus. The scrolls were found just thirteen miles east of Jerusalem in 1947, and they are directly relevant to Jewish studies; also they give us a glimpse of Jewish beliefs just at the time when Christianity was born, but to say that 'they do not match up with the gospels in the Bible' is to completely misunderstand what the Dead Sea scrolls are about.

The finds at **Nag Hammadi** in Upper Egypt in 1945 were not scrolls but rather **codices** (codex in the singular), that is, bound manuscript volumes. They are written in Coptic and date to about 350 AD, but were copied from Greek originals that date to the second century AD, though on either count they are far from being the earliest Christian records. Nevertheless these **Gnostic Gospels**, as they are known, are extremely important for the study of early Christianity, for until their discovery little was known of the

Gnostics except from the writings of their proto-orthodox opponents who branded them as heretics.

What can be described as the **proto-orthodox position** within early Christianity – that is the doctrine held by those who in the fourth century would become the victorious and therefore orthodox party – can be found in the New Testament letters of Paul and in the Gospels, particularly the Gospel of John. Together these could be read as affirming that **Jesus was divine**, that his crucifixion was followed by his **resurrection**, and that salvation lies in accepting this mystery via the **apostolic Church**, that is, the Church that gains its authority by claiming that its highest officials are the successors of Jesus's original apostles.

But as we have seen, there were other Christian views, such as that of Montanus and his followers, who claimed authority through the direct intervention of the Holy Spirit, which spoke through them as prophets, thus bypassing the apostolic hierarchy of the Church. **The Gnostics**, however, represented an even more profound divergence within early Christianity.

THE PROBLEM OF EVIL

The **existence of evil in God's world** posed a problem for early Christians. If there was only one God, and if God was the creator, and if God was good, how was it possible for there to be suffering, illness and death in his world?

In time Christians divided into two responses. On the one hand the **proto-orthodox Christians** said that it was man, not God, who had introduced evil into the world, and for this they generally put the blame on **Eve** for eating the fruit from the tree of knowledge of good and evil. A virtue of this argument was that it spoke of the great drama which found its resolution in this world. Here man had introduced evil, yes, but here Jesus had come to save him from his sins and give him eternal life. On the other hand were the **Gnostic Christians**. They lived round the shores of the Eastern Mediterranean, in Egypt, Syria, parts of Palestine, and perhaps in Asia Minor and even Greece. The Corinthians who caused Paul so much trouble may have shared some Gnostic beliefs. The Gnostics

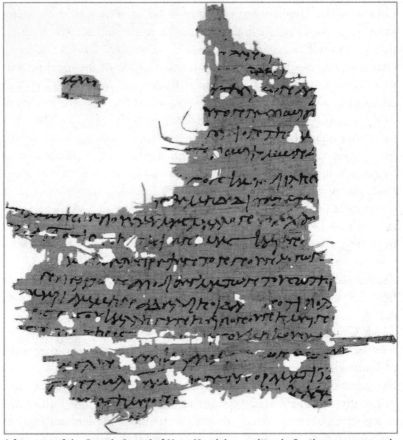

A fragment of the Gnostic Gospel of Mary Magdalene written in Coptic on papyrus and dating from the third century AD.

rejected the argument that evil originated with man; and going much further, they **rejected this world** utterly, saying it was the creation of an evil deity, the enemy of man.

THE GNOSTICS

Gnosis is the Greek word for knowledge, and it was their secret knowledge about how evil came into the world and how man could deliver himself from it that allowed the various Gnostic sects to challenge proto-orthodox Christian beliefs. One of the most prominent Gnostics was **Valentinus**, who flourished around 140 AD in Alexandria and Rome. He claimed to possess the true knowledge of how the world had been created and how evil had come into being, a story that he introduced to his followers in terms of a **cosmic myth**. He conceived of a primal God, the centre of a divine harmony, who sends out manifestations of himself in pairs of male and female. Each pair was inferior to its predecessor, and **Sophia**, the female of the thirtieth pair, was the least perfect of all. She showed her imperfection not, like the angel Lucifer, by rebelling against God, but by desiring too ardently to be united to him, so that she fell through love, and the universe is formed out of her agony and remorse. As she fell she bore a son, the **Demiurge**, who rules this world of sadness and confusion, yet is incapable of realizing anything beyond it.

The Gnostics are called **dualists** because of their belief in two worlds, the world of evil and decay inhabited by man, and the world of light where the primal God resides. But the Gnostics also knew the **secret of salvation**. At the moment of the cosmic blunder, sparks of the divine light, like slivers of shattered glass, became embedded in a portion of humankind. Therefore an aim of the Gnostics was to discover in those who were among **the elect** that inward spark which would lead them back to God.

Cosmic redemption, however, and not just personal salvation, was necessary because the whole of creation had been a mistake; it had nothing to do with God, who had never intended that there should be a universe and had never intended man. Creation was a defective work, and so man lived in a meaningless world or in the iron control of evil powers; in any case he was caught in the trap of the material world, which was sundered from the spirit of God.

Valentinus taught his followers that they could free themselves by attempting to quell their desires and by practising **sexual abstinence**. For in the polarity of the male and the female was mirrored the division, the duality, of the universe, so that the Last Judgement and the world's redemption would come – as Jesus says in the **Gnostic Gospel of the Egyptians** – 'when the two become one, and the male with the female, there being neither male nor female'.

The **crucifixion and resurrection** has no place in these Gnostic stories; instead the role of Jesus was to descend from the primal God and impart to his disciples the secret tradition of the gnosis.

JESUS, MARY MAGDALENE AND THE GNOSTICS

In *The Da Vinci Code* Dan Brown specifically mentions two of the Nag Hammadi finds, the **Gospel of Philip** and the **Gospel of Mary Magdalene**, in chapter 58. 'The Gospel of Philip', he has Teabing say, 'is always a good place to start' – the intention being to demonstrate that Jesus was married to Mary Magdalene.

> And the companion of the Saviour is Mary Magdalene. Christ loved her more than all the disciples and used to kiss her often on her mouth. The rest of the disciples were offended by it and expressed disapproval. They said to him, 'Why do you love her more than all of us?'

Sophie reads the passage and is surprised, but she notices that it says nothing about marriage. On the contrary, Teabing tells her smugly, pointing out that as any Aramaic scholar would know, 'companion' means spouse. But in fact the Gospel of Philip, like the other Nag Hammadi manuscripts, is written in **Coptic**. In any case, Gnostic writings are not conventional narratives; like the Gnostic creation myths with their dozens of descending divine pairs, and their abortion-universes, everything operates on an allegorical plane, so that the kisses on the mouth are the imparting of the gnosis.

Two pages along and Dan Brown is quoting from the Gospel of Mary Magdalene:

> And Peter said, 'Did the Saviour really speak with a woman without our knowledge? Are we to turn about and all listen to her? Did he prefer her to us?'
> And Levi answered, 'Peter, you have always been hot-tempered. Now I see you contending against the woman like an adversary.
> If the Saviour made her worthy, who are you indeed to reject her? Surely the Saviour knows her very well. That is why he loved her more than us.'

Dan Brown's purpose here is to reinforce Teabing's claim that Jesus and Mary Magdalene are married and that Peter is jealous at the preferential treatment he shows her. But he is also saying something much more. Teabing explains to Sophie that the stakes are far greater than winning Jesus's affection: 'Jesus suspects He will soon be captured and crucified. So He gives Mary Magdalene instructions on how to carry on His Church after He is gone'. Jesus is merely a mortal man, a prophet and a teacher, according to Dan Brown, and now as he faces the likelihood of an imminent death he passes the leadership of his Church to his wife – whereas the orthodox Gospel of Matthew (16:18) has Jesus say of Peter 'on this rock I will build my church'.

If the Gospel of Mary Magdalene is to be believed, Dan Brown is effectively saying, the the entire institution of the Church is built on a lie. But the lie is Dan Brown's, and deliberate, for he states that this passage describes a conversation between Jesus and Mary Magdalene before Jesus's death. In fact the Gospel of Mary Magdalene says the opposite: Jesus has already been crucified and he now appears to her after the resurrection – in other words, the Gospel of Mary Magdalene is saying that Jesus is divine.

Dan Brown seriously **misuses the Gnostic Gospels**. It is true that the Gnostics and the proto-orthodox Christians were opposed to one another, but the nature of that opposition was very different from what *The Da Vinci Code* claims. 'You're saying the Christian Church was to be carried on by a woman?', says Sophie Neveu. To which Teabing replies, 'That was the plan. Jesus was the original feminist'.

For one thing, the Gnostics were profoundly elitist. Only a few possessed the divine spark; for the rest, there was no salvation. For another, the Gnostics were unhappy about women; if proto-orthodox Christians preferred their women to be submissive, the Gnostics preferred that they were not women at all. One Gnostic gospel that Dan Brown does not cite is the **Gospel of Thomas**, where after another

Mary Magdalene, on the left, is shown telling the disciples of Jesus' resurrection. She was often known as the Apostle to the Apostles.

bout of contention between Peter and Mary Magdalene, Peter says to the disciples:

'Let Mary leave us, for women are not worthy of Life'. To which Jesus adds, 'I myself shall lead her, in order to make her male, so that she too may become a living spirit, resembling you males. For every woman who will make himself male will enter the Kingdom of Heaven'.

The bizarre logic behind this statement is consistent with the doctrine of dualism. There are two worlds, the one that we live in which is evil and an abortion; and the other world of light inhabited by the primal God along with the pre-selected few. That dualism is reflected in the difference between the sexes, the female who is 'not worthy of Life', and the male who alone can enter the Kingdom of Heaven.

In the Gospel of Mary Magdalene the text is not so explicit, but the sense is the same, as has been recognised by Karen L. King, professor of ecclesiastical history at Harvard University and a leading feminist interpreter of Christian literature. The Gospel of Mary, she says, 'expands our understanding of the dynamics of early Christianity, but it does not offer a voice that is beyond criticism. For example, the Gospel of Mary's rejection of the body as one's true self is highly problematic for contemporary feminism which affirms the dignity of the human body'.

In such remarks as Professor King's, we can see at least partly why Gnosticism eventually failed. By 150 AD it had spread all round the Mediterranean and threatened to defeat orthodox Christianity. But Gnosticism was pessimistic, esoteric and even more anti-social than proto-orthodoxy. It was not a creed that any society could adopt, and by the time of Constantine its vogue was over.

Constantine
and the Victory
of Orthodoxy

'The Bible is a product of *man*, my dear. Not of God. The Bible did not fall magically from the clouds. Man created it as a historical record of tumultuous times, and it has evolved through countless translations, additions and revisions. History has never had a definitive version of the book.'

THE DA VINCI CODE [CHAPTER 55]

Part of the appeal of *The Da Vinci Code* is the way it challenges certain assumptions and calls them into question, offering alternative notions of its own. But there is also a cheerful sloppiness about the way Dan Brown strings together people, places, incidents and ideas. It is the same technique he uses in throwing together symbols, or in rearranging the letters in words to create associations and meanings which may not be really there. Similarly *The Da Vinci Code* links together words like Rome and Roman Empire and Roman Catholic Church and Vatican and Pope, so that you almost begin to think that they were all in play at the same time or even amounted to the same thing. Before going any further, it is important to set the record straight.

WHO, WHAT, WHERE, WHEN?

The word 'catholic' means universal and all-embracing and was the word used to describe the **original Christian Church**. It was not the *Roman* Catholic Church, rather the univeral church, and it had five important centres: **Alexandria**, **Jerusalem**, **Antioch**, **Rome** and **Constantinople**. Each of these centres was the seat of a chief bishop or patriarch, sometimes called a pope. To this day the patriarch of Alexandria, who is head of the Egyptian (ie Coptic) Church, is called the pope.

Over time Jerusalem and Antioch declined, while Alexandria and Constantinople challenged one another for supremacy in the **East**, the victory ultimately going to Constantinople, while Rome exercised supreme authority in the **West**, where 'pope' became the familiar title of its chief bishops. A gradual estrangement developed between East and West, with a final breach occurring in **1054**, at which point the term **Catholic** became associated with Rome, **Orthodox** with Constantinople. The fall of Constantinople to the Turks in 1453 eliminated it as a rival to Rome, just as the Arab invasion of Egypt in 641 eliminated Alexandria as a rival to Constantinople.

The growing estrangement between the ecclesiastical authorities in Rome and Constantinople was not unconnected with the **division of the Roman Empire** in into eastern and western parts. This took place in 395 – nearly sixty years after the death of the **emperor Constantine (274-337)**, during whose reign the capital of the empire was Constantinople, not Rome. As for the **Vatican**, it became the official residence of the popes in Rome only in 1377. Therefore Dan Brown is wrong when referring to events during the reign of Constantine to talk about Rome and the Roman Empire and the Roman Catholic Church and the Vatican and the Pope as though they were all interrelated and in existence at the same time. But that is something Dan Brown routinely does throughout *The*

Da Vinci Code, as when he writes in chapter 55 that 'establishing Christ's divinity was critical to the further unification of the Roman empire and to the new Vatican power base. ... Now the followers of Christ were able to redeem themselves *only* via the established sacred channel – the Roman Catholic Church' – which even when leaving aside the issue of Jesus's divinity is a mishmash of historical nonsense.

The Roman Emperor Constantine the Great who legalised Christianity and presided over the Council of Nicaea in 325.

CONSTANTINE AND THE CHURCH

After Constantine defeated the last of his rivals in 323 AD to become sole ruler of the Roman Empire, his task was to weld its heterogeneous elements, both territorial and cultural, into a coherent unity. Rome had long been unsuitable as the capital of the empire as it was too distant from the far-flung imperial frontiers whose defence was the chief concern of emperors in command of their armies. Thus Constantine chose a spot exactly where Europe and Asia meet, the ancient city of **Byzantium**, which despite its commanding position on the Bosphorus had remained in the shadows of history since its founding in the seventh century BC. In November 326 Constantine personally paced out the line of the city's new defence walls, enclosing an area four times greater than that encompassed by its second century walls, and in May 330 at a dedication ceremony in the Hippodrome, **Nova Roma**, as he renamed Byzantium, was declared the new imperial capital.

Constantinople, the city of Constantine, as it at once became popularly known, was perfectly positioned for the strategic task confronting the empire, the defence of the Danube and the Euphrates frontiers. It also permitted the establishment of an effective civil service, for Rome, prey to its unruly mob and vulnerable in its need to import all its food, could no longer be a stable administrative capital. Moreover, the new capital stood astride the flow of goods and culture emanating from the East, that part of the empire richest in economic resources, most densely populated and the home of fertile intellectual and religious activity, whose great cities such as Alexandria and Antioch could rival Rome itself.

Earlier, in 313, Constantine had given **official recognition** to the **Christian Church**. Here again Constantinople was important, for while Rome's pagan traditions could not yet be disturbed, the new capital was consciously conceived as a Christian city, its patronage

This Byzantine mosaic over the narthex door of Haghia Sophia cathedral in Constantinople (Istanbul) shows the emperor Constantine (right) dedicating the city to Jesus and the Virgin in 330, and on the left the emperor Justinian (left), two centuries later, likewise dedicating the church of Haghia Sophia (Holy Wisdom).

ensuring that within a century Christianity would be established as the official religion of the state. It was a remarkable about-face from the time when the emperor Hadrian had written of the Christians in 134: 'As a race of men they are seditious, vain and spiteful; as a body, wealthy and prosperous, of whom nobody lives in idleness. Some blow glass, some make paper and others linen. Their one God is nothing peculiar; Christians, Jews and all nations worship him. I wish this body of men was better behaved'.

The Christians' preoccupation with salvation and their apparent detachment from the common and patriotic cause had long made them **scapegoats** at times of natural disaster, economic crisis and military setback. They were blamed when Rome burned in 64 AD during Nero's reign, the historian Tacitus explaining that they 'hate the human race'. Even so, the authorities preferred not to seek confrontation, and though Pliny the Younger, a Stoic who was governor of Bithynia in Asia Minor early in the second century, complained to the emperor Trajan about the 'depraved and extravagant superstition' of the Christians, the emperor instructed him that 'they are not to be hunted out'.

But the near collapse of the empire during the third century and the struggle to restore it corresponded with mounting **persecution**, most especially in the East, which reached a peak with the reign of the **emperor Diocletian** (284-305). Christians were ordered to sacrifice to the pagan gods and were massacred if they refused. At Antioch, martyrs were roasted over braziers; at Nicomedia in Asia Minor, while Diocletian was himself there, a number of servants in the royal household were discovered to be Christians and had 'many kinds of death invented against them', while the persecution reached its most awful climax in Egypt in 303, where hundreds of thousands were martyred in a final holocaust.

> So many were killed on a single day that the axe, blunted and worn out by the slaughter, was broken in pieces, while the exhausted executioners had to be periodically relieved. No sooner had the first batch been sentenced, than others from every side would jump on to the platform in front of the judge and proclaim themselves Christians. They paid no heed to torture in all its terrifying forms, but undaunted spoke boldly of their devotion to the God of the universe and with joy, laughter and gaiety received the final sentence of death.
>
> — **EUSEBIUS (AN EYEWITNESS), HISTORY OF THE CHURCH**

CONSTANTINE'S CONVERSION

At the **Battle of the Milvian Bridge** outside Rome in **312**, which gave Constantine control of the Roman Empire in the West, he had undergone some form of profound spiritual experience, comparable to Paul's on the road to Damascus, and if it did not mark his actual **conversion to Christianity** (he was baptised only on his deathbed in 337), from that moment he became 'god's man', as he called himself, and protector of his Christian subjects.

The following year, 313, he issued in Milan the **edict declaring toleration of Christianity**. 'Men now lost all fear of their former oppressors', wrote Eusebius, historian of the early church. 'Day after day they kept dazzling festival; light was everywhere, and men who once dared not look up greeted each other with smiling faces and shining eyes. They danced and sang in city and country alike, giving honour first of all to God our Sovereign Lord, as they had been instructed, and then to the pious emperor'.

If it was a cynical move by Constantine, as Dan Brown has his characters claim, it was a very popular one among Christians. Certainly, by allying himself with the Christians, Constantine won for himself the support of the strongest single group in the Roman world. Perhaps only one in seven of the empire's population were by then admitted Christians, but persecution had if anything enhanced their sense of solidarity. Well organised and admired for their charity towards the more needy among them, their influence extended further than their numbers suggested.

Constantine himself had previously been a follower of **Mithraism**, the worship of the Undying Sun, but its bloody rituals (initiates stood in a pit while a bull was sacrificed above their heads) had little appeal beyond the legions and none at all to women. Preaching equality of the individual soul and redemption through the death and resurrection of Jesus, Christianity could appeal to everyone: men and women, rich and poor, freemen and slaves.

ARGUMENT OVER THE DIVINE NATURE OF CHRIST

But no sooner was Christianity tolerated than it was threatened by doctrinal splits. The problem began in about 318 in Alexandria, where it was raised by **Arius**, a prominent priest. The argument was not, as claimed in *The Da Vinci Code*, over whether Jesus was divine or not – his divinity was almost universally agreed. Rather it concerned the **nature of that divinity**.

Christ is the *Son* of God, and so surely he is *younger* than God, argued Arius. The notion was appealing, for it brought Christ closer to mankind and emphasised his human nature. The proof of its comfort was the wide popularity of **Arianism** throughout most of the fourth century. But another Alexandrian, a deacon called **Athanasius**, saw a danger. If Christ was younger than God, so there must have been a time when Christ was not. This endangered the **unity of the godhead** – the Father, the Son and the Holy Spirit – and opened the way to regarding Christ's nature as being not of the same substance as God's and even being inferior to God's. Indeed, in time, Christ might be seen merely as a good man, as Unitarians and Muslims, or for that matter Dan Brown, see him today, while God would become less accessible and more remote. The counter-argument of Athanasius, which he fought for tenaciously all his life, was that **no distinction could be made between Christ and God**, for they were of the same substance.

THE COUNCIL OF NICAEA

In 321 a synod of Egyptian and Syrian bishops met in Alexandria and excommunicated Arius, but his views continued to gain ground. Seeing the Christians within his empire divided between the arguments of Arius and Athanasius, in 325 Constantine summoned and presided over the **First General Council of the Church at Nicaea** (now Iznik), not far from his intended capital of Nova Roma, or Constantinople.

Two hundred and twenty bishops were in attendance, from Egypt and Syria in the East to Italy and Spain in the West. The divine nature of Christ was argued from both the Arian and Athanasian points of view, and when the bishops voted on the issue, it was decided in favour of Athanasius by 218 votes to two – not the 'relatively close vote' claimed in *The Da Vinci Code*. This **Nicene Creed** became the official position of the universal Church and remains the creed of both the Roman and Orthodox Churches to this day.

THE NICENE CREED

Here is the text of the Creed as originally passed by the Council of Nicaea in 325. The final paragraph is specifically directed against the Arians.

'*We believe in one God, the Father Almighty, maker of all things, both visible and invisible.*

'*And in one Lord, Jesus Christ, the Son of God, begotten of the Father God of God and Light of Light, very God of very God, begotten and not made, being of one substance with the Father, by whom all things were made; who for us men and for our salvation came down and was made flesh, made man, suffered and rose again on the third day, went up into the heavens and is to come again to judge the quick and the dead;*

'*And in the Holy Spirit;*

'*But the Holy Catholic and Apostolic Church anathematises those who say that there was a time when the Son of God was not, and that he was not before he was begotten, and that he was made from that which did not exist; or who assert that he is of other substance or essence than the Father, or is susceptible of change.*'

The Council of Nicaea was a political victory for Constantine. Presiding over its procedings in the guise of both supreme and spiritual authority, his position was much enhanced, not only as Roman emperor but as the newly acclaimed **'thirteenth apostle'**. Constantine became Jesus Christ's vice-regent on earth, and his empire took on a sanctity and a mission that would give it the resilience to survive in the East for more than a thousand years to come. That coalescence of Roman authority, Hellenistic culture and the transcendental spirit of the East that we now call the **Byzantine Empire** first began with the twin events of the Council of Nicaea and the founding of Constantinople, which he dedicated on May 11 330: 'O Christ, Ruler and Master of the World, to You now I dedicate this subject City, and these Sceptres, and the Might of Rome, Protector, save her from all harm'.

EDITING THE BIBLE

The Council was also a victory for **Athanasius**, who on his return from Nicaea became patriarch of Alexandria. Once Christianity was tolerated by the state early in the fourth century and was set fair to becoming the official state religion by the century's end, so domination not only by Christianity over paganism but by one Christian tendency over the others became a realisable ambition and attracted the energies of the politically adept, men of intellectual ability and unstoppable determination like Athanasius.

For all the importance that must be granted to the development of a Church hierarchy and its alliance with the most supreme of patrons, the Roman emperor, the real and most lasting triumph of orthodoxy would lie in establishing the **canon of sacred literature**, that is, the **New Testament** as it is unquestioningly accepted today. Christianity is divided into numerous dominations, each with their own hierarchies, some of whom will hardly talk to others, and yet they all share the New Testament. It is read by people around the world and is widely accepted as inspired Scripture, directly or indirectly the word of God. The **27 books** of the New Testament

Jesus is shown enthroned in the heavens surrounded by the creatures of the Apocalypse in this early Coptic painting.

serve as the basis on which hundreds of millions of people conduct their lives and frame their attitudes. Yet as Dan Brown rightly has Sir Leigh Teabing say, 'The Bible did not arrive by fax from heaven'.

In fact the New Testament canon was first set out in **367** by Athanasius in an annual letter sent round to all the Egyptian church-es under his jurisdiction, saying 'in these alone the teaching of god-liness is proclaimed. Let no one add to these; let nothing be taken away from them'. Three hundred years had passed since Paul had first written to the Corinthians and others, and since the authors of those gospels attributed to Matthew, Mark, Luke and John had set down their reminiscences and beliefs concerning Jesus. During the course of those centuries other gospels had been written and had circulated widely, among them the **Nag Hammadi Gospels**, which were hidden away in a sealed jar and placed in a cave overlooking the Nile in Upper Egypt, probably by monks from a nearby monastery, at just about the time Athanasius was instructing his churches as to what was and was not part of the canon.

The Church's accommodation with the Roman Empire ushered in an age of confidence, stability and, above all, order. But it was not Constantine or any other Roman functionary who established what was deemed canonical, nor even was it Athanasius. Rather there had been a long fermenting of Christian beliefs, many arguments and disputes, and people had taken sides. More had taken the side of the proto-orthodox party, those who since the time of Paul had declared that Jesus was God, had died on the cross and had risen on the third day. No council was ever called to set its seal on Athanasius's selection of canon scripture; rather, they are ratified even to this day by consensus. There were some, like those monks at Nag Hammadi, who instead of burning their gospels of Thomas, Philip and Mary Magdalene, put them aside until the climate changed. Except it never changed.

The Holy Grail

THE CRUSADES, KNIGHTS TEMPLAR AND GNOSTIC SURVIVALS

'When Christianity came along, the old pagan religions did not die easily.
Legends of chivalric quests for the lost Grail were in fact
stories of forbidden quests to find the lost sacred feminine. Knights who
claimed to be "searching for the chalice" were speaking in code as a way to
protect themselves from a Church that had subjugated women, banished the
Goddess, burned nonbelievers and forbidden the pagan reverence for the
sacred feminine.'

THE DA VINCI CODE [CHAPTER 56]

I n 395, after the time of Constantine, the **Roman Empire** was divided into eastern and western halves. In 476 the empire in the West fell to Germanic invaders, but it continued in the East, still calling itself Roman though its capital was Constantinople, an Eastern Christian state Greek in language and culture, usually known to us today as the **Byzantine Empire**.

In the early seventh century in the obscurity of Arabia a man called **Mohammed** announced himself as the prophet of God and united the Arabian tribes by a combination of warfare and faith. Within a decade of his death at Mecca in 632, the whole of the Middle East, until then Christian and part of the Byzantine Empire, had fallen to Arab armies afire with the faith of **Islam**. North Africa and Egypt and Palestine were lost, but the Byzantines held on to Asia Minor and recovered portions of Syria. Then new armies appeared from the East, this time Seljuk Turks who also were Muslim, and they not only occupied Syria but invaded deep into Asia Minor. Also in Egypt and up into Palestine the Fatimid sultan al-Hakim was carrying out pogroms against the Jews and Christians.

The Crusades

Various events, including al-Hakim's widespread destruction of churches in the Holy Land, the harrassment of pilgrims and the Byzantines' appeal for help against the Seljuks, prompted **Pope Urban II** at Clermont-Ferrand on November 27, 1095 to call for a **crusade to restore Christian authority in the East** and most particularly to **reclaim Jerusalem**.

After marching across Europe the Crusader armies arrived in the spring of **1097 at Constantinople**, their numbers between 60,000 and 100,000, almost all French and including a large proportion of rabble and non-combatants. Fighting their way across Turkish-occupied Asia Minor, they came to **Antioch** in Syria that autumn. The Byzantines had recaptured Antioch in the tenth century and had lost it to the Turks only in 1085. Now it was in the hands of a Seljuk vassal. Laying siege to the city, the Crusaders finally took it in June 1098, by which time fighting, disease, famine and defections had greatly reduced their numbers.

Antioch was left in the possession of **Bohemond**, and in January 1099 the remainder of the army set out for **Jerusalem** under the command of **Raymond de Saint-Gilles**, Count of Toulouse. Passing down the Orontes valley, then through the Homs Gap to

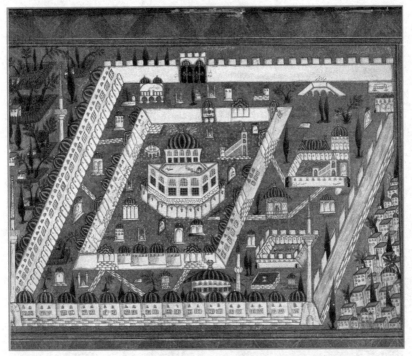

The Dome of the Rock mosque was built on the Temple Mount, once the site of Solomon's temple. The area gave its name to the Knights Templar who were quartered in the vicinity.

the Mediterranean coast, the army continued southwards through Tripoli, Beirut, Sidon and Tyre to near Jaffa, from where it wound up through the Judaean hills, arriving before the walls of Fatamid-held Jerusalem on June 7 1099. The Crusaders' numbers now were about 12,000 foot soldiers and 1200 or so mounted knights, in addition to numerous camp followers. On July 15, Jerusalem fell in a fury of bloodlust, its Muslim and Jewish inhabitants slain (the latter because they were thought to have helped the former), an event that shocked the world, both East and West.

The First Crusade created three Latin (ie Frankish or Western) enclaves in the East, the **County of Edessa** (present-day Urfa in Turkey), the **Principality of Antioch**, and the **Kingdom of Jerusalem**, none adjoining another. These were augmented by the creation of the **County of Tripoli**, so that by 1144 there was a continuous belt of Crusader states running from Cilicia and Edessa in Asia Minor down to Eilat on the Gulf of Aqaba. But in 1144 Edessa fell to the Muslims, prompting **St Bernard** to preach the **Second Crusade** in **1146** at the great abbey-church at Vézelay with its famous relics of Mary Magdalene.

Some went by sea, but those who went by land through Asia Minor suffered heavy losses. The attempt to recapture Edessa was abandoned, and an attack on Damascus proved a failure. These setbacks dampened enthusiasm in the West, and the defence of the Latin states was now left primarily in their own hands. Their

Young noblemen wanting to prove their valour and fulfill their religious obligations eagerly joined the Templars. Their original task was to protect the pilgrimage routes.

numbers being few, they relied increasingly on formidable castles, such as Margat, Saone and Krak des Chevaliers, all in Syria, which were usually manned by autonomous orders of knights, the **Hospitallers** and the **Templars**.

THE PRIORY OF SION

The Da Vinci Code gives conflicting accounts of the purpose of the Crusades. On the one hand they were intended to destroy records proving the bloodline of Jesus, while on the other hand **Godefroi de Bouillon**, who is described as the leader of the First Crusade and a king of France, wants to find the documents that make up the Holy Grail to prove that the blood of Jesus runs through his family's veins. To this end he founds the **Priory of Sion**, which in turn establishes the **Knights Templar**, who are not really in the Holy Land to protect pilgrims, but rather to dig away at the Temple site, looking for the **grail papers**.

There are several problems with this account. First, Godefroi was not the leader of the First Crusade, nor was he a French king. But he was a French duke, and he was offered and accepted the position of **Advocatus Sancti Sepulchri** – Defender of the Holy Sepulchre – which effectively made him king of Jerusalem, a position taken in both spirit and name by his brother **Baldwin** when Godefroi died soon after he arrived in 1100. A further difficulty is that nineteen years would then have passed between his death and the **founding of the Templars in 1119**. And that event did not take place during the Second Crusade in the reign of Baldwin II, as Baldwin died in 1131 and the Second Crusade did not arrive in the East until 1148.

But the chief problem with this is that there was **no such thing as the Priory of Sion** at the time of the Crusades. The Priory is a nonsense invented by a disagreeable little French fascist called **Plantard** in the **1950s**. As any sort of organisation has to be registered with the government in France, Plantard registered his – as a social club, though it was never very social as he was the only member. But then the claim was made that papers purporting to trace various genealogies supporting the Jesus bloodline thesis had been 'discovered' at the Bibliothèque Nationale in Paris, where they are catalogued as **les Dossiers Secret** under Number 4º 1m1 249. But a surrealist who was in on the plot with Plantard has admitted to planting the dossier as a joke. Needless to say the **list of Grand Masters** of the priory is likewise bogus, meaning that you have to strike Leonardo da Vinci, Sandro Botticelli, Sir Isaac Newton, Victor Hugo, and all the others, right down to Jean Cocteau, from membership. Which rather puts paid to *The Da Vinci Code*'s '**Fact:**' **statement** preceding the novel, where it is stated that the Priory, founded in 1099, is a real organization, and that *les Dossiers Secrets* identify these members.

THE TEMPLARS

The two great **orders of knights militant** in the Holy Land were the **Knights Hospitaller** and **Knights Templar**. The Hospitallers derived their name from the Hospital of St John in Jerusalem, where their original function was to care for Christian pilgrims, but by the 1130s they had taken on military duties. A similar military order, the Templars, taking their name from their headquarters in the Temple quarter of Jerusalem, had been founded in about 1119, its original duty to protect the pilgrimage routes. Both Templars and Hospitallers received donations of property in Europe which soon made them wealthy, while young men of noble families seeking to fulfill the moral and religious obligations of knighthood rushed to their standards.

Very quickly the undermanned and under-financed Crusader states were selling or giving **frontier strongholds** to the Orders, the

Hospitallers defending the narrow waist of coastline at Baniyas from the heights of Margat and manning castles in the Bekaa Valley and the Homs Gap, including Krak des Chevaliers, and the Templars undertaking the defence of the passes through the Amanus mountains north of Antioch and the coast around modern-day Tartus in Syria, or Tortosa as it was known in Crusader times.

The Templars' walled city of **Tortosa**, with its magnificent early Gothic Cathedral of Our Lady, was the last Crusader toe-hold on the Levant mainland, apart from Château Pelerin in modern-day Israel. Tortosa was abandoned by the knights on August 3, 1291 and Château Pelerin a few days later, though the Templars clung to the offshore island of **Arwad** for eleven years longer. As the Templars made the crossing to Arwad and looked back along the receding mainland, the devastation was already beginning. For some months after the fall of Tortosa, Mameluke troops laid waste to the coastal plain. Orchards were cut down and irrigation systems wrecked, while native Christians fled into the mountains behind. Anything that might have been of value to the Crusaders should they ever attempt another landing was destroyed.

Muslim bitterness towards the Crusades was matched by recriminations in Europe. With the Mameluke seizure of Arwad in 1302, the Templars became little better than refugees in Cyprus, France and elsewhere. Soon they became hunted men. Their purpose had been the defence of the Holy Land, yet in 1291 they had lost, as well as Tortosa, Christendom's last great stronghold of **Acre** in present-day Israel. They had, however, grown powerful and wealthy – far more so than the Hospitallers, for the Templars had long been the chief **money-lenders** in the East, a role that won them many enemies among the Christians, even as it earned them Muslim friends.

The interest many Templars took in **Muslim learning and religion**, and perhaps in some of the **heterodox cults** which then as now found a home in Syria, helped fan the rumours that their Order

Tried and condemned for heresy, the last of the Templars were burnt at the stake in 1314. As the chief money-lenders in the East they became very wealthy but also made many enemies at home.

conducted secret, obscene and blasphemous initiation rites which obliged entrants to deny Christ, his crucifixion, the Virgin and sometimes God, to spit on the cross, to worship cats and idols, and to kiss each other on the buttocks and the penis. In October 1307 **King Philip IV** of France arrested and charged the Templars there with **heresy**, and a year later Cyprus followed suit. Under torture, most of the knights confessed, though many retracted later, and not one was willingly prepared to be martyred for his supposed beliefs, unlike the early Christians or the Cathars who were their contemporaries. In 1312 the **Pope suppressed their Order** and granted their property to the Hospitallers, and in Paris, two years later, the **Templar Grand Master Jacques de Molay** was burnt at the stake.

Europe was scandalised by the affair; many European rulers, as well as the educated and literate population, were unconvinced of the Templars' guilt and suspected that the case had more to do with King Philip's greed. Two-thirds of the Templars' properties lay within the territory of the French monarchy and were located in rich agricultural regions or on the vital and prosperous trade routes to the Mediterranean. Altogether they represented a very rich prize. The trial of the Templars is unlikely to have been about more than that, unless there was something going on about the penis and the cat.

Gnostic Survivals in the East

Mountains have always been a refuge for **heterodox cults** because the authorities, representing the dominant religious tendency, are usually unable to enforce their will in remote places. One of the great refuges of heterodox cults are the mountains along the Mediterranean coast of **Syria, Lebanon and Israel**. Here the **Druze**, the **Alawis** and the **Ismailis** can be found.

THE ISMAILIS

Unlike the Druze and the Alawis, whom many Muslims deny are part of Islam, the **Ismailis**, though extremely heterodox, are accepted as Muslims even though they subscribe to the **dualist belief**, shared by the Christian Gnostics, that there are two separate worlds, one which is good and the other, the world we inhabit, which is evil. Those Ismailis who live in Syria for the most part inhabit the southern end of the Jebel al-Sariya. Among local orthodox Sunni Muslims the Ismailis have a reputation for **worshipping women**, with every female child born on the twenty-seventh day of the Muslim month of Ragab held to be an incarnation of the divinity.

Such a girl-child is called the **Rozah**, and while the Ismailis read the Koran, they also are said to have other sacred books, one of which is in praise of the Rozah, eulogising every part of her body. This aspect of their heterodox belief appears to be a survival from the traditions of **Astarte worship**, and beyond that to the much older veneration of a universal mother goddess.

THE DRUZE

The **Druze** trace the origins of their faith to the Cairo-based **Fatimid caliph al-Hakim** (died 1021), whose behaviour was erratic, to say the least. The Fatimids, who were Muslims of the Shia sect, had shown themselves tolerant of other religions, and the caliph himself was born of a Greek Orthodox mother and raised by Christians. But suddenly al-Hakim reacted against his early influences, and in the course of ten years, from 1004 to 1014, he ordered the destruction of thirty thousand churches in Egypt, Palestine and Syria, including the **Church of the Holy Sepulchre in Jerusalem**, an outrage that became a contributory cause of the Crusades. Jews were similarly dealt with.

Then the persecutions stopped, al-Hakim instead outraging his co-religionists by allowing himself to be proclaimed divine by his follower **Mohammed ibn Ismael al-Darazi** in 1016. While restoring freedom of worship to Christians and Jews, the caliph forbade Muslims to fast at Ramadan or undertake the pilgrimage to Mecca, and substituted his own name for that of Allah in the mosque prayers. As the fury of Cairo's Muslims turned against al-Hakim, and the caliph in turn burnt half the city to the ground, claiming the assistance of Adam and Solomon in angel guise as he lopped off the heads of the well-to-do, al-Darazi fled to Lebanon where he founded the Druze sect in his own name.

Al-Hakim's departure from this world is cloaked in mystery. Each night in the company of a mute slave he would ride a donkey in the Moqattam Hills outside Cairo to observe the stars for portents or possibly for souls. One dawn in 1021 he failed to return, some historians suspecting he was assassinated by his ambitious sister Sitt al-Mulk, whom he was threatening to bed. The Druze, believing al-Hakim to be a manifestation of the divine, say that he did not die but underwent **ghayba**, a concealment from the world, and that he will return as their messiah. This belief is similar to that of the Gnostics who attached no significance to the resurrection, their argument being that Jesus as a divinity gave only the appearance of dying on the cross. Also Gnostic in inspiration is their belief that emanations of divine principles are made incarnate in the higher levels of the Druze hierarchy, which may also explain the origin of their belief in reincarnation.

Many Muslims say that the Druze are not Muslims at all but are a departure from Islam, with which they have no more than a historical link. The Druze reject much of Sharia, that is, the canon law of Islam. They assemble on Thursdays, not Fridays, and non-Druze are forbidden to enter their places of worship. Their sect is secretive, with several stages of initiation in which guidance towards **divine enlightenment** is given as the will of al-Hakim.

They are monogamous and will marry only fellow Druze. Obedient to their elders and tightly knit, they have been remarkably successful in preserving their identity against outside pressures. Twenty years after the death of al-Hakim, entry to their sect was closed, and they believe that their numbers have remained the same every since. There are perhaps 600,000 Druze, living chiefly in southern Lebanon but also in Syria and Israel, while some have emigrated to the United States.

At one time the blue eyes and fair hair of many Druze gave rise to the fanciful European belief that these must be the descendants of Crusaders, notwithstanding that their sect came into being seventy years or more before the First Crusade. Nevertheless, many Druze women wear costumes straight out of troubadour times. They do not veil their faces, but instead they wear wimples beneath high conical headdresses, while from long tight bodices, which give charm and slenderness to their figures, their brilliantly coloured voluminous skirts gracefully sweep the ground. It may be that their style influenced medieval Europe rather than vice versa. The older men, the **Initiates**, wear a white turban and are often magnificently moustached. Perhaps too these Initiates influenced the Crusaders who encountered them in the East, planting Gnostic notions in them which they carried back to Europe.

THE ALAWIS

The northern end of Syria's coastal mountains, the Jebel al-Sariya, is the home of the **Alawis**. Their name reflects their belief that Ali, the son-in-law of Mohammed the Prophet, was an emanation of God. They are an extremely heterodox variant of **Shia Islam**, and there are many Muslims who do not accept that they are Muslims at all.

Alawi religious practice has been variously described as including elements of **Pheonician paganism**, **Babylonian star-worship** (they are said to believe that the Milky Way is made up of the deified souls of true believers), **Ismailism** and **Christian Gnosticism**. The early twentieth-century English traveller and Arabist Gertrude Bell reported what she had been told by an orthodox Sunni qadi of Homs: 'Some of them pretend to worship Ali and some worship the sun. They believe that when they die their souls pass into the bodies of other men or even animals, as it is in the faiths of India and China.'

Typically, ill is spoken of that which is not understood, and in fact no one can be entirely sure of Alawi beliefs and practices, for they worship in secret, meeting at night in secluded places. It is said that they celebrate certain Christian holidays, including Christmas and

Easter, though in their own way, and that they perform a Mass-like ceremony which includes a reference to 'body and blood' being 'eternal life'. **Initiates** ascend through three stages to the inner knowledge of the sect, often also joining the ruling oligarchy of the community, which is dominated by clans. The rest of the community constitute the uninitiated mass, among which, unlike the Druze, are women, who can never be initiates and who indeed are not credited with having souls (one of the downsides of Gnosticism if you are a feminist).

The Alawis, being a small ethnic group, perhaps originating as a south Arabian tribal people who mingled with the local population, have relied on their clan solidarity and the mountain fastnesses of coastal Syria to fashion a cult from every religion they have come into contact with over the past two thousand years, whether paganism, Christianity or Islam, even while professing the dominant religion of the times in order to escape persecution.

The Egyptian Mameluke sultan Baybars forced the Alawis to build mosques in their villages, but he could not force them to pray in them. Instead, they used the buildings as stables for their cattle and beasts of burden. Nor did the Ottomans have greater success, and they allowed them to enjoy a certain geographical toleration, the toleration of necessity accorded to people living in remote mountain areas. That also meant, however, that the Alawis were excluded, far more than Christians, from all important official and professional positions in Syria. Comprising about six per cent of the Syrian population (and found also in Lebanon and Turkey), they remained an almost entirely peasant people with no hope of advancement.

Exclusion turned out to be the making of them. Impoverished and denied other routes of advancement, Alawis joined newly independent Syria's armed forces in disproportionate numbers, and through a series of coups have since the 1960s supplanted the majority Sunnis as the holders of military and political power, their exceptional communal solidarity helping them to maintain their dominance in a country of religious and ethnic factions. The late Syrian dictator **Hafez Assad** was an Alawi. As an air force general he overthrew the civilian government and installed himself as president. His son, a one-time ophthalmologist at London's Queen Mary Hospital in Paddington (the hospital to which the wounded Bishop Aringarosa is taken in *The Da Vinci Code*), assumed the presidency on his father's death. The new president's British-born wife, who was educated at Queens College, Harley Street, a top private girls' school, is of Syrian descent and is likewise an Alawi. This seems very much a case of crypto-Gnostics not only surviving but flourishing.

Gnostic Survivals in the West

Whereas the East was a hothouse of heterodoxy where all sorts of weird religious ideas and cults flourished, often of a dualist kind, there was far less of it in the West, where **religious nonconformity** tended to be spontaneously Montanist, with charismatics hopping up and down asserting some directly received divine truth.

One incident recorded in **sixth century France** tells of a small army of men and women advancing on the bishopric at **Le Puy** in the Upper Loire; their leader announced himself as Christ, and all of them were naked and doing somersaults. This was all very well when only small numbers were involved, but armies of people feeding on the Holy Spirit tended to think of social structures as corrupt, including the Church itself, and were liable to get out of hand and smash things up. In this case the Christ-leader was killed on the spot and his female companion, called Mary, was tortured until the devil popped out. In later centuries people like these would be directed eastwards on a crusade. Yet that remedy soon proved dangerous too, as all too often Crusaders returned from the East infected with some elaborate gnostic belief.

BOGOMILS AND CATHARS

The **Bogomils** in the **Balkans** were dualists who some trace back to the Gnostics of Egypt with their belief that only a portion of oneself came from God, while the material world and all its acts was evil, so that marriage, procreation, meat, work and possessions were renounced so far as possible, as was the Church and its preachings about the cross, which the Bogomils rejected because they saw the cross only as the instrument of Jesus's torment.

Bogomil means *Loved Ones* or *Friends of God*, and as in Syria they found refuge and freedom in the mountains, but only for a while. Their rejection of the Church invited a vicious reaction from the authorities, who despatched thousands of soldiers and priests into the mountain regions, where they plundered, burnt and killed everything in their path. In this the Bogomils were different to the dualists of the East, who adapted their colouring to the prevailing religion while keeping to their secret inner faith. But not Gnosticism in Europe, which stood by the logic of its conviction that if this world was evil, there could be no compromise with it. Meanwhile, even as they were being exterminated, their heresy spread westward during the eleventh century, principally taking root in southern France, where the Gnostics went under the name of Cathars, the pure ones.

The **Cathars** were numerous and well-organised in southern France, where they elected bishops, collected funds and distributed money to the poor. The ideal of renunciation was obviously impractical for everyone, and while most lived outwardly normal lives, only a very few lived the strict life of the **perfecti**, abstaining from eggs, milk, meat and women (again the Gnostic lack of tolerance for women), also denying the Trinity and rejecting the Church.

By 1200 the heresy had become so widespread that the papacy was alarmed and in 1209 a crusade was launched against them – it was called the **Albigensian Crusade**, as so many Cathars lived around Albi – and an **Inquisition** was introduced. In that year the core of Cathar resistance withdrew to the castle of **Montségur** atop a great domed hill in the eastern Pyrenees, where they withstood assaults and sieges until capitulating in 1244. Some two hundred still refused to abjure their errors, were bound together within a stockade below the castle and were set ablaze on a huge funeral pyre.

The last of the Cathars, who were the heirs of Gnosticism in the East, sought refuge from their persecutors in the castle of Monségur in the French Pyrenees.

The Holy Grail

The Grail was invented in the mid-twelfth century by the writer **Chrétien de Troyes**. No mention of a grail had ever been made before. Chrétien was not only the inventor of the Grail but of **Arthurian literature** as we know it today, those tales of knights and ladies and of courtly romance.

There was nothing necessarily holy about Chrétien's grail; he did not write about it as the cup or chalice at the Last Supper, nor did he give it any other religious association. For that matter he did not describe it as a cup or chalice at all, but rather as a **serving dish**, which is the usual and original meaning of the Old French word *graal*. But there is something wonderful about the grail's first appearance in the pages of Chrétien's story at the beginning of a rich man's feast, and all the more wonderful and strange because Chrétien never finished what he began, so we do not know what the secret of the grail was meant to be.

This is how the grail makes its first appearance on the page:

> Then two other squires entered holding in their hands candelabra of pure gold, crafted with enamel inlays. The young men carrying the candelabra were extremely handsome. In each of the candelabra there were at least ten candles burning. A maiden accompanying the two young men was carrying a grail with her two hands; she was beautiful, noble, and richly attired. After she had entered the hall carrying the grail the room was so brightly illumined that the candles lost their brilliance like stars and the moon when the sun rises.

> *Arthurian Romances* (Penguin, London 1991)

What is tantalising about this appearance of the grail is that **Perceval**, the hero of the romance, knows exactly what it is, but he fails to tell us before the story breaks off (when Chrétien dies). Is the story allegorical? People have argued over that point for more than eight hundred years. And if allegorical, is the allegory religious? That too has never been resolved. But what we do know is that the appearance of this mysterious and haunting image was soon

This medieval illustration shows King Arthur and the Knights of the Round Table. At the centre is the Holy Grail.

inspiring writers to try their hands at completing the original story or writing new ones – and in the process inventing the prose romance genre which evolved over the centuries into the modern novel. So no grail, no *The Da Vinci Code*.

Chrétien de Troyes was writing when medieval Western society, so attached to its tradition, was opening onto a wider world, the world of the Mediterranean, the world of the East, to worlds of ideas and beliefs that it was discovering or rediscovering, not least on account of the **Crusades**. Writing about the grail meant writing about this **cultural and spiritual quest**, and yet strangely it has always been a genre, regardless of its religious overtones, that has belonged to **secular writers**, never to the Church. And so, free from doctrine and canon, the Grail has been endlessly reinvented down to the present time.

The Grail legend was first introduced to a wide range of English readers by **Sir Thomas Malory**, who drew the chapters of his **Morte d'Arthur** from the mass of French Arthurian romance and gave it epic unity. Malory was an English knight born about 1400 of an old Warwickshire family. He served in the French wars under **Richard Beauchamp**, Earl of Warwick, who was recognised throughout all Europe as embodying the knightly ideal of the age, and it is probably because of his close association with Beauchamp that Malory developed his enthusiam for chivalry.

Certainly it was Malory's admiration for **chivalrous ideals**, combined with the noble rhythm and simplicity of his prose, that have given the Morte d'Arthur such an enduring place in English literature. Malory died in 1471, and fourteen years passed before the *Morte d'Arthur* was published by the first English printer William Caxton. The event and the date were significant alike, for 1485 has become conventionally accepted as the **end of the Middle Ages** in England, and as the Grail romance passed through the printing press, so a new age had begun.

THE GRAIL IN MODERN TIMES

Interest in the legend of the Holy Grail revived at the beginning of yet another age, in the **nineteenth century** when the Industrial Revolution seemed to have altered and destroyed so much of Britain's past. As if in compensation there was a sudden revival in all things medieval, including architecture, painting and literature. The poet **Tennyson** and the artists of the **Pre-Raphaelite Brotherhood** drew heavily on Malory for their Arthurian inspiration. The death of Arthur and his passage to Avalon, a world of mysterious and enchanting ladies, the flawless **Sir Galahad and his search for the Holy Grail** were among the favourite subjects of the Pre-Raphaelites. William Morris was a guiding spirit of the Pre-Raphaelites, and his wife Jane was the model for his painting of **Guinevere**, a sensual beauty with long dark waving hair and melancholy eyes, an image repeated with variations in the paintings of the Brotherhood, not least by **Dante Gabriel Rossetti**, who was having an affair with Morris' wife.

Originally in Chrétien de Troyes and Sir Thomas Malory, the Holy Grail had symbolised an unattainable object of desire, but by the twentieth century it came to represent the **perfect object or solution**, material rather than ethereal, something that was attainable with any luck. An early example came from the pen of William Thomas Stead, an Englishman who crusaded for peace and spiritualism and went down with the Titanic, and who wrote of the characters in his 1894 novel *If Christ Came to Chicago* that 'the quest of the Almighty Dollar is their Holy Grail'.

Then towards the end of the twentieth century the Grail concept took on a life entirely independent of literature or of historical context, as in **physics** where the search for a unified theory has recently been described as the Holy Grail, or in **mathematics** where the solution of the Riemann hypothesis, which would explain the apparently

The Attainment of the Grail, a tapestry by the Pre-Raphaelite artist Sir Edward Burne-Jones, reflects the nineteenth-century revival of interest in the Arthurian romances.

random pattern of prime numbers, has likewise been described as the Holy Grail – because random prime numbers are the key to internet cryptography, and anyone cracking the code would gain unlimited access to online banking and credit card transactions. Indeed as one Oxford mathematician told *The Guardian* on 28 October 2004, 'Most mathematicians would trade their soul with Mephistopheles for a proof'. Also, in the world of **computing** there are at least five 'languages' or applications whose acronym is GRAIL.

Indeed 'Holy Grail' has become an increasingly frequent buzz phrase in the past ten years or so, as a search for it through online newspaper archives reveals. *The Washington Post* now annually uses the phrase six times more than it did twenty years ago; *The Times* of London uses it twelve times more than fifteen years ago; and in *The New York Times* its frequency has increased by five times in five years.

Perhaps what lies behind this newfound popularity of the phrase has been the rise in the late 1970s and the 1980s of the **fantasy film genre** which only really work if they are built on coherent secondary worlds – which happens to be exactly how the Pre-Raphaelites depicted the Middle Ages, as an idealised romantic time, a coherent world of fantasy. In such films as *Excalibur*, *Robin Hood*, *Sword of the Valiant* and *First Knight*, the female lead has many features in common with the ideal Pre-Raphaelite woman – in fact they all look just like the sensual and enigmatic Jane Morris with those wonderful eyes. And then of course there have been films like *Monty Python and the Holy Grail* (1975), a low-budget but immensely successful search for the Grail during which many very silly obstacles are encountered, and *Indiana Jones and the Last Crusade* (1989) in which the hero's search for the Holy Grail is complicated by the Nazis' interest in the same prize. The teenagers who enjoyed those films have grown up to be the brain surgeons, physicists, journalists and indeed bestselling thriller writers of today, and they put the phrase around.

How else to explain this usage from *The Guardian* in 2002, that 'Nude tights are something of a holy grail' (notice the lower case letters), or again from the same paper a year earlier: 'One day in 1997, Kim Cattrall received a script for *Sex And The City*. Darren Star, the producer, wanted her to audition for the role of Samantha, a premier-league slapper who chases blokes around Manhattan looking for the holy grail of the Modern Miss – an enormous willy ("Ding ding ding, jackpot!" she says when she finds it)'.

Leonardo da Vinci

L eonardo da Vinci (1452–1519) is the principal historical character in *The Da Vinci Code* and – Dan Brown's own art notwithstanding – probably accounts for much of the novel's global appeal. There is simply no other artist like Leonardo. His *Mona Lisa* in the Louvre is the world's most iconic painting; his fresco of *The Last Supper*, even in its ruinous state, is one of a half dozen key images of Christian art; his pentagrammic *Vitruvian Man* is virtually a symbol of science. And if you want to introduce an artist of genius and mystery to a thriller, Leonardo has no real rivals: he drew flying machines (famously, a helicopter) centuries before they were made; he devised everything from siege engines to a putative robot; he could write in mirror image; he conjured endlessly with riddles and codes. If there had been a Priory of Sion, protecting the world's greatest mysteries, the man from Vinci, in Tuscany, would surely have been its Grand Master.

But is *The Da Vinci Code*'s Leonardo remotely for real?

PENTACLE AND PENIS

The disturbing image of Jacques Saunière sprawled on the ground naked and with arms and legs spread wide is given meaning by Robert Langdon when he remembers that the shape corresponds to that of a **pentacle**, a symbol representing the sacred feminine. This illustration, known as the **Vitruvian Man**, is among the most readily recognisable works of Leonardo da Vinci.

So does this pentacle – a five-pointed star formed by the head and outstretched arms and legs of a man – really represent the harmony of the male and female principle when it is enclosed within a circle? And can we deduce from this and other information in *The Da Vinci Code* that Leonardo believed enlightenment may be achieved only when these elements are harmonised within the human soul? Maybe, but the truth is that we cannot arrive at this conclusion from the evidence Dan Brown gives us. In his version of the Vitruvian Man there is an element missing: the **square** which in the original sat within the circle. This arrangement of square and circle is vital to the meaning of the illustration as it would have been understood by Leonardo.

So, too, is its context. The illustration is the most famous of a number of similar works made by various artists during the Renaissance that attempted to illustrate the anatomical proportions of the human body as defined by **Vitruvius**, an architect of the Roman Empire, after whom the drawing is named. In his treatise on architecture, *De Architectura*, Vitruvius set out his ideal architectural proportions, alongside his ideas on what he deemed to be the correct human proportions.

The concept of **Divine Proportion** ran as the link between the two. Vitruvius believed that when a correctly proportioned body was placed within a square (*homo ad quadratum*), which in turn was placed within a circle (*homo ad circulum*) in such a way that the corners of the square were just touching the arc of the circle,

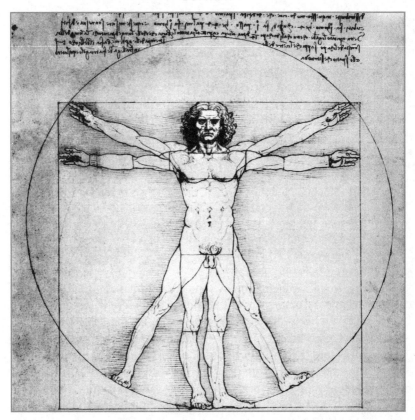

Squaring the circle – Leonardo's Vitruvian Man

then the precise centre of both circle and square would be at the belly button of the man (*umbilicus ad circulum et ad quadratum*). Frustratingly, all attempts by Renaissance artists to draw a human figure in accordance with Vitruvius's instructions resulted in the most bizarre distortions, most notoriously a woodcut by the Milanese surveyor Cesare Cesariano showing an outstretched man with enormous hands, elongated feet and startling erection.

Leonardo went about the creation of his Vitruvian Man in an entirely different way. Instead of forcing his human figure to suit Vitruvius's geometric principle, Leonardo rearranged the geometry to suit the man. So what we see in Leonardo's illustration is a well-proportioned man set within both a circle and a square, except that the square is not centred on the circle, rather on the man's penis. What the exact symbolism of this is – if there is any, beyond the genius of the exercise – Robert Langdon neglects to tell us.

A ROUGH GUIDE TO LEONARDO DA VINCI

Leonardo's achievements make an even more remarkable story when seen within the context of his origins. He had virtually no formal education, and his independent vision was forged, it seems, on observation and natural genius. Below is a brief **chronology of his life and works**.

1452 Leonardo is born (Saturday 15 April, 10.30pm) in Vinci, Tuscany. The illegitimate son of a Tuscan notary named **Ser Piero da Vinci** and a woman named **Caterina**. It is generally assumed he grew up with his father's family in the small Tuscan town of Vinci.

1466 Having earlier moved with his father to Florence, Leonardo is apprenticed to the sculptor **Andrea del Verrocchio**. There he met and perhaps worked under Botticelli and Ghirlandaio.

1473 Leonardo, by now registered in the painters' guild, assists Verrocchio on his **Baptism of Christ**, painting the angel and backdrop.

1476 Along with a Medici family member and two others, Leonardo is accused twice, anonymously, of **sodomy** with Jacopo Salterelli, a model in Verrochio's workshop. The charges are later dropped.

1481 First known commission – **The Adoration of the Magi**. He never completes the work, which is today 'awaiting restoration' at the Uffizi Gallery in Florence.

1482 Leonardo enters the court of **Ludovico Sforza** in **Milan** as painter and engineer. He remains in Sforza's service until 1498.

1482–83 Designs various artillery weapons. Receives commission to paint **The Virgin of the Rocks** (Louvre version).

1484–85 Works on church designs with Bramante, as well as on **town planning**. Designs a parachute and the **'helicopter.'**

1487 Completes the **Vitruvian Man**. Also designs a tank, a deep-sea diving suit and a number of flying machines. Begins first **anatomical sketches** and models: he is the first person to draw correctly the uterus and vagina.

1490 Apprentices and adopts ten-year-old boy, whom he nicknames **Salai** (little devil), and who becomes his lifelong companion.

1495–98 Works on **The Last Supper** in Milan.

1499 Returns to **Florence**. Studies mathematics and, at Santa Maria Nuova hospital, **human anatomy**, working to understand the action of muscles, and the respiratory system. Designs glider.

1502 Engaged as a military engineer by **Cesare Borgia**. Meets and begins friendship with **Machiavelli**.

1503 Paints second version of **Virgin of the Rocks** (now in London's National Gallery), and the **Mona Lisa** (now in the Louvre).

1506 Returns to **Milan** to work as an architect and engineer for Charles d'Amboise, and is later appointed court painter by Louis XII (of France). Paints **St Anne, Mary and Child** (now in the Louvre).

1507 Forms a second lifelong companionship, with **Francesco Melzi**. In the following years, works on cardio-vascular system.

1513 Brought to Rome by the Medici pope **Leo X**, for whom he paints **St John the Baptist** (the only artwork he did for the Vatican, despite the claim of 'hundreds of Vatican commissions' in *The Da Vinci Code*), as well as architectural and engineering projects.

1516 Invited by **Francois I** to become 'First painter, architect and mechanic of the King', moves to France, settling in the castle of **Cloux**, near Amboise. There he (partially) edits his scientific papers.

1519 Leonardo **dies**, aged 67, at home in Cloux, leaving his studio paintings to Salai, and everything else to Melzi.

EERIE ECCENTRICITIES: THE REPRESENTATION OF LEONARDO IN *THE DA VINCI CODE*

'Despite the visionary's genius he was a flamboyant homosexual and worshipper of divine order, both of which placed him in a perpetual state of sin against God … Da Vinci exhumed corpses to study human anatomy; he believed he possessed the alchemic power to turn lead into gold and even cheat God by creating an elixir to postpone death; and his inventions included horrific, never-before-imagined weapons of war and torture.'

So claims the narrative of *The Da Vinci Code*: quite an array of charges, or tokens of admiration, depending on how you read them. And all of them with some basis in fact.

It is generally accepted that Leonardo was predominantly **homosexual** – though that 'despite' seems distinctly bizarre, with its implied contradiction between genius and homosexuality. The historical record is that Leonardo was publicly accused of sodomy, along with other men, in an action designed to incriminate a boy named **Saltarelli**. However, the charges were eventually dropped, and the incident confirms little about Leonardo's sexuality. In his manuscripts, scribblings have been found expressing his affectionate feelings for one young man, and he had two life-long male companions – one of whom, his assistant **Salai**, he adopted.

Details like this have led most Leonardo researchers to conclude that he had a sexual interest in men and boys. However, his notebooks also contain drawings of the **male and female sexual organs**, and sexual intercourse, noting its unattractiveness, and stating that without pretty faces, mankind would become extinct. Certainly, the notion of being flamboyantly homosexual seems fanciful – for to be so at a time when one could literally be burnt at the stake for sodomy would have been reckless.

Human dissection in Leonardo's time was an equally dangerous and controversial issue, though it was permissible under licence.

Leonardo describes working at the hospital in Florence, so he must have at times obtained such a licence, although other notes suggest he was doing his grisly work on an unlicensed basis. He expresses some fear of being alone with bodies, though he also seems proud of his work with the scalpel.

During the Renaissance, the inner workings of the body were not considered the business of the mortals who inhabited them, and Leonardo was denounced by one individual before the Pope, and at the hospital in 1515. This may have been related to his work on **embryos** which, then as now, caused the greatest controversy by bringing up issues on the nature of the soul of the unborn child. There is no clear evidence, though, that Leonardo had to personally **exhume corpses** – he would have been able to work on the bodies of those who had been executed or who had died in the hospital.

In his anatomical work, Leonardo also pioneered an attitude and spirit of intellectual progress. Rather than remaining content to accept the findings of the ancient Greeks – who dissected and observed the human body, and whose books (by Galen, Aristotle and Hippocrates) were the learning resources of Renaissance medics – he insisted upon re-evaluating their work through his own observations. The anatomical drawings that resulted were among his greatest contributions to art as well as to science, and included pioneering work on the whole system of the body, which he described as 'the ultimate machine'.

No evidence exists for any belief that the maestro thought he could perform **alchemic miracles** or that he was working on a **death-postponing elixir**. There is one peculiar note that shows he paid six soldi to a fortune teller. Elsewhere he seems terribly unimpressed by any form of **superstition**, warning that Nature seeks revenge on anyone who tries to perform miracles – such as alchemists who attempt to create gold and silver, as well as necromancers and sorcerers.

As to the **inventions**, they were in part, at least, a practical course in order to make a living. Leonardo had no private means and was obliged to depend upon patronage. Writing to **Ludovico Sforza**, the governor of Milan, he outlined the talents he imagined would appeal most to a man frequently involved in one conflict or another. To this end, Leonardo promoted himself as one who knew how to manufacture cannons, build bridges, and make siege engines as well as other instruments of war.

For a man of curiosity with a developed knowledge of the mechanical workings of devices, as well as a visionary mind unbounded by the limits of contemporary technology, the allure of inventions of all types, including military, comes as no surprise. Combine that with the financial rewards that came from designing instruments of **war and torture**, and Leonardo's activities were not so eccentric or surprising after all. It is worth noting, too, that his vicious-looking illustration of a *Battle Cart with Mobile Scythes* (1485) was made from a contemporary military treatise, Roberto Valtario's *De re militari* of 1472.

And a **pagan**? Leonardo indeed comes across as a man who trusts his own judgement and will not bow to the irrational doctrines of the Church, nor as a rule will he give his trust to the charlatans of society. He obeys the rule of the empirical observation of nature with a worshipful fervency. So it is a neat step by Dan Brown to enlist him as a pagan goddess worshipper, for there is almost enough overlap between the worship of the sacred feminine and the Leonardian '**worship' of Nature** for the two to be mistaken.

THE VIRGIN OF THE ROCKS

After gaining employment as an engineer to Ludovico Sforza, some years passed before Leonardo gained a place as the court painter. In the meantime he was given a commission from The Confraternity of the Immaculate Conception to paint **The Virgin of the Rocks**. This is the painting that is described in *The Da Vinci Code* as containing a plethora of **pagan symbolism**.

These supposed symbols include the menacing gesture of the angel Uriel's hand, which slices across the neck of the infant John the Baptist; the talon-like fingers of the Virgin Mary spread out above Jesus's head; and the mysterious fact that a 'watered down' version was later given to the Confraternity in lieu of this one. These are interpretations raised about the painting by Lynn Picknett and Clive Prince in their book **The Templar Revelation** – one of the key sources of Dan Brown's backdrop to his novel.

A little mystery does indeed surround this painting, which was rejected by the **Confraternity of the Immaculate Conception** and now hangs in the Louvre. According to the contract made with the Confraternity on April 25, 1483 Leonardo was supposed to be producing an altarpiece the central panel of which was to include a few angels and two prophets. The final product plainly ignores the stipulations of the contract by leaving out these figures but adding an infant **John the Baptist**. Why Leonardo did so is open to speculation. Conventional art history suggests that, as the piece was due to be delivered in time for the Feast Day of the Immaculate Conception on December 8 – a relatively tight eight-month sched-ule from the contract – Leonardo may have used a piece of work he had already started on back in Florence. According to *The Da Vinci Code*, however, the painting was rejected because the **'nuns' of the Confraternity** were shocked at its details. That doesn't quite wash, for there were actually no nuns to be shocked; the Confraternity was comprised of some of Milan's wealthiest families.

More significantly, *The Da Vinci Code/Templar Revelation* reading peculiarly misunderstands the painting, asserting that it is the infant **Jesus on the left** with the Virgin Mary, and the infant **John the Baptist on the right** with the angel, rather than vice versa. Read the

The original version of Leonardo's Virgin of the Rocks is at the Louvre. The gestures made by the Virgin Mary and the Angel Uriel are described in *The Da Vinci Code* as threatening. The novel also mistakes Jesus (right) for John the Baptist (left).

The later 'watered down' version of Leonardo's Virgin of the Rocks hangs in London's National Gallery. John the Baptist is still on the left near the Virgin Mary; he is being blessed by Jesus, who sits near the Angel Uriel.

correct way round, the seemingly 'threatening' hand gestures can be appreciated as part of an interplay of hand movements contributing to the aesthetic unity of the piece. The **hand of the Virgin Mary** hovers in a protective manner above the head of Jesus, who is blessing John, rather than the other way round. The hand of the angel Uriel points towards John, marking him out as the one who will recognise Jesus as the Messiah.

The choice of **landscape** deserves a mention. While some may say that the background is reminiscent of Scottish topography, linking the painting to the **Rosslyn Chapel** (and thus the idea that Leonardo, as Grand Master of the Priory of Sion, was aware that the bones of Mary Magdalene had been interred there), there are more immediately relevant reasons for this particular setting. The primitive rocky background which creates a shelter for the travelling holy figures tells a story of protection in the midst of an isolated area. In addition **rocks** are a part of the symbolism associated with Mary and her Immaculate Conception of the Son of God. More religious symbolism appears in the carefully-wrought **plants** which soften the rocky crags. Columbine represents the dove of the Holy Spirit, cyclamen symbolises love and devotion, primrose stands here for virtue, and the acanthus for resurrection – all conventional affirmations of orthodox doctrine, yet at the same time in harmony with Leonardo's passion for drawing his lessons from nature. Certainly there is nothing in *The Virgin of the Rocks*, either in the first or second versions (the latter is now in London's National Gallery), that could ever have been construed as subverting a Christian painting with **pagan symbols**.

One **last note on the rocks**. Lynn Picknett and Clive Prince – who hold as good a claim as any to be the model for Robert Langdon, for their book stands at the heart of *The Da Vinci Code*'s ideas – made an even wilder claim in a 2003 article. 'Rocks', Picknett wrote, was contemporary Italian slang for **testicles**, and Leonardo was thus delivering a piece of Damien Hirst-style, heretical shock-art, full of sexual imagery, even down to 'a giant penis growing out of [the Virgin's] head'. His message, to those in the know, was that 'this is no Virgin'.

EVERYONE LOVES A CONSPIRACY: THE ADORATION OF THE MAGI

Dan Brown must have been a happy man when – revising *The Da Vinci Code* just a few months before publication – he opened *The New York Times Magazine* to find an article entitled 'The Leonardo Cover-Up'. The basic story is genuine, as he re-tells it in Chapter 40, preceded by a line of italics: *Everyone loves a conspiracy*.

It concerns an Italian art diagnostician called Maurizio Seracini, who has pioneered use of infrared reflectography and X-ray technology in order to identify layers of painting underneath the surface. His work is useful to art restorers, when considering how much of the surface of a work, often restored or repainted many times before, to remove. Seracini was enlisted by the Uffizi Gallery in Florence to take a look at Leonardo's **Adoration of the Magi**, which the artist had begun in 1481 in Florence, but left unfinished when he moved to Milan the following year. The painting depicts the Magi among a crowd of people, on foot and on horses, sur-rounding the Virgin and Child, against a backdrop of ruins that are thought to symbolise the death of paganism. It is also thought to include a self-portrait of Leonardo, as a shepherd. Art historians have long admired the painting for its composition, its complex emotions and iconography, and the physical representation of its figures – for which Leonardo made many preliminary sketches.

When Seracini examined the painting, however, he concluded that 'None of the paint we see today was put there by Leonardo' and that beneath the painting was a quite different scene, includ-ing a clash of horses, and the construction of a staircase. Dan Brown can't resist leaving out these details, suggesting that the Uffizi has 'banished' the work for fear of revealing some mystery. As often, the truth is rather more mundane. The Uffizi authorities simply have no idea how to proceed with their restoration.

THE LAST SUPPER

When Leonardo finally got an appointment to the court in Milan he worked on various commissions, including **The Last Supper**. The character of Sir Leigh Teabing, again following closely the theories put forward by Lynn Picknett and Clive Prince in *The Templar Revelation* (which is the first book Sophie notes on his bookshelves), notes a number of details in the painting which he regards as clues to the true nature of the Holy Grail.

Before taking Sophie through these particularities he notes that no chalice appears on the fresco as he calls it – or rather the mural, to accurately describe the painted tableau. Jesus and his disciples each have a cup before them. The significance of this is apparently that the **absence of the chalice**, considered along with other 'clues', leads the viewer to the conclusion that the Grail is in fact none other than Mary Magdalene and the bloodline descending from Jesus via the child she bears him. Through the eyes of Sophie we learn, too, that the figure of John the Evangelist, to the left of Jesus, is in fact **Mary Magdalene** and is identified as such by her 'flowing red hair, delicate folded hands, and the hint of a bosom'. Teabing takes Sophie further with this realisation by telling her that the painting 'practically screams that Jesus and Mary Magdalene were a pair'. He points out how the Jesus and the 'Mary' figure are dressed in mirror-image colours, how they are supposedly 'joined at the hip', yet lean away from one another to create a V-shaped space between them. This 'indisputable' V-shape is supposedly representative of the chalice and of a woman's womb and, we are told, appears at the focal point of the picture. Keeping on with the compositional 'evidence', Teabing declares the existence of a huge 'M', created by the figure of Jesus and the figure to his right, which may be there to stand for *Matrimonio* or Mary Magdalene.

Finally Teabing implies that the hand **Peter** has raised in the air is slicing blade-like across 'Mary Magdalene's neck'. This is apparently an expression of his jealousy at the prospect of Mary becoming the head of the church that Jesus was to leave behind after his death. The so-called **disembodied knife** which appears in the mural is also considered by Langdon to be ominous.

Each of these theories is drawn directly from Lynn Picknett and Clive Prince's book, *The Templar Revelation*.

Among the few facts we can establish about the painting is that it was undertaken and completed between 1495 and 1497 in the refectory of the **Monastery Santa Maria delle Grazie** in Leonardo's capacity as court painter for Ludovico Sforza, the Governor of Milan. Before arriving at this particular version of the Last Supper, Leonardo toyed with alternative moments in the biblical episode. Ultimately he picked the moment in the **Gospel of St. John (13:21)** when Jesus says that one amongst them will betray him. The three other gospels all describe the Last Supper, but John's account begins when the supper is over and the table has been all but cleared. No mention is made of a cup or a chalice of wine, and so understandably none appears in the mural. Sophie is thinking of the synoptic gospels and not of John's when she remembers the words, 'And after dinner, Jesus took the cup of wine, sharing it with His disciples'. The thirteen cups still left on the table are there perhaps as reminders that while the mural focuses on the moment when Jesus reveals the shocking truth that one of his disciples will betray him, the moment has been preceded by the famous and important Last Supper.

Leonardo was experimenting with an **oil and tempera mix** as he worked on the Last Supper. This medium allowed him the option of making changes to his piece as he went along, which would have been more difficult to do with traditional oil paints. The disadvantage of this experiment was that the painting began rapidly to decay soon after its completion. The work has been restored on several occasions since then and, as Teabing points out, we have now been able to see clearly the actual paint laid down by Leonardo and his apprentices.

This does not, however, mean that at last we are able to see that the figure on Jesus's right hand is a woman, though it does mean we are able to see the features of this individual more closely and we can more easily make the comparison between this figure of John the Evangelist and a painting assigned to Leonardo of *Saint John the Baptist* in an effort to draw some conclusions about style. In the portrait of John the Baptist that shows him coming out of the darkness, his flowing red hair is clearly visible as are his soft feminine features. There is controversy as to whether this painting can actually be attributed to Leonardo da Vinci but whomever the artist, it shows that at this period there existed a convention for portraying John in a feminised style, and that the feminine John in the Last Supper is not an anomaly. Moreover, Leonardo used a female subject to make studies for his male angel Uriel in *The Virgin of the Rocks*.

Perspective studies drawn by Leonardo show that it is Jesus who appears in the centre of the painting, yet *The Da Vinci Code* refers

John the Baptist was routinely depicted as an effeminate figure in Renaissance art. Here Leonardo paints him with long curling red hair, a tilted head and fay smile, very similar in fact to the John shown at the Last Supper, which *The Da Vinci Code* claims is really a woman.

to the space between Jesus and his right hand person as the 'focal point' of the painting. Whether the centre is the same thing as the focal point is a moot point, but as these studies show, the eye of the viewer is drawn by the lines of perspective toward the figure of Jesus. As the central focal point, Jesus is reinforced by the large luminous space behind him created by the doorway. The space between Jesus and John is neither central nor the focal point, and a casual glance at the painting shows the figures are certainly not 'joined at the hip'. However, the space on this side of Jesus creates quite a gap in the composition, larger than on the other side. The **mirror-image colour scheme** of Jesus and John thus makes sense as a means of creating a little continuity in an otherwise rather disrupted group of disciples.

The whole point of the **composition** is to dramatise the effect of the astounding statement Jesus has just made about his betrayal. Leonardo has made a break with the Middle Ages convention of the Last Supper, which has the disciples sitting in an orderly line. Here they are separated out into groups of three, thrown out of line by the alarm and confusion of the moment. Seen in this light, the movement of John away from Jesus would be better understood as a turning toward his natural compositional home – in a group of three just like all the others at the table. The alleged 'M' shape – which, once pointed out, is the only thing Sophie can see – is an untenable idea unless you choose to ignore the whole artistic and historical background to the painting.

Part of the dynamic **arrangement of the disciples** is created by the way the disciples have their hands outstretched in different directions – some of them pointing towards Jesus and further enforcing his centrality. The hand of Peter extended towards Jesus can be seen in this light not as a menacing, jealous gesture. And as for the **disembodied hand** wielding a dagger, the hand in fact belongs to Peter and the dagger is really a breadknife. There exists in the Windsor Castle collection a **study by Leonardo** of an arm bent in just the same way. A passage of notes on the disciples' reactions to the news describes the figure who has turned with a knife in his hand and who has knocked a glass over on the table. Taken by itself this note may not persuade the reader away from the view that the knife is there as a means expressing threatening intent toward Mary Magdalene. But a look at the rest of the notes on the reactions shows that the emphasis is on the particular physical movements of each individual figure which was so important in creating the dramatic effect Leonardo was striving to achieve. The raised knife tells of the intense emotion felt by Peter, the same intense emotion expressed in a variety of other gestures by the other disciples.

Hidden Knowledge

THE DA VINCI CODE [CHAPTER 3]

There is a nicely ironic passage in *The Da Vinci Code* where Robert Langdon confesses: 'a career tendency of symbologists was to extract meaning from situations that had none'. This endearingly honest self-appraisal could well apply to the plot of the novel, which, ingenious though it is, is premised on the thinnest of facts and a wealth of loosely associated symbols. Indeed, it seems that Langdon and Dan Brown have added the word '**symbologist**' to the dictionary. Correctly, a person who studies symbols is called a symbolist. The word 'symbology' is usually taken to mean the study of theological and mystical symbols, but there is no academic discipline called symbology at Harvard where Langdon is said to teach the subject, although that is perhaps a matter of time. Likewise Sophie Neveu's named profession is a little odd seeing as a **cryptographer** is one who invents codes rather than breaks them. The word for a code-breaker like Sophie is a **cryptanalyst** and the umbrella term for these would be cryptology. But, hey, that's semantics...

Anagrammatic Action

One of the enjoyable features of *The Da Vinci Code* is its author's fondness for **anagrams** and **double-entendres**, which is given free reign throughout the narrative.

ODDEST HAND IN COW VIBRANCE

As a simple starter take the names of the characters:

BEZU FACHE

Bezu Fache presumably derives from Mount Bezu in Rennes-le-Château, the village where the story began for the authors of the book *Holy Blood, Holy Grail*, upon whose ideas much of this book is based (and **Sir Leigh Teabing** combines the names of two of that book's authors: Richard *Leigh* and, anagramatically, Michael *Baigent).* **Fache** hints – via the French word for angry – at the character of the inspector in charge of solving Saunière's murder.

SOPHIE NEVEU

Sophie Neveu's first name refers to wisdom, which is Sophia in Greek, while in French her surname means 'descendant', a telling clue, and also unravels hints at New Eve (Nu Eve). In Christian tradition the Virgin Mary is the new Eve who makes up for the sins of the original Eve. In this book it is Mary Magdalene who can be seen as the true New Eve. The feminist theology which promotes Mary Magdalene sees her as the lost-bride.

GETTUM... AND RED HERRING

On a less lofty level of punning we have **Pamela Gettum**, the Librarian with a passion for getting those books out. And then there's **Bishop Aringarosa**, whose surname translates as Red Herring, a fitting monicker considering his role in the plot.

SO DARK THE CON OF MAN

Dan Brown also likes to mix around epochs in his anagrams, which can be misleading, as for instance when the book claims that the Romans referred to the study of anagrams as 'Ars Magna' – the Great Art. That would be rather splendid, but he is just rearranging the English letters of the word 'anagrams' to create a Latin phrase.

Nonetheless, superstitious traditions were an established part of Roman beliefs, and playful **anagrams in Latin** have been found. And moving on a millennium, **Louis XIII** actually appointed an anagrammatist named Thomas Billon to pep up dull days in the King's Court with word play, perhaps finding cheeky alternative names for the upper crust. On a more serious level, the mystical Jewish teachings of the **Kabbalah** drew heavily on anagrams to find new meanings. The Hebrew Old Testament was reinterpreted by Kabbalists and the search did not stop with letters – the manipulation of Bible texts worked on a **numerical basis** too. Each letter of the Hebrew alphabet was assigned a numerical value which allowed further interpretation of the texts.

LA LINGUA PURA

As noted, much of Dan Brown's wordplay works only if the English language is being used. To keep the fictional reality in place while still managing to make up anagrams that work, Brown has Teabing introduce a bizarre notion that English is **la lingua pura** by virtue of its distance from the nasty old Vatican (he has Galileo use English for similar reasons in his earlier novel, *Angels and Demons*). This allows him to circumvent the problem of writing for an English language audience and using clues that rely on real names from foreign languages. No matter that English is the least pure language in Europe on a linguistic level. And one can only hope that the book's French, Spanish and Italian readers take in good heart being told they are speaking languages tainted by Rome's 'propaganda machine'.

The secret of the Mona Lisa's smile, according to *The Da Vinci Code*, is that really she is a self-portrait by Leonardo da Vinci.

Of course the anagrams in *The Da Vinci Code* are part of what makes the plot so intriguing. A closer look at the clues will show that Brown has had to stretch the truth a bit to get the desired result. When Sophie flashes Langdon a triumphant smile having cracked the third anagram – **So dark the con of man = Madonna of the Rocks** – she might have wondered at her grand-père's name for the painting, as both versions of the painting commissioned by the Confraternity of the Immaculate Conception usually go by the name of *The Virgin of the Rocks*, as the curator of the Louvre would surely have known. But it's an excellent anagram clue, for all that.

Amon l'Isa (4, 4)

Another Leonardo code receives a bit of linguistic manipulation. Langdon is teaching his class about the supposed fusion of masculine and feminine in Leonardo's **Mona Lisa**. The clue, he says, is in the title *Mona Lisa* which can be reformulated as *Amon L'Isa*. If Amon is the ancient Egyptian god of fertility and if L'Isa refers to Isis, the Egyptian goddess of fertility then we have here a title which brings home perfectly the idea of androgyny or fusion of the sexes which apparently smiles out of the painting. So the theory goes.

And a lovely theory it is until you remember that Leonardo was an Italian, so his giving the painting an English name would be odd. In any case, since the painting went without a name at the time of its creation there was no name out of which to create a meaningful clue. The painting was known in Italy as *La Gioconda* and in French as *La Joconde* – both of which mean 'the playful woman'. These unofficial titles play on the name of the woman who is generally assumed to be the sitter – Lisa Gherardini, wife of wealthy Florentine Giocondo. The English name *Mona Lisa* was attributed at a later date.

Another little flaw lies in the reference to *L'Isa* as an ancient **pictogram of Isis**. The goddess Isis was always represented as a goddess with either horns or with a sun disc resting on her head and has always been known as Isis. The statement that her ancient pictogram was once called L'Isa is, alas, nonsense.

The Missing Cryptex Mystery

Sadly, the **cryptex** does not number among Leonardo's many blueprints: Dan Brown is its creator, and like so much of the book, it is an interesting device with a couple of design flaws.

DON'T SMASH THE PHIAL!

Once Sophie and Langdon have gained access to the safe box in the Deposit Bank of Zurich by entering the **Fibonacci sequence** security number they reckon they have the keystone at last. But no, they have a device which as Sophie explains is called a cryptex and which preserves **messages on papyrus**. To access the papyrus one must line up the dials correctly. To smash open the device would be futile as this would also smash the phial of vinegar contained within, which would dissolve the papyrus. It's a fun idea but it wouldn't work. The cellulose fibres from the papyrus plant make a pretty tough material which can and has survived for centuries. Vinegar would not destroy the fibres in any way.

There is also a little confusion needing to be cleared up about the difference between **paper and papyrus**, which are used interchangeably. We derive our word for paper from the word papyrus but the two are completely different materials. Likewise elsewhere in the novel there is confusion between the words **codex and scroll**. A scroll is a rolled up piece of paper or papyrus or parchment while a codex is an early form of book.

ILLEGIBLE ILLEGITIMATE

For the sake of the plot, you need to accept that cryptexes do exist – and work. To open one of these things the message's recipient must choose the correct line up of letters on the five dials consisting of 26 letters each. As Sophie correctly calculates, this would add up to almost **12 million possibilities**. This pair don't have that kind of time and fortunately Langdon remembers that the rose inlaid on the box may lead to another clue and so he peels it away to reveal an illegible message. Sophie is quick to register that this script is in English and has simply been written or rather made to look as if it was written out backwards.

The message they find written right to left and as if it were seen in a mirror has obviously been written as a sort of code by Saunière. This **mirror writing** was utilised by Leonardo and is found all over his many manuscripts. Whether Leonardo himself was using this script as a kind of code to make it a little more difficult for people to steal his ideas is open to debate. Brown's suggestion that this type of writing may have amused the eccentric Leonardo is a possibility. Those who emphasise Leonardo's dangerously unorthodox interests may lean toward the code theory; and since Leonardo had concerns about other people taking his ideas there is a logic to his disguising his ideas and designs. It was highly probable, however, that Leonardo was left-handed and for lefties this kind of writing comes quite naturally as a speedier and more comfortable way of putting ink to paper. Some art historians further suggest that he was dyslexic – a condition that is often linked with highly original thinking.

ATBASH CIPHER

Once Sophie has established the cryptex's mirror writing, it is revealed that the key to the password will be found using the **atbash cipher** as

Codes and symbols were used by early Christians to communicate secret meanings to one another, as in this third-century epitaph. At the centre is an anchor, used as an alternative to the cross and symbolising hope and life. The fish are a cryptogram; the initial letters in the Greek word for fish are also the initial letters for the profession of faith: Jesus Christ, Son of God and Saviour. Also the image of fish comes into the Gospels, as when Jesus spoke of making his disciples fishers of men. Above the fish and anchor is the legend 'The Fish of the Living'.

the key. This system is based on the substitution of the last letter of the Hebrew alphabet for the first, the second letter for the second to last and so on. The word *atbash* is itself an example of the system at work: the first letter of the Hebrew alphabet, *aleph* is followed by the last letter, *taw*, then comes *besh* the second letter, and finally *shin* the second to last letter.

According to some the cipher of the atbash is used widely within the Old Testament. No genuine code has been found at work though, and the use of the cipher was more likely placed there as a means of generating a sense of mystery. Research by Brendan Mckay, Professor of Computer Sciences at the Australian National University, has shown that the apparent cipher messages in the Bible as 'found' by the author of *The Bible Code*, Michael Drosnin, are just what one might expect to be thrown up by chance rather than by intention.

Bearing this in mind, a cautionary lesson can be drawn against the temptation to get further meaning out of the Old Testament now that you know a cipher makes the occasional appearance. The use of the Cipher to encrypt the odd word like Babel so that it becomes Seshnach, as Dan Brown notes, is not evidence for a sustained code system throughout the texts.

CAESAR AND MARY QUEEN OF SCOTS

If it is disappointing to learn that the cryptex exists only on the plane of fictional reality, some comfort lies in knowledge of the reality that both Julius Caesar and Mary Queen of Scots did actually devise **cryptologic solutions** to solve their data protection problems – with differing degrees of success.

Gaius Julius Caesar used what is known as the **Caesar Substitution** during the Gallic wars. His method was to first mask the Latin plaintext with Greek letters. The Latin would be rearranged and then the cipher alphabet (the Greek in this case) would be shifted a predetermined number of steps along the plaintext alphabet. This is the **shift substitution** system – although whether a box was involved, as Brown implies, is obscured by the mists of time.

Mary Queen of Scots was rather less fortunate with her cipher substitution system, which consisted of a **nomenclator** – a codelike list of words and names – and a **cipher alphabet**. By the sixteenth century, the renaissance of cryptanalysis meant that Walsingham's official cipher secretary, **Thomas Phelippes**, was readily equipped to detect the weaknesses in the system and decipher the code. Believing their code to be safe, Mary's conspirators were explicit in their plans to overthrow Queen Elizabeth. The help of a double agent and the cryptanalyst revealed more than enough evidence to try the conspirators, who were put to death by being hung, drawn and quartered. Mary Queen of Scots was saved this appallingly grisly fate by being beheaded.

A little poetic licence is detectable in *The Da Vinci Code's* description of the Arab scientist **Abu Yusuf Ismail al-Kindi** who, it is asserted, protected his secrets with a **polyalphabetic substitution cipher**. This ninth-century Arab philosopher was more given to elucidation than encryption – as for example is the case with his 'Manuscript for Deciphering Cryptographic Messages'. This contains the earliest known description of how to break ciphers using the technique of frequency analysis. Mary Queen of Scots' persecutors cetainly benefitted from this cryptanalysis of centuries before.

The Ancient Art of Symbology

'The symbolism of the clues meshed too perfectly – the pentacle, The Vitruvian Man, the goddess and even the Fibonacci sequence. A coherent symbolic set, as iconographers would call it.'

Sophie is remarking on the clues left behind by her grandfather, but she could just as well be referring to Dan Brown's plethora of symbols, piled one upon another throughout the narrative to create the illusion of coherence. The novel's fictional reality depends for a large part on this use of symbols and their alleged association to one another and to historical fact.

The notable symbols used in *The Da Vinci Code* are the **Rose**, the **Pentacle**, the **Fleur-de-Lis** and various ancient symbols of **feminine and masculine**. Again and again these symbols come up, each apparently corroborating the central thesis of *The Da Vinci Code* – that Jesus and Mary Magdalene were man and wife – and enshrining the principle of the sacred feminine in harmony with the masculine force of the universe, the great truth that the Templars and then the Priory of Sion were put in place to protect. The story exists everywhere if you open your eyes to it, Langdon tells Sophie. This is the kind of trick you may notice Brown employs frequently throughout the narrative as his means cleverly blunting readers' critical faculties and carrying them beyond the framework of the narrative into apparent realms of reality and history.

THE FLOWER OF LISA?

The special key belonging to her grandfather which Sophie comes across has on it a flower, a type of lily known as the **Fleur-de-Lis.** Langdon, whose speciality is the symbolism of secret societies is taken aback to hear of it as this confirms for him that Saunière was involved in the **Priory of Sion.** This lily is their 'Official device. Their coat of arms. Their logo'. Of course, long before the phoney Priory (see p.93) was ever started up this lily was adopted by Clovis, the first Christian king of France, as an emblem of his spiritual purity through baptism and the purity of France. Then the emblem was taken on by the kings of France and from this comes the idea that the Fleur-de-Lis signifies the bearer's right to kingship whether deserved or not. The popularity of the flower as a Christian symbol is explicable in part because of its **three petals** – signifying the Holy Trinity – and because of its **white** colour denoting purity.

The right to kingship aspect of the flower is particular telling when we see it in relation to the Priory of Sion's fraudster founder **Pierre Plantard.** In the late 1930s, as a teenager of radical fascist and anti-semitic persuasion, he was eager to have France purified, believing that the Jews had in fact started the war. Naturally the way to get the country back in order was to make himself king by posing as a descendant of the long-since extinguished Merovingian bloodline. Since getting himself reified was the main aim of the self-conceived Priory, he naturally chose the Fleur-de-Lis as his secret society's symbol, with its implication of rightful kingship. So the background to Plantard's use of the Fleur-de-Lis tells a more sinister tale of twentieth-century fascism than that told by the original Christian association of purity. Or at least it would be sinister if it weren't for the fact that this loopy imposter was so far off the mark. The kings of France were long-gone and the Merovingians had no claim to the throne even if one was available to claim. Truth is rather more absorbing than fiction in this case.

As for the implied connection between the Fleur-de-Lis and the Mona Lisa, there is none – or virtually none. For as well being the symbol of France it is also the flower representing Florence, the home of the woman thought to be the subject of the *Mona Lisa*. You can find connections anywhere if you look hard enough.

A ROSE IS A ROSE IS A ROSE

The rose symbolism is a prime example of the way that Dan Brown takes various traditions of symbolism, interconnects them whether or not there are any real links to be made, and thus creates a sense of reality out of a bunch of interesting loose ends.

In Christian legend the thornless rose represents the **absence of original sin** in the Mother of God, while in Christian symbolism the red rose represents **martyrdom**. To the Romans, the rose was associated with **Venus**, the goddess of love, and it was also employed as an emblem of secrecy – the phrase Latin phrase **sub rosa** has come from this association to mean something treated in confidence.

Then there is the **compass rose** – so named simply because the direction indicators splay out in a pattern reminiscent of a rose.

And the **Rose Line**, an unofficial name some people have decided to give to the **Meridian Line**. The line, whether or not one wants to call it a rose, did run through Paris from the time of the French Revolution as a statement of France's newfound sense of importance. The Greenwich Meridian Line ultimately took primacy as the official Meridian line, some say because Britain was where the top cartography was taking place. The **Rosslyn chapel** has nothing to do with the Rose Line, as Dan Brown claims. Ross means hill and lyn means water.

The Da Vinci Code replaces the Christian association of the rose with the Virgin Mary with **Mary Magdalene** by telling us that since the bride of Jesus could not be openly referred to, other symbols like the grail, chalice and rose were used instead. Brown also links up the idea of the rose's association with Venus, which he has already imbued with specifically feminine meanings by association to the pentacle (feminine priciple) to create a strong overall association with the feminine – an association which the flower did not previously possess in any specific way. All of this is in turn linked up to the idea of secrecy, both in the plot where the rosebox is the container of secrets and through the *sub rosa* anecdote. Finally the compass rose and the rose line are thrown in as a link to the idea of guidance toward secret truth. With the various components of symbolism in place the rose becomes 'the feminine chalice and guiding star that led to secret truth'. You have to take your hat off.

Pentacles and Tarot

There is no one correct way to read a symbol. Its meaning depends upon the religious, historical and cultural context. The **pentacle** illustrates this very well, being a geometrical figure whose dimensions have meant different things over thousands of years. The figure appears to have been used in some way by the Sumerians, and later it aquired a mystical significance for the Pythagoreans who drew meaning from geometry and numbers. It was used as a protection against evil in the Middle Ages and represents the five wounds of Christ in Christian symbolism. By using the ancient **astronomical explanation** for the pentacle, Brown stretches the meaning to include the theme of the sacred feminine. Because Venus appeared to trace a pentacle-like movemement across the skies, the symbol becomes associated with this planet. By combining that with the idea of Venus worshipped as the goddess of love, *The Da Vinci Code* somehow draws the general conclusion that the pentacle was also worshipped as the female half of all things.

This nineteenth century French Tarot card shows the devil with a fallen woman, a reminder of Eve.

As anyone who has played with **tarot cards** will know, a suit of pentacles does indeed figure in the pack. The general consensus is that the game was introduced into Europe in the fifteenth century by gipsies. Some think it was used simply for gaming purposes. These days the esoteric mystique that surrounded these cards has turned into a belief in the cards as a means to explore the unconscious aspect of the psyche. It is no wonder that in another period the Tarot gained occult status as the spirit was essentially a matter for the Church – any other kind of investigation would be considered 'occult'. With this mysterious status attached it is not difficult to see how any conspiracy theorist might take the opportunity to laden the game with an even more obscure meaning, hence the tale in *The Da Vinci Code* of the 'lost-bride and her hidden subjugation by the Church'.

In his efforts to squeeze one last drop of meaning out of the number five and the pentacle of Venus, Brown reaches for a pagan interpretation of the **iambic pentametre**, the metre in which the mirror-image poem is written. There is nothing mystical or pagan about the metric arrangement: iambic pentametre simply mirrors the natural rhythm of speech. And as such became the 'preferred poetic metre of outspoken literati across the globe', or, put another way, pretty much standard through the whole history of English poetry.

Blade and Chalice

Societies throughout the ages have developed their own **ideogramatic representations** of the **female and male sexes**. Langdon correctly informs Sophie that the symbols in current usage, which derive from astrological symbols, were not always the signs for male and female. Brown could have chosen any number of signs depending upon the period and culture he was looking at: the V shape for the female and the ^ for the male simply fit into the plot. Later *The Da Vinci Code* will imply that the **Star of Solomon** (or David) traced by the footsteps of visitors walking around **Rosslyn Chapel** is there as a representation of the fusion of the two signs – a symbol of harmony in the universe and between the sexes. Alas, if you go to Rosslyn Chapel you won't find any evidence of this attractive concept.

There is no dominant male and female symbol in ancient cultures, though in Egyptian hieroglyphs, variations on the V shape do appear to be taken from the shape of the **female pubis**. Brown uses the interpretation that the shape in fact represents the womb, an interpretation used primarily to take in the idea that the Holy Grail – as bloodline – can be coded by using this ancient V sign. It is a theory that he has adopted essentially from **Riane Eisler**'s book **The Chalice and the Blade** – a bestseller on publication in the US in 1988 – the central thesis of which is that the world will resume order when the sexes achieve harmony.

Of course Brown's choice of symbols comes in handy when it comes to finding a fitting resting place for Mary Magdalene's relics: the **pyramid inversée** and the **larger pyramid** as versions of these male-female symbols create the ideal resting place. The fact that the shapes and symbols, riddles and plot tie up with seeming perfection is a testament to Brown's weaving together of plots, but speaks little of any real connection.

Fibonacci and Divine Proportion

The **Fibonacci sequence** makes an appearance right at the start of the action. The dying Saunière managed to scrawl the sequence out on the floor in scrambled form as part of the clue for Sophie and Langdon. This, they later realise is the security number to gain access to Saunière's safebox in the depositary bank of Zurich.

This famous sequence was derived by the Italian mathematician **Leonardo Fibonacci** (c.1170–c.1240) in his *Liber Abaci* (Book of the Abacus). He was addressing a problem: how many rabbits would be produced from a pair of rabbits in one year if every month that pair begets another pair which becomes productive from the second month onward. The outome was the number sequence 1, 1, 2, 3, 5, 8, 13, 21, 34, 55. Each number is the sum of the two preceding numbers. It was the first **recursive number sequence** (in which the relationship between two or more successive terms can be expressed by a formula) known in Europe.

For Langdon the most interesting feature of the Fibonacci sequence is that as the numbers increase in magnitude, the ratio between succeeding numbers approaches **Phi**, also known as the **Golden Ratio**, whose value is approximately 1.618. This relationship between Phi and the Fibonacci sequence was worked out by the mathematician **Robert Simson** at the University of Glasgow in 1753.

As Langdon tells his class, examples of this ratio are to be found in nature, in art and in architecture. The best known examples in nature are the ratio of spirals on sunflower heads or in the arrangement of buds on a stem. The Phi or Golden Ratio was noted and found to be aesthetically pleasing well before the Fibonacci sequence was worked out. For example, the Classical architecture of the **Parthenon** at Athens famously bases its design upon the **Golden Rectangle** – the sides of the rectangle conform to the proportions of the Golden Ratio. The **Eden Project** in southwest England also incorporates this Golden Ratio into its design as a tribute to nature – proof that the Golden Ratio is found to be just as aesthetically pleasing across the centuries. Endless examples of its usage can be found in music and art.

It is a clever extension of the realm of *The Da Vinci Code*, particularly since it has a Leonardo link. When the mathematician **Luca Pacioli** came to the Florentine Court and worked on his masterpiece **Divina Proportione** (1509) it was **Leonardo** who provided the geometric illustrations. In addition Leonardo's fascination with the divine proportion is shown in his work on the **Vitruvian Man** illustration.

Leonardo, most likely an atheist, explicitly states in his manucripts that Nature is the finest teacher. The divine proportions found in nature might well have been the kind of thing which prompted this kind of statement. For a religious adherent God the creator can be found in the numbers. And if you're a physicist you'll be unsurprised at what others see as the amazing recurrence of a divine number in nature, believing that a few simple rules govern the nature of things and thus only so many variations that can occur. Langdon's excitement over Phi naturally comes to a head when he's describing the way it works in his favourite geometric shape, the pentacle.

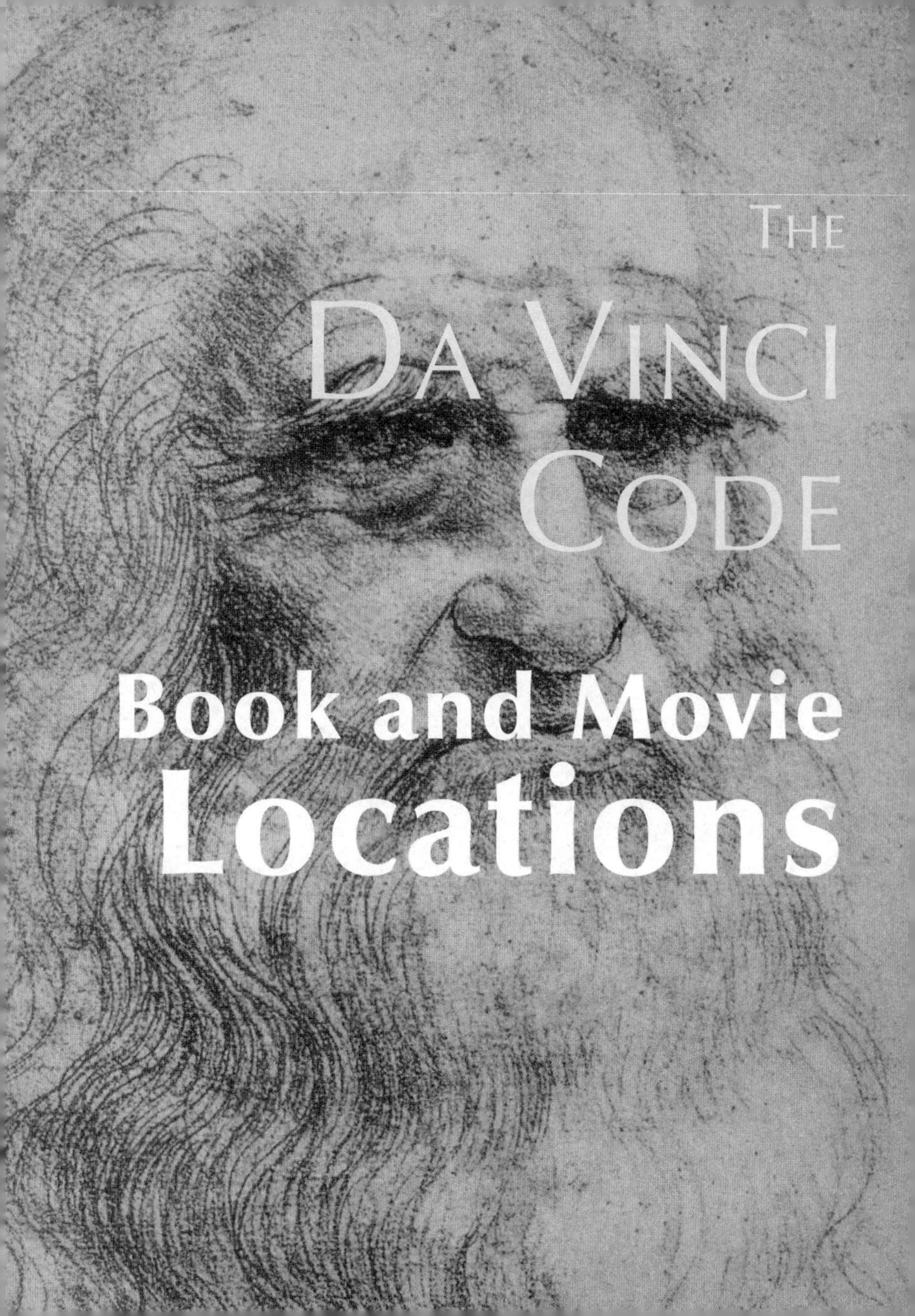

THE

DA VINCI
CODE

Book and Movie
Locations

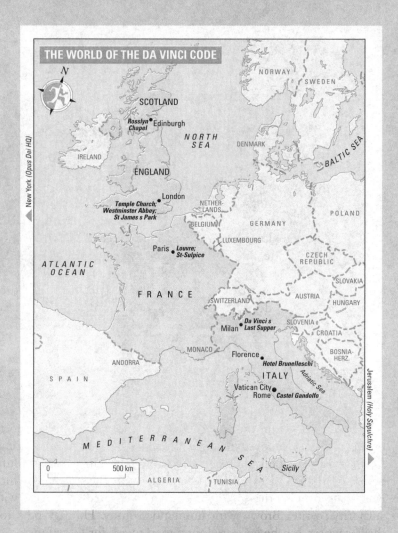

THE WORLD OF THE DA VINCI CODE

New York (Opus Dei HQ)

N

SCOTLAND

Rosslyn Chapel • Edinburgh

NORTH SEA

NORWAY

SWEDEN

DENMARK

BALTIC SEA

IRELAND

ENGLAND

London •

Temple Church;
Westminster Abbey;
St James s Park

NETHER-
LANDS

BELGIUM

GERMANY

POLAND

LUXEMBOURG

Paris • *Louvre;*
St-Sulpice

CZECH
REPUBLIC

ATLANTIC
OCEAN

FRANCE

SWITZERLAND

AUSTRIA

SLOVAKIA

HUNGARY

SLOVENIA

Milan • *Da Vinci s*
Last Supper

CROATIA

MONACO

Florence •

Hotel Brunelleschi

ANDORRA

SPAIN

ITALY

Vatican City •
Rome • *Castel Gandolfo*

BOSNIA-
HERZ.

Adriatic Sea

Jerusalem (Holy Sepulchre)

MEDITERRANEAN SEA

0   500 km

Sicily

ALGERIA   TUNISIA

Paris

The Da Vinci Code – book and movie – does a magnificent job of turning Paris into the stage backdrop for a thrilling chase through the city's history and streets: a circuit that you can follow, book in hand. Starting in the most astounding of all its monuments, the **Louvre**, you can walk through the Grande Galerie and view the Leonardo paintings, and from there it's a pleasant walk south to the church of **St-Sulpice**, to examine the real gnomon. For the full *Da Vinci Code* Paris experience, you could also pay a visit to the **Paris Ritz**, where Robert Langdon makes his first appearance in the novel, drive through the **Bois de Boulogne** at night, get yourself a fake ticket to Lille at the **Gare du Nord**, and take a tour of the **Château de Villette** – or even stay there, if you can afford to do the whole thing in style. We've also detailed one further site Dan Brown could have featured: the **Basilica of St-Denis**, just north of the city, where you'll find the tombs of almost all the Merovingian kings of France.

A word of caution: don't use *The Da Vinci Code* as a guidebook, as its **map-reading** is ropey. For example, Langdon recalls following the Meridian Line 'from Sacré-Cœur, north across the Seine, and finally to the ancient Paris observatory', which would be quite some feat, as the lofty ice-cream domes of Sacré-Cœur stand in the far north of the city, and the observatory lies in the south. In another scene, Dan Brown has a police Citroën skimming round in a circular route, before heading west from the Tuileries towards the Louvre – which is actually over to the east; 'the Citroën navigated the chaos with authority', writes Brown with unintended irony. He may be a top thriller writer, but he is clearly not a man to ask for directions.

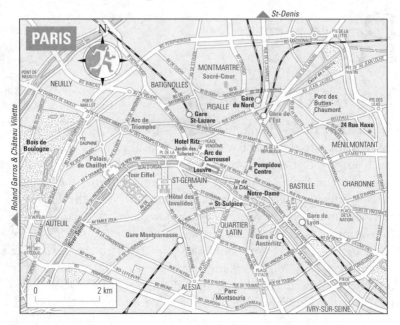

Paintings and Pyramids: The Louvre

The Louvre is, as Dan Brown describes it, the most famous art museum in the world. It is also correctly described as the longest building in Europe, as long as three Eiffel Towers stretched end to end, with a three-mile perimeter – which Langdon has, for some reason known only to himself, walked all the way round – and a staggeringly expansive plaza. As for it being 'a monolithic Renaissance palace', it's true that it has an extraordinary uniformity of symmetry in the grand French Classical style, though only one small wing, in the southwestern corner of the Cour Carée, or inner court, is technically Renaissance. The rest of the complex is made up of later additions, spanning several centuries, although following basically the same style.

The **Musée du Louvre**, which occupies the palace, is as overbearing as the building, with more than 60,000 works of art – the largest collection in the world. Fewer than half are on display at any one time, but it would still take at least Brown's estimated five weeks to 'properly appreciate' them all. Even getting round the most acclaimed masterpieces requires repeat visits.

SOME LOUVRE HISTORY

The original Louvre was little more than a feudal fortress, begun by Philippe-Auguste in 1200. Charles V was the first French king to make it a royal home, rebuilding in elaborate late-Gothic style, but it wasn't until the reign of François I, in the first flowering of the Renaissance, that the foundations of the present-day palace were laid – right on top of the older fortress. From then on, almost every sovereign added to the Louvre, though it had a couple of close shaves. Louis XIV toyed with the idea of destroying it altogether, and commissioning a new design from Bernini, but ended up just copying François I's original design round the other three sides of the Cour Carée. Even as late as the nineteenth century, Napoleon III's architects were still following the original design theme.

LES PYRAMIDES

The Louvre's glass **Pyramid** erupted from the centre of the main Cour Napoléon in 1989 like a visitor from another architectural planet. Conceived by the Chinese-born American architect **Ieoh Ming Pei**, it was an extraordinary leap of imagination that initially appalled many Parisians – who experienced the addition as 'fingernails on a chalkboard', in Dan Brown's words. These were the conservatives who, like Bezu Fache, saw the pyramid as 'a scar on the face of Paris'.

The Pyramid at the Louvre reawakens the power of this ancient symbol of the sun and its rays casting a heavenly light upon the earth.

Nowadays, however, only the most reactionary Parisians can fail to be proud of their city's daring, seeing the Pyramid, as Brown puts it, as 'a dazzling synergy of ancient structure and modern method – a symbolic link between the old and new – helping usher the Louvre into the next millennium'.

The Pyramid has successfully acted as a giant glass beacon, encouraging millions of visitors into the Louvre and signalling the museum's ambitions as a cathedral of light and colour, rather than a dusty old stone warehouse. This was President Mitterrand's aim when he authorized the Grand Louvre project: to revitalize Paris's heart. Mitterrand may have had a dubious reputation – Brown includes an aside that he was 'rumoured to move in mysterious circles' – but these rumours were more to do with his political or sexual peccadilloes than anything else. The idea that there are **666 panes** of glass in the Pyramid is based on an urban myth that did the rounds in Paris nearly twenty years ago; the Louvre officially states that there are 673 – which fits our own count – while the office of I.M. Pei (an architect interested in light and geometric abstraction, rather than symbology) counted 698. It's not far off the Number of the Beast, but then a near miss is as good as a mile with numerology.

Much less well known – at least before *The Da Vinci Code* – is the **Pyramide Inversée**, or Upside-down Pyramid, which stands in the middle of the open expanse of **Place du Carrousel**, hidden by a roundabout and circular hedges. Brown claims this was 'once the site of Paris's primeval nature-worshipping festivals', which is a flight of fancy. This smaller pyramid extends down from ground level into the modernized bowels of the Louvre, bringing light into the giant underground shopping complex and car park created beneath Mitterrand's museum plan. At its base, a miniature, black marble pyramid does indeed extend upwards like a swollen, geometric stalagmite to meet its inverted sister, but you'll get some odd looks if you fall on your knees, like Robert Langdon, to worship at it. In

Beneath the Louvre is the mysterious Pyramide Inversée which descends from the Place du Carrousel. A smaller pyramid rises beneath it.

season, however, when the fashionistas use the Carrousel complex for their haute couture fashion shows, anything goes.

Just beyond the Place du Carrousel, the pink marble **Arc du Carrousel** stands in forlorn isolation. Again Brown conjures 'orgiastic rituals' once being held here. The more mundane history is that it was a militaristic triumphal arch built for Napoleon, and orginally formed a gateway for the Palais des Tuileries, the Louvre's lost twin, which burnt to the ground during the Paris Commune uprising of 1871.

OH LAME SAINT: LEONARDO'S MONA LISA

Like so many visitors to the Louvre's biggest celebrity, Sophie Neveu has high expectations when she stands in front of the **Mona Lisa** for the first time. But she feels 'no jolt of amazement. No instant of wonder. The famous face looked as it did in books'. She finds it 'too little' and 'foggy' – 'she looks like she knows something'. Sophie doesn't like the image. Some visitors have the same reaction: disappointment or a let-down feeling; others find it strange to see something so familiar as if for the first time. And there is the further problem of its popularity. For most of the day, the painting is mobbed: something exacerbated by the success of *The Da Vinci Code* which brought an estimated half million additional visitors to the museum in 2005. However, on the positive side, 2005 also saw the portrait rehung, with much improved visibility, in the superbly restored Salle des Etats, off the Grande Galerie.

If you can ignore the crowds, and the colours yellowed and darkened by varnish that no one dares to clean, if you can banish Jacques Saunière's spurious explanation of the smile, then you are left with a masterful painting that you might think lives up to its reputation. However, the fame of Leonardo's *Mona Lisa* rests as much on the controversies that have long surrounded it as on its aesthetic qualities. Its early history is revealed in its name, an English corruption of Monna Lisa, which was historian Giorgio Vasari's polite way of referring to *madonna* (my lady) Lisa Gherardini, whose portrait he documented in the sixteenth century. She was married to one Francesco del Giocondo, from whose surname the Italians get their name for the painting, **la Gioconda**, and the French **la Joconde**. Dan Brown therefore cheats a bit to work in his Anglocentric anagrams 'oh lame saint' and 'Amon/L'Isa'.

It's not actually certain that the *Mona Lisa* depicts Monna Lisa. The portrait Vasari described, having never seen it himself, had eyebrows where the hair 'grows thickly in one place' (the *Mona Lisa* has none) and 'parting lips', (she smiles, but her mouth is closed). The only other contemporary description is by a secretary of Cardinal Louis of Aragon, who visited Leonardo at Amboise and was shown three pictures that the artist had brought with him to France, including 'one of a certain Florentine lady, done from life'. The only real certainty is that the *Mona Lisa* turned up in the bathroom of the Palace of Fontainebleau, which Henri IV decided to restore in the 1590s. She remained largely neglected by public and art historians alike, and her early days in the Louvre were restricted to the curator's office. But in the 1830s, the Romantic poet and novelist Théophile Gautier created the myth of the picture as femme fatale, writing of how her 'sinuous, serpentine mouth, turned up at the corners in a violet penumbra, mocks the viewer with such sweetness, grace and superiority that we feel timid, like schoolboys in the presence of a duchess'. From then on, her fame grew and grew, augmented when the picture was stolen by an Italian security guard on August 21, 1911, and recovered in December 1913.

So Dark the Con of Man: the Grande Galerie

The thrilling, intriguing opening scene of *The Da Vinci Code*'s Louvre sequence takes place in what Dan Brown calls the 'Grand

The *Mona Lisa* was returned to the Salle des Etats in 2005 – this was its previous, temporary home; photography, thankfully, has now been outlawed.

Gallery'. Strictly speaking, its name is really more like 'Big Gallery', as the French term is simply *La Grande Galerie*. Built on the orders of Catherine de Médici to link the Louvre and Tuileries palaces, the **Grande Galerie** stretches into the distance on an endless carpet of perfect parquet flooring (a wonder in itself, as Brown points out), while its walls parade all the great names of the Italian Renaissance – Mantegna, Filippo Lippi, Raphael, Correggio, Titian and, of course, Leonardo da Vinci.

It's in the Grande Galerie that you'll find Leonardo's *Vierge aux Rochers* or **Virgin of the Rocks**, in Salle 5. Dan Brown has stretched the truth a little in order to get an anagram out of this name, as the painting is never referred to as the *Madonna of the Rocks*, even in English. But it was indeed rejected by the Milanese Confraternity that commissioned it, though apparently more on the grounds that it was judged to be unfinished and to lack overtly Christian references, than

Here in the Grande Galerie the dying Jacques Saunière spent his last moments scribbling clues and arranging his naked body in a symbolic position on the parquet floor.

for any supposedly heretical symbolism. As *The Da Vinci Code* asserts, Leonardo painted a second version, now in London's National Gallery, while this one found its way over the Alps with Leonardo to the court of François I, and thus into the royal collection in the Louvre.

Close at hand is Leonardo's wonderful **Virgin and Child with St Anne**, again little troubled by crowds. And a short way beyond, in Salle 8, are some fine Mannerist paintings and the **Caravaggios** – you can try to guess which one the dying Saunière might have used to trigger the Louvre's alarms. Perhaps the *Death of the Virgin*?

FILMING THE LOUVRE

Filming began at the Louvre on the night of 30 June–1 July 2005. The *Da Vinci Code* producers had spent three solid months wooing the museum's directors and the French culture ministry. They even enjoyed a leisurely coffee with President Jacques Chirac, who supposedly offered to oil the wheels of French bureaucracy. The Culture Ministry eventually agreed to allow on-location filming, albeit with a reported €1million location fee and some tight restrictions.

The Louvre insisted that all shooting had to be done at night, after the museum had closed to regular visitors – not much of a problem, as all the book's scenes are set at night anyway. Lights were not to be shone on the more precious paintings, and the crew were banned from using fake blood on the precious parquet floor of the Grande Galerie. Scrawling 'So Dark the Con of Man' across the Mona Lisa's new, multi-million-euro glass case was presumably out of the question, too, so all shots featuring the painting were done in the studio, using a mock-up. That said, the Salle des Etats, the gorgeous and newly restored room where the Mona Lisa hangs, apparently made a convenient place for the crew to store equipment during shooting in the adjacent Grande Galerie. 'You turn a corner', recalled Tom Hanks, 'and you see this room holding all the stuff you make movies with – boxes, tools, camera stands, disassembled cranes ... and the *Mona Lisa*'.

LOUVRE PRACTICALITIES

The Louvre is **open daily** except Tuesdays from 9am–6pm, with late opening till 9.45pm on Wednesdays and Fridays. Admission costs €8.50 (€6 for the 'nocturnes', after 6pm; free to under-26s on Fridays after 6pm). See *www.louvre.fr* for details. **Tickets** can be bought in advance by calling ☎0892.683.622; from branches of FNAC and Virgin Megastore; or online at *www.louvre.fr*

Tips on visiting

Tales of queues for tickets and miles of energy-sapping corridors can leave you feeling somewhat intimidated before you've even set foot in the Louvre. The best advice is to go early or late in the day, and not to attempt to see too much – as it says in *The Da Vinci Code*, it would take five weeks or more to see the lot. And pick up a free **floor plan** from the information booth in the Hall Napoléon, which makes sense of the building by colour-coding its various sections, and highlighting a few of the best-known masterpieces.

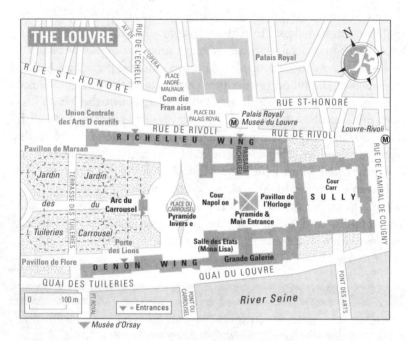

THE LOUVRE

Palais Royal

AV. DE L'OPERA

RUE DE L'ECHELLE

PLACE ANDRÉ-MALRAUX

RUE ST-HONORE

RUE ST-HONORÉ

Com die Fran aise

PLACE DU PALAIS ROYAL

Union Centrale des Arts D coratifs

Palais Royal/ Musée du Louvre (M)

RUE DE RIVOLI

RUE DE RIVOLI

Louvre-Rivoli (M)

R I C H E L I E U   W I N G

RUE DE L'AMIRAL DE COLIGNY

Pavillon de Marsan

Jardin   Jardin

des   du

PASSAGE RICHELIEU

TERRASSE DES TUILERIES

Arc du Carrousel

PLACE DU CARROUSEL

Cour Napol on

Pavillon de l'Horloge

Cour Carr

S U L L Y

Pyramide Invers e

Pyramide & Main Entrance

Tuileries   Carrousel

Porte des Lions

Salle des Etats (Mona Lisa)

Grande Galerie

Pavillon de Flore

D E N O N   W I N G

QUAI DU LOUVRE

PONT DES ARTS

QUAI DES TUILERIES

0   100 m

PT ROYAL

PONT DU CARROUSEL

▼ = Entrances

River Seine

▼ Musée d'Orsay

The main **entrance** is via the pyramid, but if it's raining or the queues look too long then try the entrance directly under the Arc du Carrousel – this can be accessed from 99 rue de Rivoli and from the line #1 platform of the Palais Royal-Musée du Louvre métro stop. If you've already got a ticket you can also enter from the Passage Richelieu – where Langdon breaks into a jog as he nears the denouement. The passage also offers a free view of the dramatically glazed-over sculpture courtyards.

If you're planning on making a short visit, you might consider confining yourself to the **Denon section** of the museum, rightly lauded by Dan Brown. As well as the *Mona Lisa*, Denon houses all of Italian painting, some tremendous French nineteenth-century canvases, and the great Italian and Classical sculptures. Rewarding and less crowded alternatives would be to focus on the grand chronologies of French painting and sculpture or stroll through the sensual collection of Objets d'Art.

If you're attempting a longer visit, remember that the entry ticket allows you to step outside. Or for a change of scene, you can burrow down to the lowest level, where you'll find the Louvre's **medieval foundations**, including the huge stump of Philippe-Auguste's medieval keep, dramatically revealed beneath the hangar-like concrete roof. Alternatively, try one of the museum's **cafés**: the relatively quiet *Café Richelieu* (first floor, Richelieu), the cosy *Café Denon* (lower ground floor, Denon), and the busier *Café Mollien* (first floor, Denon), which has a summer terrace, are the nicest.

The Rose Line: St-Sulpice

The Da Vinci Code's second key Paris location is undoubtedly the church of **St-Sulpice**, site in the novel of the 'Rose Line'. It has long been a popular Paris sight, set as it is in the quartier of St-Germain – once famed for Left Bank intellectuals, although the handsome eighteenth-century town houses, celebrity cafés and boutique shops are these days home to a much more affluent community, many British and American expatriates among them.

If you head down rue Bonaparte from Boulevard St-Germain, you'll come to the chestnut-tree-shaded expanse of Place St-Sulpice, centred on a dramatic fountain. As one of Paris's loveliest spots, it's somehow

St-Sulpice – an essential stop on the Parisian Grail trail.

The Rose Line set into the floor of St Sulpice leads to the base of the obelisk where Silas hopes to find the key to the Holy Grail.

appropriate that French actress Catherine Deneuve maintains an apartment here. Looming up on the square's east side is the giant bulk of the **church** (open daily 7.30am–7.30pm), an austere classical edifice erected either side of 1700, with a Doric colonnade surmounted by an Ionic, and Corinthian pilasters in the towers – uncut masonry blocks still protrude from the south tower, awaiting the sculptor's chisel. *The Da Vinci Code* has it 'built over the ruins of an ancient temple to the Egyptian goddess Isis' – a claim that has prompted the church authorities to post a notice inside, asserting 'this is NOT a pagan temple'. It is in fact built on the same footprint as Notre-Dame de Paris, though it's some ten metres shorter.

Occult associations

Dan Brown is not the first writer to use St-Sulpice as a literary location. The Decadent novelist Joris-Karl Huysmans' strange 1891 novel *La-Bàs* features the bell-ringer of St-Sulpice carrying on a secluded existence at the heart of a late-nineteenth-century Paris gripped by a fever for the occult. Meanwhile, the novel's hero, Durtal, is writing a biography of the Satanic, child-murdering, fifteenth-century nobleman Gilles de Rais, a legendarily monstrous figure better known in the English-speaking world as Bluebeard. Given this literary background, it's perhaps understandable that the authorities at St-Sulpice weren't too pleased to feature in *The Da Vinci Code* as well, and they refused permission for the movie to be filmed on location.

THE GNOMON

Prior to *The Da Vinci Code*, the church's gloomy **interior** was best known for three **Delacroix murals** found in the first chapel on the right – notably one of St Michael slaying a dragon – and for the huge, eighteenth-century, five-manual **organ**, which is put through its paces in regular recitals. But these days it is the **gnomon** that pulls in the visitors. There's no sign of Sister Sandrine's dwelling on the left of the choir balcony, but head to the transepts and you can't miss the line, which begins as a strip of brass on the south side. Sadly, the lens that once filled the oculus in the south wall is no more, so this is not a working gnomon. In the rose windows of the transepts, you can see the notorious stained-glass windows marked 'P' and 'S'. They stand for Peter and Sulpice, the church's main saints.

Far from being some kind of pagan vestige of solar-worship, the gnomon was set up in 1727 by one Henry Sully, an English clock-maker, to allow the church's priest, Jean-Baptiste Languet de Gergy, to establish the exact date of Easter. *The Da Vinci Code* departs from accuracy once again in its passage about the copper measuring track marking the Meridian. 'Long before the establishment of Greenwich as the prime meridian,' it asserts, 'the zero longitude of the entire world had passed directly through Paris'. True so far, but it then claims: 'The brass marker was a memorial to the world's first prime meridian… the original Rose Line'. Unfortunately, a quick glance at a map of Paris shows that while the Meridian passes close to St-Sulpice – it was designed deliberately to run right through the city centre – it doesn't actually run through it.

If you're keen to find out more, you can head southeast through the delightful Jardin du Luxembourg and across the Boulevard de Montparnasse to the **Observatoire de Paris**, where the astronomical measurements establishing the Meridian were first made in the 1660s, and where you can try to spot some of the little brass medallions that mark the **'Arago line'**, named after the astronomer.

Merovingian Paris

The traces of **Merovingian Paris** are not documented in Dan Brown's novel, but deserve to be a part of any *Da Vinci Code* trail.

St-Germain and Notre-Dame

Just a couple of minutes' walk to the north of St-Sulpice – on the sunny side of Boulevard St-Germain, beside the famous Existentialist cafés *Flore* and *Les Deux Magots* – stands the venerable church of **St-Germain-des-Prés**. There may or may not have been a pagan temple here, but the site is certainly very ancient. The earliest known church here dated back to the sixth century, when the **Merovingian dynasty** – the supposed descendants of Jesus and Mary Magdalene – used it as an early royal burial place. You can still see some marble columns from the old church, but the only tomb of note nowadays is that of the rationalist philosopher **René Descartes** – who some would think a far worthier object of veneration than the incestuous, murderous Merovingian dynasty…

However, if there is a true Merovingian centre in Paris, it lies under the great cathedral of **Notre-Dame**, which was built right on top of St-Etienne, the original church built by the son of Clovis, the founder of the Merovingian dynasty. The site's sanctity actually dates right back to the Romans, who had a temple here, but there's little left now other than a few broken stone fragments and bits of wall, visible in its **Crypte Archéologique**.

St-Denis

For actual Merovingian remains, the key site is **St-Denis**, just outside the northern perimeter of this city. Its stone effigies are far more impressive than London's Temple Church, as this abbey basilica was the burial place of all but three of the French monarchs, from Hugh Capet in 996 to the Revolution. What's more, the history of St-Denis is intertwined with the Merovingian dynasty, as it was founded by the Merovingian **King Dagobert**, of mysterious reputation, who died in 639. Dagobert was the first French monarch to be buried here – or, more accurately, the first Frankish king, as France had not yet come into being, and the old Roman province of Gaul had dissolved into the warring territories of Neustria, Burgundy and Austrasia.

According to *The Da Vinci Code*, the blood of Jesus and Mary Magdalene once flowed through the veins of the Merovingians in the Abbey church of St-Denis.

When Sir Leigh Teabing explains the secret history of the grail lineage to Sophie at his Château de Villette, in Chapter 60, he asks her if she has heard of Dagobert. Good student of esoteric lore that she is, she replies that he was stabbed in the eye while sleeping. Or, as Teabing puts it, he was 'assassinated by the Vatican in collusion with Pepin d'Heristal. With Dagobert's murder, the Merovingian bloodline was almost exterminated.' Which is half, or perhaps more accurately, quarter-true. The murdered king was actually Dagobert II, who ruled some forty years after the first Dagobert, or rather failed to rule, as he spent much of his life in terrified exile in Ireland. His murderer was indeed Pepin 'the Fat' of Heristal, though the Vatican link is pure fancy. Teabing's phrase 'almost exterminated' is another of those *Da Vinci Code* not-quite-links, as he goes on to state that Dagobert's son Sigisbert survived. In fact, Pepin subsequently ruled in Dagobert's place, so the 'extermination' was less the near-end of a mystical bloodline and more the last act in a ruthless political tragedy of Merovingian decline. After Dagobert's death, the palace mayors grew in power until, under Pepin's great-grandson, Charlemagne, the Merovingians were finally and definitively replaced by the new 'Carolingian' dynasty.

THE TOMBS

Dagobert was both the first king to be interred in St-Denis, and the last Merovingian king of any significance. His tomb still stands in the basilica, along with all the other **royal tombs** – refined and melancholy structures that fill the transepts and ambulatory. Dagobert's own extravagant, canopied monument is, sadly, not contemporary; it was commissioned by Louis IX of the Capetian dynasty, who ennobled his forebears' tombs with fine medieval sculpture in the 1260s. And it's not even entirely original, as in 1793 iconoclastic revolutionaries went on a riot of tomb-smashing. Along with the rest of the royal tombs it is partly the product of post-revolutionary restoration efforts.

Nonetheless, the **basilica** itself is one of the finest medieval churches in France, and is generally regarded as the European birthplace of the Gothic style. The credit for its building goes to **Abbot Suger**, friend and adviser to kings, who built a new church here in the first half of the twelfth century. His design set the pattern of Gothic facades to come. Suger's innovations can still be seen in the lowest storey of the choir, but the upper storeys were rebuilt in the mid-thirteenth century, at the same time as the nave was constructed, in the mature Rayonnant Gothic style.

VISITING ST-DENIS

The Basilique St-Denis (April–Sept Mon–Sat 10am–6.15pm, Sun 1pm–6.15pm; Oct–March Mon–Sat 10am–5.15pm, Sun 1pm–5.15pm) is only a short walk from the St-Denis-Basilique métro station, at the end of métro line 13. You need to buy a ticket (€6.10) to get access to the tombs – and note that these can't be visited during services.

Tea with Teabing: Château de Villette

Château de Villette – or 'The Château Villette', as Sophie Neveu calls it – really exists, though its location in a 'castle district' in the 'environs of Versailles' is a bit of a stretch. However, Versailles isn't far off, and the entire region around Paris is littered with châteaux built by French royals and nobles before the Revolution.

Château de Villette outside Paris – the home of Sir Leigh Teabing, historian of the Holy Grail.

Here in the library at Château de Villette, amid copies of the Nag Hammadi codices and the Dead Sea scrolls, Teabing reveals the truth about the Holy Grail to Sophie Neveu.

Villette was designed by the great architect François Mansart around 1668, for Count d'Aufflay, Louis XIV's ambassador to Italy, and has recently been restored to glory by an American Francophile, Olivia Hsu Decker. It is described in *The Da Vinci Code* as 'one of Paris's most significant historical châteaux' – which perhaps gives a little too grand an impression. This is not a top-rank royal château like Fontainebleau, Vaux-le-Vicomte, Chantilly or Versailles itself – all close at hand if you are visiting Paris. But it is all the more enjoyable for that: a beautiful private residence, on a sumptuous but human scale, with its own **chapel**, **lake** and **water gardens**. And it has the bonus that – if you can afford the weekly rate of €3900– €4300 a head – you can actually **stay** in one of its eighteen guest bedrooms, and indulge yourself in a luxury *Da Vinci Code* program. This includes visits to the Louvre and St-Sulpice, a tour of the Bois de Boulogne, lunch at the Ritz and a group discussion session, with opportunities to watch the film and various *Code*-related documentaries. Visitors of more modest means may just want to do a **two-hour tour** of the *Da Vinci Code* rooms at Villette itself, which include the **library**. When available, this is priced at €55 – and you need to get together a group of ten or more to book.

Most of the Villette scenes in the movie were filmed in the studio, although the exterior features in a dramatic aerial sequence, shot from a helicopter, and Ian McKellen's first entrance, descending the stairs as Leigh Teabing, complete with black walking canes and leg-brace (rather than the crutches described in the book), was filmed on Villette's actual staircase – a decision, said McKellen, which would 'help authenticate the movie'.

For details of rooms and tours, see the château's website (*www.frenchvacation.com*), or email *Villette@frenchvacation.com*

Other Paris Locations

Keep the book open: there are three further, minor *Da Vinci Code* locations in Paris that you can visit.

THE RITZ

The American University of Paris, for which Langdon is lecturing, is obviously a well-endowed institution. Robert Langdon's hotel room in the extremely snobby **Ritz Paris hotel**, on the fur-coat-and-diamonds Place Vendôme, costs a minimum of €610 a night, and you can pay up to €8500 for the top suite. Tea – or a drink at the bar – won't break the bank to the same extent. The movie's very first location shoot took place outside the Ritz, on the Place Vendôme.

GARE DU NORD

In the first edition of *The Da Vinci Code*, Brown had Sophie and Robert dashing off to the **Gare St-Lazare** to buy a ticket to Lille. Subsequent editions, no doubt after a deluge of readers' mail, have them heading to the **Gare du Nord** – the right station for departures to Lille. The Paris stations, presumably, didn't form a part of Brown's research, for he gives a peculiar description of a train 'belching and wheezing in preparation for departure'. In fact, you're more likely to see some of the most modern trains in the world: the sharp-nosed TGV, the Eurostar heading to London, or the brash, red Franco-German Thalys train.

BOIS DE BOULOGNE

The Da Vinci Code's description of the **Bois de Boulogne** – a giant wooded park just beyond the western city limits near Roland Garros tennis stadium – is more accurate, though 'Parisian cognoscenti' do not know it as the 'Garden of Earthly Delights', and in the daytime it's just one of the city's greatest and greenest lungs, a public park filled with woods, lakes, riding schools, gardens, floral displays and cycling routes. As Paris's chief night-time cruising area for prostitutes and their clients, however, its roads can indeed be 'lined with hundreds of glistening bodies for hire, earthly delights to satisfy one's deepest unspoken desires – male, female, and everything in between'.

More puzzling is the choice of the park as a route to **Rue Haxo** – which is found entirely on the opposite side of the city, in the eastern, working-class district of Ménilmontant. An odd location for a classy Swiss bank.

London

In the last third of *The Da Vinci Code* the action shifts across the Channel from Paris to London. Our heroes shun the underground possibilities of the Channel Tunnel for Teabing's ultra-speedy Hawker 731, which deposits them safely at **Biggin Hill**, celebrated as the RAF base from which the first Spitfires took off to fight the Battle of Britain in 1940, and now a private airport just south of the capital. For the film, however, homely Biggin Hill wasn't considered glamorous enough, and the 1930s Art Deco **Shoreham airport**, near Brighton, was used as a more photogenic stand-in.

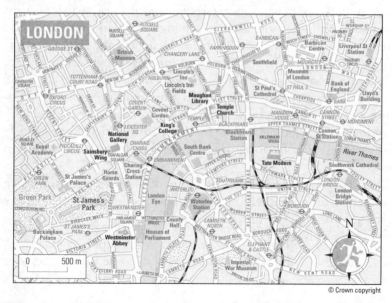

© Crown copyright

From the airport, the adrenalin-fuelled quest takes Langdon and Sophie to what was (until *The Da Vinci Code*) one of London's lesser-known sights – the **Temple Church** – and then, after a detour via the library at **King's College**, to perhaps the best known London attraction of all, **Westminster Abbey**.

If you're visiting both the religious sites, it's well worth passing through one of Brown's relatively minor but lovelier locations: **St James's Park**, where the Teacher murders Rémy. And take a detour to the **National Gallery**, where you can check out the 'watered-down' version of Leonardo's twice-painted masterpiece, the **Virgin of the Rocks**.

Temple Church

The **Temple Church**, where Robert Langdon and Sophie Neveu make a false start in their quest for 'the knight A pope interred', is the oldest building in the **Inns of Court**, a little-known and rather isolated part of London. Squeezed in between the historic City of Westminster, to the west, and the ancient City of London, to the east, the Inns of Court acts as the mother hive of Britain's industrious law trade, and has done so ever since law students slept at the original inns here, in order to be close to the courthouses.

Rather like Oxbridge colleges, the Inns are divided up into distinct institutions: Inner Temple, Middle Temple, Lincoln's Inn and Gray's Inn. The first two get their odd name from the **Knights Templar**, who had a similar collegiate-style institution at this spot, until they were suppressed by the Crown in 1312, following the European lead.

The Temple Church itself dates from 1185, when the original **Round Church** was built by the Knights Templar on the model of the Church of the Holy Sepulchre in Jerusalem. A projecting chancel was added in the thirteenth century, but otherwise the basic circular structure survives, despite Christopher Wren's major restoration of

1682. The Round Church even weathered the bombs of 1941 (not 1940, as Brown has it), though much of the actual stonework is post-war mimicry as a result. This final restoration gave the interior what Brown calls a 'stark grandeur', though it is scarcely 'original' – the interior would once have been painted in lavishly bright colours.

Sophie imagines the space as a 'theatre in the round', as if built for 'a sacred communion', and she's quite literally correct. Indeed, many modern churches have been built in a similar round shape, emphasizing the communally-shared nature of the Eucharist, as opposed to the old-style High Mass which had a priest standing at the high altar with his back to the congregation, mediating between God and Man at a safe distance. Sophie's feverish vision of 'masked people chanting by torchlight', however, is well off-beam – at least if she's imagining an erotic *Hieros Gamos* rite in this sedate, Anglican church.

The famous **stone knights** were badly damaged in the bombing, but still have an eerie presence thanks to their life-size stillness. There is in fact no missing knight – there have always been just nine, plus a coffin. The best-known effigy is of **William the Marshal**, Earl of Pembroke, who acted as go-between for King John and his rebellious barons when Magna Carta was signed in 1215. Buried alongside is his son, another William, who was a key player in forcing King John to bend to the barons' demands.

TEMPLE CHURCH PRACTICALITIES

The church's **opening hours** (☎020 7353 3470, *www.templechurch. com*) vary considerably, so check in advance. The church is hidden in a maze of courtyards and little streets, but it's easy to find your way from Fleet Street, to the north. The church's all-male **choir** makes the most of the superb acoustics with a choral mass at 11.15am on Sundays, and choral evensong one afternoon a week. The Master of The Temple Church, the Rev Robin Griffith-Jones, also gives talks on *The Da Vinci Code* every Friday at 1pm.

The effigies of Templar knights are set into the stone floor of the circular Temple church in London.

Systematic Theology: King's College

If you're heading on from Temple Church towards **King's College's Research Institute of Systematic Theology**, you could, like Robert and Sophie, take the westbound **District and Circle Line** (noting that Temple tube station is closed on Sundays), though you wouldn't be advised to 'hurdle a turnstile', as they somehow succeed in doing. It has been a good fifteen years since London Underground replaced the old, vaultable gates with the modern, ticket-dodger-proof kind…

However, if, like Robert and Sophie, you're in a hurry, you should really avoid the tube altogether. The Research Institute of Systematic Theology meets at the **Chesham Building** – on Surrey Street, just fifty yards north of Temple tube! Why you'd go there is less clear, as the institute is in fact little more than a program of seminars for academics, held in Room 2E of the Chesham Building for an hour and three-quarters on Tuesday mornings.

The 'octagonal chamber' that Brown describes at the opening of Chapter 92 is in fact the **Maughan Library**, inside the Chancery Lane campus building – itself a five-minute stroll from Temple tube, to the northeast. The Victorian Gothic building, built by a pupil of John Nash, was once the home of the Public Record Office, and dubbed 'the strong box of the Empire'. Inside, the library's **Round Reading Room** (yes, it is more nearly octagonal than round) was built as a junior version of the old British Library's famous Reading Room. It's a serene and handsome space but, sadly for *Da Vinci* tourists, open only to visiting researchers – unless you can time your visit to coincide with London's annual 'Open House' weekend, in September. You can at least find a photo at King's College's website: *www.kcl.ac.uk/college/history/campuses/chancery.html*

Knight A Pope Interred: Westminster Abbey

If you're coming from the Temple and heading for **Westminster Abbey** and Newton's monument, take that westbound District and Circle Line – the daringly modern Westminster tube station is just two stops west, and Westminster Abbey stands just on the opposite side of Parliament Square from the station, right next to the Houses of Parliament. The Abbey declined the advances of the *Da Vinci* film makers, possibly, as Ian McKellen mused, through establishment pressure (see p.256). And indeed, the church is the ancient and still just-twitching heart of Stately Britain – its pulse sustained by infusions of sublime evensong from the dedicated choir school, and by the infrequent adrenalin surges of pompous royal weddings (not, however, that of Charles and Diana, which took place in St Paul's Cathedral), coronations and funerals. And it is also, as Dan Brown states, very much a tourist trap.

The Teacher finds Westminster Abbey a 'quiet sanctuary'; Langdon feels 'the outside world evaporate with a sudden hush … just a deafening silence, which seemed to reverberate back and forth as if the building were whispering to itself'. But alas, that isn't the experience of most of its hundreds of thousands of visitors – and there is something objectionable about a national church that puts itself entirely off-limits, without a £10 ticket, unless you attend a service.

It is, nevertheless, staggeringly beautiful. Brown dates the abbey as 900 years old, though the original structure built by Edward the Confessor in the eleventh century survives only in the floor plan and crypt. The current structure was begun by **Henry III** in 1245, in admiring emulation of the Gothic design of Rheims cathedral. Henry's masons completed the east end, transept, and the first four bays of the nave, but it was another century before Richard II continued the work, and only in the sixteenth century did the great Tudor monarch **Henry VII** build the stunning **Lady Chapel** at the east end, the masterpiece of the impossibly elaborate English Perpendicular style. And the west front and twin towers are the work of **Nicholas Hawksmoor** in the eighteenth century.

NEWTON'S MONUMENT

Isaac Newton died on March 20, 1727 and was buried in the Abbey on March 28, at a spot just in front of the choir screen, where a Latin inscription explains 'Here lies that which was mortal of Isaac Newton'. Newton's coffin was accompanied by the Fellows of the Royal Society, along with the Lord Chancellor, two dukes and three earls. The event has been lavishly recreated in the movie, although the north transept of Lincoln Cathedral is standing in for the abbey.

Sir Isaac Newton, supposed Grand Master of the Priory of Sion, who is buried in Westminster Abbey. His monument is on the left.

Sadly, **Alexander Pope** wasn't there to deliver the stirring eulogy Brown attributes to him. That came much later, in the form of the poet's famous epitaph, as learned by generations of English schoolchildren: 'Nature and Nature's laws lay hid in night / God said, "Let Newton be!" and all was light'. Still, an epitaph is almost a burial, so you can forgive Brown bending the facts a little to get in his pun on 'A pope'. (It's a shame he couldn't squeeze in J.C. Squire's later riposte: 'It did not last, the Devil howling "Ho! / Let Einstein be!" restored the status quo'.)

The **monument** – or, as Brown would have it, the 'stately tomb' – is close at hand. Designed by William Kent in pale marble, with the main sculpture by Michael Rysbrack, it was finished in 1731, and is indeed stately, if not strictly a tomb. Brown's description is accurate enough, but the full text of the Latin inscription is worth quoting: 'Here is buried Isaac Newton, Knight, who by a strength of mind almost divine, and mathematical principles peculiarly his own, explored the course and figures of the planets, the paths of comets, the tides of the sea, the dissimilarities in rays of light, and, what no other scholar has previously imagined, the properties of the colours thus produced ... Mortals rejoice that there has existed such and so great an ornament of the human race!'

THE CLOISTERS AND CHAPTER HOUSE

In Chapter 98, Teabing lays his trap for Robert Langdon and Sophie Neveu, instructing them to meet him in the Chapter House. Unlike Langdon and Neveu, you don't have to go through the Abbey to get there – you can save the entrance fee if you enter via the huge enclosure of Dean's Yard, immediately south of the Abbey – but there is a route, via the south choir aisle. Either way, you have to pass through the **Great Cloister** (daily 8am–6pm), which Brown calls the east cloisters, and which Langdon found 'lived up to their Latin ties to the word claustrophobic'. In fact, they're remarkably large, though of course, closed in on all four sides. As she hurries through, Neveu doesn't have time to follow Virginia Woolf's instruction that all women should 'let flowers fall' on the funerary slab commemorating the seventeenth-century writer Aphra Behn; for, Woolf wrote, 'it was she who earned them the right to speak their minds'.

Beyond the Cloister lies the **Chapter House** (daily: April–Sept 9.30am–5pm; Oct 10am–5pm; Nov–March 10am–4pm; £1), a giant octagonal structure dating from 1255. The House of Commons met here until 1395, standing on the same decorative floor tiles, under the gaze of the same apocalyptic wall paintings which look down on modern visitors. But as Langdon and Neveu discover with dismay, this is a dead end; you have to exit the way you came in.

On leaving, you can also turn left to head through the Little Cloister, once the home of sick and old monks, to the **College Garden** (Tues–Thurs: April–Sept 10am–6pm; Oct–March 10am–4pm; free), which Langdon remembers seeing on a previous visit. It is indeed an ancient orchard and herb garden, though now used as a croquet lawn by pupils of the elite Westminster School, next door.

THE REST OF THE ABBEY

If you've got time for more than puzzling out the missing orb on Newton's monument and playing Mexican stand-offs in the Chapter House, make for the **Lady Chapel**, where you'll find Henry VII's own black marble sarcophagus, along with the giant tomb of Elizabeth I and a chapel dedicated to the RAF, where a window depicts the angels that supposedly appeared to pilots at the 1940 Battle of Britain. Just outside the chapel is the ancient, oak **Coronation Chair**, used for every royal crowning since 1308. Behind is the tomb of the soldier-king, **Henry V**.

Over in the south transept, **Poets' Corner** is another popular place to visit. You can seek out the graves or memorial stones of, among others, William Shakespeare, Samuel Johnson, William Blake – the original esoteric-cum-Gnostic poet if there ever was one, represented by a fine sculpture by Jacob Epstein – Byron, Tennyson, Charles Dickens and Thomas Hardy.

The **nave** is perhaps the grandest space of all, easily the tallest in Britain at over a hundred feet. Dan Brown nicely describes it as a 'great abyss' whose 'columns ascended like redwoods into the shadows, arching gracefully over dizzying expanses'. Close to Newton's monument you can find other scientists' graves, including those of Lord Kelvin and – some are surprised to discover – supposed archatheist **Charles Darwin**.

VISITING THE ABBEY

Westminster Abbey is **open for visits** every day except Sunday (Mon, Tues, Thurs & Fri 9.30am–3.45pm, Wed 9am–6pm, Sat 9.30am–1.45pm; £10; *www.westminster-abbey.org*), and parts may also be visited at other times if you attend a service. You need to pass through a metal detector, so unless you're Sir Leigh Teabing with an ID card declaring you're 'a modern British knight', it's best to leave the handgun at home. It's also a very good idea to visit early or late in the day, on a weekday, and outside peak tourist seasons, to avoid the crowds.

Rémy's Murder: St James's Park

In Chapter 94, the Teacher murders Rémy in **St James's Park**, which Brown describes as 'a sea of green in the middle of London'. Lovely though St James's is, this overstates its subtle charms. If handed Brown's description, most Londoners would probably imagine he was writing about the grassy ocean of neighbouring Hyde Park.

But Brown is right in that St James's was indeed enclosed by Henry VIII, and it was finally opened to the public by Charles II, who used to bathe in the canal and who did indeed receive a gift of pelicans from the Russian ambassador; these are the ancestors of the pelicans that now live happily on Duck Island. Unfortunately, the crocodiles kept here by Charles's grandfather, James I, failed to produce an equivalent dynasty.

The 'morning fog' which fails to prevent the Teacher having 'splendid views of the Houses of Parliament and Big Ben' seems to be the child of an abiding American myth about London that owes more to George Gershwin than Thameside fact. Mist or fog of any kind is rare indeed in London, and the once-famous smog has scarcely been smelt since the Clean Air Act of 1956. You will have to stand in the right spot to enjoy the Teacher's view, as the hulking Neoclassical lumps of the Foreign Office and Treasury stand in the way from some angles. But perhaps the finest panorama encompasses the back of the handsome, eighteenth-century **Horse Guards** building, overlooking the grand square of Horse Guards Parade, with the giant bicycle wheel of the **London Eye** peeping engagingly over the top.

St James's Park lies just a couple of hundred yards north of Westminster Abbey – cross in front of the elaborate stony mass of Methodist Central Hall, then continue up the narrow street of Storey's Gate, which brings you to the corner of the park.

The National Gallery

What Langdon calls the 'watered-down' version of the *Madonna of the Rocks*, more usually known as the **Virgin of the Rocks**, hangs in London's **National Gallery** (daily 10am–6pm, Wed till 9pm; free; *www.nationalgallery.org.uk*). It's one of the many masterpieces that place this gallery in the top rank, a status upheld by its authoritative position on the north side of Trafalgar Square.

The painting is housed in the postmodernist **Sainsbury Wing**, on the west side of the main façade, a sober block that fits into its surroundings cleverly, seeming to fade out the neoclassical details on its façade as it moves away from the original gallery building. It could have been very different: after a public outcry, this design replaced an earlier, more aggressively modern conception that Prince Charles famously called 'a monstrous carbuncle on the face of a much-loved and elegant friend'.

Once inside, head for **Room 51,** where you can check out the **Virgin of the Rocks** for yourself against the *Da Vinci Code* theories originally put forward by Lynn Picknett and Clive Prince (see p.202). This is the later painting, revised from the one in the Louvre before its delivery to the Milanese Confraternity of the Immaculate Conception. As if to underline the orthodox view, two words have been painted very finely on John's scroll: *ecce a[g]nvs*, or 'behold the lamb'. The painting was part of an altarpiece triptych, and the two side panels, painted by associates of Leonardo, now hang separately as *Angel in Green with a Vielle* and *Angel in Red with a Lute*.

The National's only other work from Leonardo's own hand, the slightly earlier but related **Virgin and Child with Saint Anne and Saint John the Baptist**, is hidden away just behind Room 51. Sketched in charcoal and chalk on paper, it's an incredibly fragile work, and you have to enter a specially darkened, shrine-like chamber to view it.

To get to the National Gallery, Trafalgar Square is only a ten- or fifteen-minute walk west along the Strand from the Temple Church, or you can follow Robert and Sophie and take the westbound District and Circle line, getting off after one stop at **Embankment station**, and walking up Villiers Street, turning left in front of Charing Cross station.

Stand-Ins

The refusal of Westminster Abbey's authorities to allow filming (see p.255) threw the film makers into a spin for a while, but they found the perfect stand-in in **Lincoln Cathedral**. Following is a guide to this and a few other English locations which appear in the movie, but not in the book.

Lincoln

Lincoln Cathedral was an inspired, and obvious, stand-in for Westminster Abbey: a building of almost contemporary thirteenth-century English Gothic. And its authorities were happy to help out. Over a week in August 2005, the cathedral earned itself a rumoured £100,000 for masquerading as its southern cousin. Some local Christians weren't too pleased, and the first day of filming saw a few protests (see p.258). But these were less about *The Da Vinci Code*'s heresy than the film makers' overbearing influence. The big local issue was that during filming the cathedral bell, 'Great Tom', was silenced for the first time since World War II.

The location fee, however, was a welcome boost to the cathedral's restoration fund, for Lincoln is literally falling apart; even the flying buttresses have come away at the east end, and £1 million is spent every year just keeping the thing standing. It's not exactly a new problem: earlier structures were destroyed by fire in the eleventh century and by an earthquake in the twelfth. For two centuries, a fourteenth-century wooden spire towered 525 feet above the ground

– making Lincoln the tallest structure in the medieval world, and the first building in Europe to rise above the height of the Great Pyramid at Giza – but it collapsed in 1549.

The sheer presence of the building is a major draw for visitors and film crews alike. And the cathedral has the big advantage of being relatively free of modern clutter, making their recreation of **Isaac Newton's funeral** – employing two hundred bewigged extas, plus plenty of smoke and giant Klieg lights shining through the windows – all the more convincing.

Lincoln is transformed into Westminster Abbey, with the addition of these plaster tombs.

The most alluring sights inside are the tomb of Richard Fleming, Bishop of Lincoln until his death in 1431, which shows him as a rather gruesome cadaver – the first such tomb in England. There's also the celebrated Lincoln Imp, in the Angel Choir behind the high altar, a stone gargoyle which was supposedly causing mischief in the cathedral until an angel intervened, turning him into stone, and leaving him with a petrified smile, perched atop his stone pillar. The cathedral opening hours vary seasonally (summer Mon–Fri 7.15am–9pm, Sat & Sun 7.15am–6pm; winter Mon–Sat 7.15am–6pm, Sun 7.15am–5pm; £4; *www.lincolncathedral.com*).

BURGHLEY HOUSE

One of the loveliest UK locations in the film of *The Da Vinci Code* is also found in Lincolnshire: **Burghley House** (*www.burghley.co.uk*) in Stamford features as Teabing's pad. Built by Queen Elizabeth I's Principal Secretary and Lord Treasurer, William Cecil, Lord Burghley, it is still owned and managed by a direct descendant. As one of the finest and grandest stately homes in all England, with over a hundred rooms, it's not bad going for the humble academic Leigh Teabing. The house is only open in summer (April–Oct daily except Fri 11am–5pm; £8.20).

WINCHESTER CATHEDRAL

Winchester Cathedral (open daily 8.30am–6pm; free), in Hampshire, also features in the movie, the Norman north transept acting as the setting for the **Knights Templar flashbacks**. As a crude example of early Norman church-building, it perfectly fits the bill. For more architectural sophistication, visitors can enjoy the stunning, early-fifteenth-century nave. For greater literary sophistication, there's always Jane Austen's tomb.

Like Lincoln – and unlike Westminster – Winchester didn't see itself as above a career in cinema. 'A novel that sells so many copies can afford to laugh at its critics', said the Very Revd Michael Till, Dean of Winchester, in reply to critical parishioners. "Income from one day's filming will help us in the care of this Cathedral for this and future generations." Michael Till also saw the film as an opportunity to save some souls: an exhibition and a series of lectures was timed to coincide with the film. See *www.winchester-cathedral.org.uk* for details.

Edinburgh

The Cathedral of Codes...

Rosslyn Chapel – south of **Edinburgh** – is the central locale of the closing section of *The Da Vinci Code*. And it was a strong choice: the 'Cathedral of Codes' has long been associated with grail legend, and stands close to the last Knights Templar stronghold in Britain, albeit one that was destroyed more than a century before the chapel was built. As we'll see, Brown makes a series of highly speculative claims about the chapel to drive on to the story's climax. But no matter. Rosslyn is a beautiful and deeply spiritual site, well worth its place in the book and the movie – and a visit.

Rosslyn Chapel

Rosslyn has been co-opted into every other alternative history of Britain, and Dan Brown, on his website, credits Tim Wallace-Murphy and Marilyn Hopkins' book *Rosslyn: Guardians of the Secret of the Holy Grail*, which suggests the chapel stands on an ancient, pre-Christian pilgrimage route stretching to Santiago de Compostela. In the novel, he suggests the chapel was built 'on the site of an ancient Mithraic temple', and that it stands on a 'north-south meridian' that runs through Glastonbury, on a **Rose Line** from which the chapel gets its name. In fact, Rosslyn's longitude is W3:08:41, while Glastonbury's is W2:42:52, centred on the Abbey, or W2:41:41, centred on the ancient Tor. And, like any good Scots kirk, Rosslyn's name refers simply to its location: 'Ross', meaning promontory or headland, and 'Lyn', meaning pool or stream.

Brown goes on to claim the chapel is 'an exact architectural blue-print of **Solomon's Temple** in Jerusalem'. That's a hard one. The Temple was razed to the ground by the Babylonians in 586 BC, and no one is sure what it looked like, as no plans survived into historical record. To accept the claim, you would have to believe that the original Masons built Solomon's First Temple (and this is not something the Freemasons themselves believe), and thus Rosslyn is a copy based on their secret, centuries-old knowledge. The reality is, sadly, more prosaic, and you don't have to go far to find out where the designers of Rosslyn chapel got their inspiration. Its plan is almost certainly modelled on the choir of Glasgow Cathedral, just a few miles away on Scotland's west coast.

The Masonic or **Templar connection** is equally dubious. The chapel was built by **William St Clair** in 1446 and was originally intended to be part of a much larger church dedicated to Saint Matthew, there being a fashion in Scotland at the time for the construction of ambitious private churches with live-in priestly communities. However, rather than being a Templar Grand Master, as is often claimed, St Clair was a local laird, the descendant of the St Clairs who testified against the Templars at their trial in Edinburgh's Holyrood palace in 1309. Another of William St Clair's ancestors, his grandfather **Prince Henry of Orkney**, was a sea explorer who may have seen the New World more than a hundred years before Columbus – at least if the carvings at Rosslyn apparently showing cacti and Indian corn are anything to judge by.

In July 2005, a modern-day descendant, **Dr Andrew Sinclair**, rose up to condemn the Rosslyn Trust for allowing *The Da Vinci Code* to be filmed **on location at the chapel**. 'The book is "preposterous", he said, 'its message pernicious, its history a bungle and a muddle … What it says about the grail and Rosslyn is absolute invention.' Stung, the Trustees retorted that the money would help save the chapel, and that they were expecting visitor numbers to double.

Tom Hanks on location at a rather cold, wet Rosslyn

The reported £7000 a day paid as a location fee sounds like a handsome windfall – until compared to the estimated £3 million required for full conservation of the chapel. However, canny locals are preparing to cash in on the expected stream of visitors. The chapel is offering themed guided tours, and the Original Roslin Hotel has changed the name of its restaurant to 'The Grail'.

THE INTERIOR

Even unfinished – William St Clair's death in 1448 put a halt to works – and based on Glasgow Cathedral rather than Solomon's Temple, Rosslyn Chapel remains an extraordinary place to visit. The exterior is alive with exaggeratedly decorated stone buttresses, arches,

The interior of Rosslyn Chapel is so intricately carved all over with figures and symbols that it is known as the Chapel of Codes. The Prentice Pillar is on the right.

finials and canopies, and the interior stonework is if anything even more exotic, every surface covered in richly allegorical sculpture that draws heavily on Biblical and medieval Christian symbolism – the Seven Deadly Sins, the Dance of Death and so on – and also on figurative naturalistic work and pagan mythological images. Look out for the frequent Green Men.

The most breathtaking of all the thousands of pieces of virtuoso stonework is the twisting, knotted **Prentice Pillar**, which stands at a corner of the Lady Chapel, to the right of the main altar, entwined dragons at its foot. Local legend has it that the column was created by an apprentice subsequently murdered by his master in a jealous rage. Brown's idea that a second, facing pillar is an 'exact replica' of Boaz, the pillar that legendarily stood on the left of the entrance to Solomon's Temple, is pure invention. There is a second column dubbed the **'Mason's Pillar'** at Rosslyn, but no evidence that the name relates to the Freemasons. It appears to have developed out of local legend and is almost certainly related to stone-carving rather than Freemasonry. Two carved heads in the ceiling of the northwest corner of the chapel, one with a slashed head, are supposed to represent the master and apprentice of the local stone-mason's legend. Also, despite what Dan Brown writes, there is no Star of David pathway traced in the floor, and no 'massive subterranean chamber' lurking beneath it either – though high-tech efforts to find one are unceasing.

ROSSLYN PRACTICALITIES

At just seven miles south of Edinburgh, you could walk or cycle to Roslin – as the village spells the name – but it's easier to get the bus: #37A or First Edinburgh #315 from St Andrew Square. The village itself is quiet and rather dull, its status entirely due to the chapel – and more recently to Dolly the sheep, who was famously cloned here (the first animal to be cloned) in 1997.

Note that the chapel is currently undergoing a massive restoration project, due to finish in 2008. In the meantime, a canopy has been erected over the entire chapel to allow the roof and walls to dry out. It is still visitable, though the atmosphere has suffered a little. More information can be found at *www.rosslynchapel.org. uk*, and of course donations towards conservation are willingly accepted.

Italy

MILAN, ROME, FLORENCE...

For the best Italian locations, the Dan Brown book you want is *Angels & Demons*, which adopts Rome even more than *The Da Vinci Code* does Paris, with its frantic chase around Bernini's statuary and the bomb-threatened Vatican. There's still plenty of Italian material in *The Da Vinci Code*, though, including many references to Leonardo's **Last Supper**, in **Milan**, Bishop Aringarosa's emergency flight to **Rome** and **Castel Gandolfo**, and Robert's date with Sophie in **Florence**, where he has to promise 'no museums, no churches, no tombs, no art, no relics'. Which is rather like going to the Caribbean without seeing a beach, but each to their own.

Milan: The Last Supper

Robert and Sophie don't actually go to Milan to check out Leonardo's **Last Supper** for themselves. They're happy, it seems, to be persuaded by Leigh Teabing's 'eight-foot-long print' on the wall, and a 'colourful graphic that spanned both full pages' as reproduced in his art book, *La Storia di Leonardo*. It's hard to imagine anyone reading *The Da Vinci Code* without wanting to see the Leonardo image for themselves. It's easy to check out a book, like Robert and Sophie, or visit Milan's official tourist website, *http://milano.arounder.com*, which contains a link to a high-resolution image of *The Last Supper*. But it's best of all to head to Milan and the church of **Santa Maria delle Grazie**, which is just five minutes' walk south of the main Stazione Nord railway terminus, on Corso Magenta.

The **Last Supper** is found on the walls of the monastery refectory of this former Dominican convent – signposted *Cenacolo Vinciano* (Vincian Supper). The painting is in a sorry state, partly due to Leonardo's eccentric, experimental decision to use oil paint on dry plaster rather than the well-tried fresco technique (it is not technically a fresco, as Brown describes it). Even twenty years after it was first painted, it was reportedly suffering, and it was later used for target practice by Napoleonic troops, and survived a bomb which reduced every other wall in the refectory to rubble. Worst of all, it was restored at least four times in the twentieth century – leaving almost none of the original paint intact.

Whether or not you think the figure next to Jesus is a woman – and most art historians, Christian or otherwise, think not (see p.124) – it's a fascinating painting. Leonardo had been working on it for two years when the monks asked why it was taking so long to finish **Judas's face**. Leonardo replied that he was still looking for a sufficiently evil-looking model, and hinted that if he was bothered any more perhaps the Prior might just serve. Portrait of the Prior or not, Judas is, as Vasari noted, 'the very embodiment of treachery and inhumanity'.

LAST SUPPER PRACTICALITIES

Visits aren't easy to organize, especially with the hundreds of *Da Vinci Coders* swelling the ranks of art-lovers trying to get in. You have to book weeks in advance (reservations Mon–Fri 9am–6pm, Sat 9am–2pm on ☎02.8942.1146; viewing Tues–Sun 8am–7.30pm; €6.50 plus €1.50 obligatory booking fee). And be kind to the guides. Recent press reports suggest they are losing the will to live responding to the questions 'Which one is John?' and 'Is that Mary Magdalene?'

Rome: Papal Astronomy

The principal Italian location in *The Da Vinci Code* is **Castel Gandolfo**, where Bishop Aringarosa is taken after his arrival in Rome. This is one of the loveliest day-trips from Rome, nestling in the Alban Hills and directly overlooking the calm, bluff-ringed waters of Lago d'Albano. Brown imagines that 'Gandolfo resembled a great stone monster pondering a suicidal leap', and it is poised over 400 metres above the rim of the lake.

It's a minor detail that the movie seems to gloss over in choosing England's own **Belvoir Castle** (pronounced 'Beaver Castle'; *www.belvoircastle.com*) as a stand-in exterior. The dramatic helicopter shot makes full use of the castle's hilltop location, but the blue waters of Lago Gandolfo below are conspicuous by their absence. And

Castel Gandolfo is the summer residence of the Pope. The Vatican astronomical observatory is also located here.

beautiful as the Leicestershire countryside can look, it will never be Lacio. If you decide to visit, be aware that on Sundays between July and September, the Pope traditionally gives a midday address from the Papal Palace. But you may prefer to swim below, from one of the many artificial sandy beaches. To get there, you take the old Via Appia south out of Rome, past **Ciampino airport** (not in fact a mere 'charter' airport, as Brown calls it).

One *Da Vinci Code* location you're not likely to be able to visit is the **Tyrrhenian Sea**, which lies between the Italian mainland, Sardinia and Sicily, but which Bishop Aringarosa somehow manages to fly over in his Beechcraft Baron 58, nervously clutching his air-sickness bag. A cursory look at a map shows that if you fly 'northward' from Rome, you'll be heading over the hills of Umbria on your way to Venice – that is, in exactly the wrong direction.

Florence: Honeymoon Hotel

At the end of *The Da Vinci Code*, Robert Langdon reveals that he's wangled himself another luxury conference trip. This time, to Florence, and he'll be staying at the **Hotel Brunelleschi**, if Sophie would care to join him. Those with a few euros to spare (upwards of €350, to be exact) can follow him. The Brunelleschi, centrally located off Via dei Calzaiuoli (☎055.27.370, *www.hotelbrunelleschi.it*), is one of the best in the city, its superb modern design incorporating a Byzantine chapel and fifth-century tower.

While you're in Florence, try to visit the nearby **Cappella di San Sepolcro** (June–Sept hours vary but usually Mon–Fri 10am–noon; Oct–May Mon–Sat 10am–noon & 5–5.30pm; free), which houses an exquisite funerary monument designed by the great Renaissance architect Alberti for the Florentine nobleman Giovanni Rucellai. It's a miniature copy of Jerusalem's Church of the Holy Sepulchre (see overpage).

Jerusalem

At some point, there's bound to be a Dan Brown novel that's set in **Jerusalem** itself – but for now, the city crops up peripherally in *The Da Vinci Code* in the Rosslyn episode, where the chapel is described as a copy of **Solomon's Temple**, and in the Temple Church section, as the church's design was modelled on Jerusalem's **Church of the Holy Sepulchre**. A trip to the Holy Land, then, could be in order.

Jerusalem: The Temple Mount

Jerusalem's **Church of the Holy Sepulchre** occupies one of the most controversial religious sites in the world – the **Temple Mount**, sacred to Jews as the site of **Solomon's Temple**, and to Muslims as the spot where Mohammed ascended into heaven. It was to this nexus (in an act that might itself belong to a Dan Brown thriller) that Ariel Sharon, then the opposition Likud Party leader, paid a visit in September 2000, sparking off the Palestinian uprising known as the second Intifada.

THE TEMPLE

There is nothing actually to see of the **First Temple**, which was built on Mount Moriah by Solomon, the son of King David, between 960 and 957 BC, but destroyed by the Babylonians in 586 BC. There's vigorous debate as to where exactly it stood, though the Temple Mount Excavations, just inside the Dung Gate, have revealed structures dating back to the same era.

The Wailing Wall in Jerusalem is all that remains of Solomon's Temple. On the Temple Mount, above it, stand two great mosques of Islam, the Dome of the Rock and al-Aqsa. The Knights Templar were originally based in this Temple quarter of Jerusalem.

Sixty years after the First Temple was destroyed, the smaller Second Temple was built on Solomon's ruins, but this was in turn destroyed, and the **Dome of the Rock** mosque now stands atop the mount. The only surviving temple structure is the Western or **Wailing Wall** – in fact, part of a retaining wall probably built under Herod the Great to support the mount. You can visit the Esplanade in front of it, by the Dung Gate, and watch (or join) Orthodox Jews at prayer.

The Church of the Holy Sepulchre

The **Holy Sepulchre** was the tomb in which Jesus's body was laid after the crucifixion, and on this site – or at least what was thought to be the site – the giant **Church of the Holy Sepulchre** was built in 336 by the Emperor Constantine (the man so badly maligned by Dan Brown for his Nicaean machinations). Like the Temple Church, which was modelled after it, its centre was a rotunda – Sophie reflects at the London Temple that 'the circular room seemed custom-built for a pagan rite' and Constantine's church was, unsurprisingly, built on earlier temples to Venus and Jupiter – and it was topped by a magnificent golden dome.

Constantine's basilica, however, was destroyed by fire in 614, and replaced by a succession of chapels, until the Crusaders completed a new basilica in 1168, also incorporating a rotunda over the supposed tomb site. It too was destroyed by fire, in 1808, but a new church was constructed soon after by the Greek Orthodox and Armenian community. It echoes Constantine's rotunda, with eighteen giant columns supporting a dome above.

This most holy of sites has been disputed by Jerusalem's Christian communities for centuries, with the different factions controlling different parts of the building. The Greek Orthodox, for example, maintain the chapel located on what is thought to have been the **Place of Crucifixion**. The other key sites are the **Edicule**, supposed location of Christ's tomb, which you can queue to enter (it holds only four people at a time), and the '**Tomb of Joseph of Arimathea**' – one of several burial shafts contemporaneous with Christ's death.

You can **visit** the Sepulchre (daily 4am–7pm). It is located in the western, Christian quarter of Jerusalem.

New York

Once you've read *The Da Vinci Code* you will surely want to see the **Opus Dei HQ** for yourself – and you'll find it in one of the swishest parts of Manhattan.

Opus Dei HQ: Manhattan

Opus Dei's World Headquarters is just where Dan Brown says it is, at 243 Lexington Avenue, Manhattan, filling the brash new Murray Hill Place building on the northeast corner of East 34th Street. If you can't make it there yourself, the best thing to do is check out the website of its architects. Click on *http://maypinska.com/pages/projects/ buildbodylex.htm* and you'll find out that the **May & Pinska** design included 'seven chapels and sacristies, and their service requirements' and 'bedrooms, living rooms, and offices for approximately 100 residents'.

More spooky is the provision for 'separate entrances for men and women, on separate streets; separate on-site parking for men and women; separation visually and acoustically of men and women within the building'. Different streets?! This division is even reflected on the exterior, where 'the vertical slot on the south in the tower is symbolic of the separation of men and women'. If you visit, you can scan the outside for other troubling kinds of symbolism, but you'll need to enlist if you want to get anywhere near the interior.

The American national headquarters of Opus Dei on Lexington Avenue, Manhattan. Women are kept strictly separate from men, and though both are encouraged to punish themselves severely, women are expected to try harder.

THE

DA VINCI
CODE

Author

Where does
Dan Brown get his
ideas from?

THE DA VINCI CODE SOURCES

When interviewed, Dan Brown makes a point of the research he undertook to write *The Da Vinci Code*, and on his website he lists the chief sources he used. In this chapter, we look at these books – and how their ideas have been put to use in Dan Brown's novel. But these sources alone do not tell the whole story. Few of the titles represent original research; instead their materials and ideas are derived from academic and other sources which Dan Brown does not acknowledge and may not even be aware of. We take a look, too, at where these debates have emerged.

THE TWO KEY SOURCES: *THE TEMPLAR REVELATION* AND *HOLY BLOOD, HOLY GRAIL*

Two key books which are namechecked by characters in *The Da Vinci Code*, and which have contributed to much of the story line of the novel are *The Templar Revelation* and *Holy Blood, Holy Grail* (which is its American title; it is published in Britain as *The Holy Blood and the Holy Grail*).

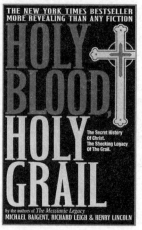

Just about everything that Dan Brown has to say about Leonardo da Vinci comes from **The Templar Revelation**. It is in this book that we learn of 'the secret code of Leonardo da Vinci' found throughout his works, and particularly in **The Last Supper**. So when Dan Brown writes about *The Last Supper* and asserts that the figure of John is really that of Mary Magdalene, that this figure and Jesus are 'joined at the hip', that together they describe the shape of the letter M, that there is a disembodied hand holding a dagger – all this and more comes from *The Templar Revelation*. In addition to regurgitating whole this plethora of distortion, Dan Brown also uncritically repeats the remark of *The Templar Revelation* that there is no chalice, no grail upon the table, as related in the New Testament – ignoring the fact that Leonardo was painting a scene from the *Gospel of John* in which the supper was over and the table had been cleared.

From **Holy Blood, Holy Grail** Dan Brown unloads the great secret hidden within the code, that Jesus was married to Mary Magdalene, who after his crucifixion escaped to France, where she gave birth to their child and propagated his bloodline. This is the explosive secret that would 'crumble up the Church', as Sophie Neveu puts it, though in fact there is no reason why it would. The faith of no one in the Church would be fundamentally affected by the revelation that Jesus had a child, as

Christianity positively vaunts the human aspect of Jesus, which is an essential part of his significance as God-in-man.

THE SACRED FEMININE DEBATE

In any case, the energy that drives *The Da Vinci Code* does not reside in some 'explosive' secret such as a marriage between Jesus and Mary Magdalene or whether the holy bloodline runs through Jacques Chirac. Rather it is contained in the engaging notion of the **sacred feminine**, of a time when harmony ruled the world through a balance of the male and female principles. No such harmony is with us now, proof enough that for two thousand years the sacred feminine has been suppressed. And that is where **Mary Magdalene** comes in, the archetypal abused and oppressed woman, a goddess made to play the role of penitent. But what is the highest goal of a knight in search of the Holy Grail in *The Da Vinci Code*? To kneel at the bones of Mary Magdalene.

So where does this **new Mariolotry** come from? What we know about Mary Magdalene has not much changed in two millennia. She was a witness at the crucifixion and the resurrection, an independent woman who has long been honoured as the Apostle to the Apostles. Pope Gregory's sixth-century slander that she had been a prostitute stuck with her until the 1960s when it was withdrawn by the Vatican (it had never been accepted in the Eastern Church), and probably it still sticks to her now in the popular imagination, but scholars have long known better.

All the same, within the past twenty years or so, this new cult of Mary Magdalene has percolated into popular culture through the New Age writings of people like **Margaret Starbird** – and then into the mainstream through *The Da Vinci Code*. That it has much and maybe everything to do with **feminism** is obvious enough. The equality of the sexes and a sharing between them is now widely

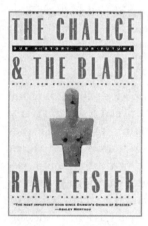

accepted as the way things should be. Yet in this supposedly secular age, why Mary Magdalene? Who has promoted her, and who is using her, and how?

If anyone doubts the power of small elites to create a mass effect, they should observe this case, for the answer is located in the religious studies departments of several of America's most prestigious universities, where a small circle of feminist scholars – such as **Elaine Pagels** and **Ann Graham Brock** – have turned Mary Magdalene into an icon of their cause. The discovery of the **Nag Hammadi codices** in 1945 presented an alternative Christian tradition, one that was opposed to the proto-orthodoxy that eventually became dominant and formed the institutional hierarchy of the Church – a hierarchy that was and has remained overwhelmingly male. Scenes of Peter's anger or jealousy towards Mary Magdalene in these **Gnostic Gospels** are taken as proof of an early sex war. Peter may be the rock upon whom the Church is built, but Mary Magdalene is the one whom Jesus kisses. Jesus has been betrayed by the Christian Church. As a device for a feminist assault on the whole of Western culture and practice, it is brilliant.

But whatever one thinks of the feminist argument, it is unfortunate when history is misrepresented for the sake of narrowly advancing a cause. The **argument between Peter and Mary Magdalene** was not about male authority – that is to entirely miss the point – rather it was about how to attain knowledge of the authentic spirit. Peter seems to be arguing that authority is passed down through a hierarchy, as in apostolic succession, whereas Mary Magdalene has been inspired directly by Jesus. That is clear from the fact that he appears to her in a vision and not to the male apostles, and it is also clear from the kisses he would give her, the kisses of inspiration, of divine breath, before his crucifixion. That is the Gnostic argument. But it is hard to argue that Mary Magdalene was important because she was a woman, that Jesus had intended to launch a feminist Church, when in fact the Gnostic Gospels talk about eliminating the female and forcing it to become male. Indeed if any people were antipathetic to the sacred feminine, it was the authors of the Gnostic Gospels. To say otherwise is to prostitute the truth in the way that the Church once prostituted Mary Magdalene.

But putting the ins and outs of that aside, if you are searching for the ultimate sources of *The Da Vinci Code* you should be reading the Gnostic literature of the first three centuries AD and the serious books written on that subject. There, more than in potboilers like *The Templar Revelation* or *Holy Blood, Holy Grail* or even *The Woman with the Alabaster Jar* (another Dan Brown namecheck) begins the path that leads ultimately to the Pyramide Inversée.

THE BOOKS DAN BROWN READ AS RESEARCH

Dan Brown lists on his website, *danbrown.com*, **27 key books** that he made particular use of in writing *The Da Vinci Code*. We've listed these in Brown's own order, below; the comments on the books, and their influence on his novel, are our own.

The History of the Knights Templars
Charles G. Addison *Originally published 1842. Reprinted by Adventures Unlimited Press, 1997 (US); RA Kressinger Publishing, 1998 (UK).* Addison was a member of the British Society of the Knights Templar – an inner branch of Freemasonry – and his history of the Templars includes interesting contemporary material on the 1816 rebuilding of the Inner Temple in London, as well as their medieval origins and activities, and their suppression by Pope Clement V in 1307. As a Templar initiate, Addison suggests a continuity in the Order and the 'modern' Templar society, hinting that the Knights were never entirely suppressed. He is perhaps the first 'modern' writer to do so. But the book is very much of its time, wearing its learning on its sleeve with a lot of (untranslated) Latin littered about.

Rosslyn: Guardians of the Secret of the Holy Grail Tim Wallace-Murphy & Marilyn Hopkins *Element (UK/US), 1999.* Rosslyn Chapel, near Edinburgh, is, of course, a key locale in the climax of *The Da Vinci Code* – and it was an obvious choice, as a long-favoured site, among alternative 'historians', for the resting place of the Holy Grail. Wallace-Murphy and Hopkins introduced their own spin on the story, proposing the chapel as one of seven pre-Christian sites, forming a route of initiation and enlightenment for Druids that was later adopted by – who else? – the Knights Templar, whose Scottish headquarters was close by the site, albeit destroyed a century before the chapel was built. The authors' speculate a 'voyage of discovery' that began at Santiago de Compostela in northwest Spain, and passed through Toulouse, Orleans, Chartres, Paris and Amiens, before ending at Rosslyn.

The Woman With the Alabaster Jar: Mary Magdalene and the Holy Grail Margaret Starbird *Bear & Company (US), 1993.* Margaret Starbird is a self-described theologian (she has a master's from the University of Maryland) and a prolific writer on the concept of the sacred feminine and Mary Magdalene. She has half a dozen books to her name and two of them – The Woman With the Alabaster Jar and The Goddess in the Gospels: Reclaiming the Sacred Feminine – get a namecheck in *The Da Vinci Code* when Sophie Neveu spots them in Leigh Teabing's library at Château Villette. Starbird believes that God is 'beyond gender' and that 'His' masculine attributes were wrongly characterised by the early Church. She also contends that Mary Magdalene's status as the bride of Jesus – and in particular their sacred union, or Hieros Gamos (which *The Da Vinci Code* has Jacques Saunière sexually re-enact, to Sophie's distress), has been denied in Church teachings. As Starbird tells it, Hieros Gamos is a Greek mythic concept of conferring kingship and she suggests that the story of the woman anointing Jesus with the alabaster jar would have been recognized by contemporaries in this context. Even more central to *The Da Vinci Code*, however, is Starbird's contention that the Holy Grail or Chalice was Mary's womb, and her carriage of Jesus's bloodline to Egypt and then France: the theory proposed in Holy Blood, Holy Grail (see below). The discussion in *The Da Vinci Code* of the Sangraal as sang raal – blood royal – is clearly derived from the theories put forward in this book, as are the rather obtuse references to the hidden Grail-related symbols in the Tarot, which are widely illustrated here, and are explored further by Starbird in her book, The Tarot Trumps and the Holy Grail: Great Secrets of the Middle Ages.

The Templar Revelation: Secret Guardians of the True Identity of Christ Lynn Picknett & Clive Prince *Simon & Schuster (US), Corgi (UK), 1997.* 'One of the most fascinating books I have read since *Holy Blood Holy Grail*,' trumpets Colin Wilson on the cover of this book – still in print in paperback editions in both the US and UK. And it is indeed a cracking art-detection story – as well as a central inspiration for *The Da Vinci Code*. The London-based authors set out on an investigation of Leonardo da Vinci's possible involvement with the Turin shroud, and claim to discover not just a 'dangerously heretical' artist but a whole underground religion, encoded in works of art and forging a continuous link from the first century AD through to the Knights Templar, Freemasonry and – inevitably – the Priory of Sion. Global conspiracy aside, there is much interesting material here on Christianity's incorporation of earlier religion – in particular of the Egyptian goddess Isis and its supposed transformation in southern France into the cult of the Black Madonna, and on the extraordinary reverence of John the Baptist in the Early Church. And this is a highly entertaining book – written more like a thriller than anything else.

The Goddess in the Gospels: Reclaiming the Sacred Feminine **Margaret Starbird** *Bear & Company (US), 1998.* One of the reasons many readers give for their engagement with *The Da Vinci Code* is its focus on the sacred feminine in Christianity. The popular feminist theologian Margaret Starbird (see above) is in large part responsible, as Dan Brown acknowledges in crediting two of her books on his website and featuring them in the novel. In this book, Starbird writes about the image of the Virgin and Child being modelled on that of Isis and the sacred

child Horus, about the Black Madonnas of the Mediterranean, and the role of Mary Magdalene within Christianity, whose centrality she regards as being 'downgraded' (in favour of the Virgin) following the Albigensian crusade against the Cathars. But this book is also a personal account of the author's own spiritual journey 'from patriarchal reason to feminine intuition, faith, authority and wisdom.'

Holy Blood, Holy Grail. Michael Baigent, Richard Leigh, Henry Lincoln *Dell (US), Arrow (UK), 1982.* It would be wrong to say that without Holy Blood, Holy Grail there would be no Da Vinci Code – but without any doubt this book by a trio of British authors, a bestseller in its own right when first published twenty years ago, is a key source; it was responsible for the whole idea of the Grail as bloodline, as well as the emergence into Premier League conspiracy theory of the Priory of Sion. It was so key, in fact, that in October 2004 Baigent and Leigh issued a writ against Dan Brown's publishers, claiming that 'the whole jigsaw puzzle' of their book had been lifted in *The Da Vinci Code*. It was an odd – although understandably opportunistic – claim, given the assertions of the Holy Blood, Holy Grail authors that their book is non fiction, based on sound research. After all, nobody holds the copyright on genuine history. At the time of its release, it was panned by most critics as 'pseudo history', although Anthony Burgess praised it highly as an entertaining thriller (and it was neatly parodied in Umberto Eco's novel, *Foucault's Pendulum*). In *The Da Vinci Code*, it is mentioned just once, when Leigh Teabing (whose name is a playful take on two of the Holy Blood, Holy Grail authors – Teabing is an anagram of Baigent) pulls the book off his library shelf and says: 'To my taste, the authors made some dubious leaps of faith in their analysis, but their fundamental premise is sound.'

In Search of the Holy Grail and the Precious Blood: A Traveller's Guide Deike Begg and Ean Begg *Harper Collins, 1995 (out of print). Danbrown. com* gets the title of this useful Grail travel guide slightly mixed up – the one above is correct. It's just what it claims to be: a guide to the many buildings – cathedrals, chapels, ancient sites – around Brtain and Europe that have connections to the Grail legend. The foreword is by Holy Blood, Holy Grail co-author, Michael Baigent.

The Messianic Legacy Michael Baigent, Richard Leigh, Henry Lincoln *1987. Arrow (UK), Delta (US).* The *Holy Blood, Holy Grail* trio returned to literary controversy with this book, asking a number of big, bold questions: notably 'Did Jesus actually found Christianity?' and 'Was there more than one Christ?' As ever, their stamping ground is the shifting terrrain between the Early and medieval church, and once more they enlist the Prieure de Sion, those secretive Grail guardians, for contemporary revelations. The authors claim the Priory has been preparing suitable Messianic candidates for the leadership that the world craves.

The Knights Templar and their Myth Peter Partner *1990. Inner Traditions International (UK), Destiny Books (US).* Despite the New Age-ish appearance of its publishers, this is a serious and rather specialist book by a British journalist and historian. It breaks into two parts: first a (surprisingly hostile) history of the Templars, second a (sceptical) analysis of the myths around them. You would need a decent knowledge of the Crusades to appreciate Partner's arguments on the history, and would have to be pretty well versed in conspiracy and Templar lore to follow all his treatment of the myths. But that said, there's a lot of interesting, original discussion, particularly on how the Masonic Lodges appropriated the Templars to give them the appearance of ancient foundation. And – relevant to *The Da Vinci Code* – Partner looks closely at the claims of Templar heresies, including their supposed worship of 'Baphomet', which he says was a medieval French rendering of 'Muhammad' and was probably a desperate invention by some Knight undergoing torture.

The Dead Sea Bible: The Oldest Known Bible Martin G. Abegg (Editor) *Harper (US), 1999.* The Dead Sea Scrolls predate the previous earliest-known Old Testament manuscripts by a thousand years. They were discovered between 1947 and 1956, amid a cache of 800 scrolls in a series of caves overlooking the Dead Sea at Qumran. The scrolls had been used by the conservative Jewish Essene sect, from around 150BC to 68AD. This scholarly edition highlights the differences – and perhaps more so the lack of differences – between the Dead Sea text and the later canonized (Masoretic) Bible. The book's introduction discusses how at the time of Jesus, there was no definitive 'Bible', but a number of sacred books recognized by Jewish communities as the foundation of their religion and practice, and looks at the process of canonization, and the different arrangements of the books in the Jewish Tanakh and Christian Old Testament. There is little of direct relevance here for *Da Vinci Code* readers – the Dead Sea Scrolls 'Bible' has no bearing on the New Testament – other than its questions of just how did the Bible come to be created and edited.

The Dead Sea Deception **Michael Baigent, Richard Leigh** *1993. Arrow (UK), Simon & Schuster (US).* If you thought for a minute that the Dead Sea Scrolls were lacking in controversy, here are our Holy Blood, Holy Grail authors back to prove otherwise. Indeed, that we are firmly back in conspiracy land. The thesis is that for four decades, from the discovery of the Dead Sea Scrolls in 1947, a small cabal of Catholic scholars successfully blocked access to 75 percent of the 800 Scrolls, and co-opted them to Vatican propaganda purposes. The authors claim that the Habakkuk Commentary and other non-Bibilical scrolls refer to the events in the New Testament Book of Acts, and by

Josephus, and suggest that Saint Paul may have been a Roman agent, briefed to use Christianity to undermine an anti-Roman, Jewish messianic nationalist movement comprised of Zealots, Nazarenes and the Essenes of Qumran. Access to the Dead Sea Scrolls in fact seem to have been blocked more by the rivalry of scholars, than any institutional conspiracy, and photographs of the 'secret scrolls' from Cave 4 (about 40 percent of the total) were made available in 1988 by Huntington Library in California, one of the depositories of copies. If you want to read a (non-conspiratorial) modern account of the Scrolls' history, content and context, the most accessible book is Jonathan Campbell's *Deciphering the Dead Sea Scrolls* (Blackwell, UK, 2002).

The Nag Hammadi Library in English **James M. Robinson** *1978. Harper Collins (UK/US), rev. edn. 1988.* The 1940s were good years for ancient manuscripts. In 1945, outside the Egyptian city of Nag Hammadi, a large stone jar was unearthed, containing nine 'books', written in Coptic by fourth-century Gnostic Christians. The so-called Gnostic Gospels comprised a selection of texts relevant to the heretical Gnostic philosophy – which on one view believed in heaven as an immediate, internal state ('When your leaders tell you that God is in heaven, say rather, God is within you, and without you'). They include a number of texts that failed to make it into the New Testament, among them The Gospel of Thomas, The Gospel of Philip, The Gospel of Truth and The Gospel of Mary. This is reckoned a superb edition of the Gospels, with an introduction from Robinson and a fascinating afterword by Richard Smith discussing the influence of Gnosticism on writers from Voltaire and Blake to Kerouac and Philip K. Dick.

Jesus and the Lost Goddess: The Secret Teachings of the Original Christians Timothy Freke, Peter Gandy *Harmony (UK), Three Rivers Press (US), 2001* Freke and Gandy made their name with The Jesus Mysteries, a book that expounded, in a popular and persuasive way, the parallels between the life of Jesus and that of earlier and contemporary mythic and pagan figures, such as Osiris, Dionysus and Mithras. The ideas were not original but the book, drawing heavily on the Gnostic gospels of Nag Hammadi, had a coherence and a faith in Gnostic philosophy that created something of a cult following of its own, with author seminars and a splendidly-addressed website, *www.jesusmysteries.demon.co.uk*. In Jesus and the Lost Goddess, the duo – who are not professional academics – turned to a more strident Gnostic position, asserting that the original Christian teachings had been brutally suppressed by the Roman Church, due to their portrayal of Jesus and Mary Magdalene 'as mythic figures based on the Pagan dying and resurrecting Godman and the fallen and redeemed Goddess … [and] because they show that the gospel story is a mystical allegory encoding the profound philosophy of Gnosis – Knowledge of Truth.' As that

suggests, it is a more mystical and less historical-based book than its predecessor.

When God was a Woman Merlin Stone *Harcourt (US), 1976.* Originally published by UK feminist house Virago, as The Paradise Papers, this was a groundbreaking book that has been referenced by most of Merlin Stone's successors in the field of the Sacred Feminine, such as Margaret Starbird and Lynn Picknett. It is a somewhat plodding read but Stone, a sculptor and art history professor, prepares her ground with care, documenting the pre-monothestic worship of the creator Mother Goddess, and her 'transformation into a wanton, depraved figure by invading patriarchal tribes' – most notably in the Hebrew suppression of religions practised in Canaan. As her argument goes, female goddess images are the oldest religious imagery and posessed a magic based on fertility, in a time (prior to much animal husbandry) when the relationship between men and pregnancy was little understood. Then along came the notion of male gods, the story of Adam and Eve, and three millenia of monotheism. Stone explores how this came about, with female goddess figures acquiring first a son, then a consort, then a husband and father, to which she played a secondary and eventually extraneous role.

The Chalice and the Blade. Our History, Our Future Riane Eisler *Harper (US), 1988.* 'The most important book since Darwin's Origin of Species' boasts the cover of this 500,000-copy American bestseller. That seems pushing the frontiers of hype, even in publishing. Eisler, a self-proclaimed 'scholar, futurist and activist', has written a tendentious, shallow (but highly readable) account of women's significant role in early Christianity, of the pagan goddess tradition of ancient Hebrews, and of the corruption of male-dominated societies. Her message is that society should return to its supposedly non-hierarchical, non-violent, humane roots.

Born in Blood: The Lost Secrets of Freemasonry John J. Robinson *Evans & Co (US), 1993.* Were the Knights Templar the true founders of the Freemasons? Robinson believes they were, in an evaluation of Masonic and Templar history, language and symbols. Among his claims is an interesting take on the Peasants' Revolt of 1381, which has always been characterised as a spontaneous uprising of the people. Not at all, according to Robinson: this was a revenge by Templars – officially disbanded 65 years previously – upon their bitter rivals, the Knights Hospitaller.

The Malleus Maleficarum of Heinrich Kramer & James Sprenger Montague Summers (ed) *Originally published 1489. Dover edition (UK/US), 1971.* This is one of history's most awful texts: a fifteenth-century witchhunters' handbook, published soon after the invention of the printing press, and used to condemn thousands of innocent women to torture and death. Its spur was the papal bull, five years earlier, legitimising the belief in witches, and granting permission to bishops and secular authorities to

prosecute them, if there were no representatives from the Inquisition. There are three parts to the book: first, a debate on whether witches exist in the face of God; second, about their powers and practices and how to counter them; and third, how to bring them to justice. The text was originally in Latin. This translation dates from 1900, and its arcane language only adds to the chilling tone.

The Notebooks of Leonardo da Vinci Leonardo da Vinci *Dover (UK/US), 1970.* There are various editions of Leonardo's Notebooks, but the Dover 2-volume set is the one to go for. Together, the books include 1566 extracts, ranging across Leonardo's writings on painting, music, anatomy, architecture and inventions, along with more than 500 drawings.

Prophecies Leonardo da Vinci *Hesperus Press (UK), 2002.* Here is Leonardo much in the mode that Dan Brown conjures him – in an assembly of his fables, sayings, thoughts and riddles. The latter are often disguised as apocalyptic prophecies and fantasies and their 'solution' may simply be the image of an animal or beast. All in all, a top candidate for the Priory of Sion.

Leonardo da Vinci: Scientist, Inventor, Artist Otto Letze *Hatje Cantz (Germany), 1996.* We've not been able to trace this out of print German art book – nor any particular influence on *The Da Vinci Code.* But if you want books on Leonardo, you are not exactly bereft of choice: more than a hundred are reviewed at the website *www.leterrae. com/Leonardo.htm*

Leonardo: The Artist and the Man Serge Bramly, Sian Reynolds *Penguin (UK), 1995.* Bramly's book is a much more obvious choice for anyone wanting to know more about Leonardo – the artist and the man, as the subtitle promises. This is, simply, the best biography of Leonardo in print: a hugely engaging work, brilliantly written and translated, with excellent art, historical and psychological analysis of all the major and minor works, and an eye ever open for revealing anecdote. And while Bramly is as good an art historian as you could hope to find, he also responds superbly to the breathtaking range of Leonardo's pursuits as an inventor, architect, military engineer, pioneer of anatomy, and creator of wordplay and riddles. You get a strong sense, too, of the artist's life – his illegitimate birth, his homosexuality, his relationships with friends, patrons and other artists. In respect of *The Da Vinci Code*, there is fascinating coverage of the key commissions – the *Last Supper*, the *Virgin on the Rocks, Mona Lisa* – and how these came about and were executed.

Their Kingdom Come: Inside the secret world of Opus Dei Robert A. Hutchison *Doubleday/Corgi (UK), Thomas Dunne Books (US), 1997.* Opus Dei is almost as central to *The Da Vinci Code* as Leonardo, and indeed there is no other modern religious organization better suited to a conspiracy thriller. Just as Dan Brown depicts them, Opus Dei are secretive, wealthy and powerful, the only Personal Prelature of the late Pope John

Paul II. Hutchison, a Swiss-Canadian journalist, delved deeper than anyone before him into the history and workings of the sect whose self-declared mission is to save the Catholic Church. He doesn't always seem to worry unduly about the strength of his sources, and the book has a strong current of global conspiracy, with its 'exposure' of links with everyone from the Mafia to the FBI, and its 'octopus' hold over a whole network of international political, financial and educational institutions. A central thesis of the book is that Opus Dei is preparing a Crusade against Islam, a claim that might have been dismissed out of hand on the book's publication in 1997, though less so today, as Hutchison identified Opus Dei's targets – the most dangerous figures in the Islamic world – as Hassan al-Turabi and 'his chief of staff, Saudi entrepreneur Osama Bin Laden'. A chapter directly relevant to *The Da Vinci Code* discusses Opus Dei's financial operations, including its loans to the Vatican.

Beyond the Threshold: A Life in Opus Dei Maria Del Carmen Tapia *Continuum International Publishing (UK/US), 1998.* Tapia was a former numerary of Opus Dei – a full-time member, similar to being a nun or monk – but after twenty years, she left the sect, disillusioned and troubled. Her account of life in Spain within Opus Dei is probably the most detailed and vivid in print, and will have been good background for Dan Brown's creation of the Silas character. She is not wholly negative about the organization and its religious observances, but is deeply critical of its cult-like tactics, isolating recruits from family and friends, and paints a predominantly hostile picture of Monsignor Josemaría Escrivá de Balaguer, whom she met personally on several occasions.

The Pope's Armada: Unlocking the Secrets of Mysterious and Powerful New Sects in the Church Gordon Urquhart *Prometheus Books (US), 1995.* Perhaps the main surprise of this book on the new Catholic sects is that Opus Dei hardly get a mention. Instead, Urquhart focuses on the workings of a trio of evangelical and Catholic organizations, actively favoured by Pope John Paul II: *Focolare, Communione e Liberazione* (*CL*) and *Neocatechumenate* (*NC*). Their global membership, he claims, is 30 million, and together they represent the Pope's own 'armada', the frontline of (theologically conservative) Catholicism. Urquhart himself was a former member of Focolare, which numbers 80,000 core members around the world, and his book is in large part an attempt to discredit and warn against its cultist methods, its fanaticism, indoctrination and 'ego-destruction'.

Opus Dei: An Investigation into the Secret Society Struggling for Power Within the Roman Catholic Church Michael Walsh *Harper Collins (UK/US), 1992.* This is again highly critical of Opus Dei. It is less wide-ranging than Their Kingdom Come, and perhaps its chief interest is in discussion of the criticisms of Escriva that emerged upon his Beatification in 1992, and the organiza-

tion's own attempts to defame the adversatial witnesses.

I. M. Pei: A Profile in American Architecture Carter Wiseman *Harry N. Abrams Inc. (US), revised edition 2001.* Even without *The Da Vinci Code*, Ioeh Ming Pei, the Chinese-born, American-educated architect, would be famous primarily for his landmark glass pyramid at the Louvre. This beautifully illustrated book, by New Yorker architecture critic and devoted Pei enthusiast Carter Wiseman is as good an overview of the architect's career as you could hope to find. It doesn't specifically answer the questions thrown up by Dan Brown's novel, in particular the claim by Robert Langdon that President Mitterrand explicitly requested that the pyramid should comprise 666 panes of glass – a claim that seems likely to enter broad conspiracy lore. But Pei's office has subsequently clarified that the Pyramid actually contains 698 panes. And as for the pyramid's symbolism as chalice and dagger – Wiseman has been quoted as stating that Pei is an architect concerned almost exclusively with geometric patterns and abstractions and 'to think he was concealing symbolic content in his work would be to miss the whole point of his aesthetic.'

Conversations With I.M. Pei: Light Is the Key Gero Von Boehm *Prestel Publishing (US), 2001.* Pei discusses his work, including the Louvre Pyramid, in a series of interviews with film maker Gero Von Boehm. As he asserts, people and light, and the interactions between them, are at the centre of his vision.

Dan Brown

A Rough Guide

THE AUTHOR AND HIS BOOKS

'In 1994, while vacationing in Tahiti, I found an old copy of Sydney Sheldon's *Doomsday Conspiracy* on the beach. I read the first page ... and then the next ... and then the next. Several hours later, I finished the book and thought, 'Hey, I can do that.' '

DAN BROWN, INTERVIEW

Dan Brown's *The Da Vinci Code* is currently the world's bestselling adult novel – a book that proved just as popular in China and Japan as in the USA, Italy or Bulgaria, long before the arrival of a major Hollywood movie. Its appeal is three-fold: it's a top-grade, page-turner of a thriller, it packs in more conspiracy per page than almost any other novel you can name, and it has a backdrop of religion, art and secrecy that somehow hits a vein in our supposedly secular modern world.

This chapter takes a look at Dan Brown the author, and checks through his back catalogue – the *Da Vinci Code* 'prequel' *Angels & Demons*, featuring Robert Langdon, and his two earlier thrillers, *Digital Fortress* and *Deception Point* – and takes a look at what might be coming next.

Who is Dan Brown?

Dan Brown was born on June 22, 1964, and grew up in Exeter, New Hampshire, where he attended Phillips Exeter Academy, the wealthiest private school in the United States. His father taught mathematics at Exeter, while his mother is a 'professional sacred musician' (as he puts it on his website, *danbrown.com*). Brown attended Amherst, a venerable Massachusetts liberal arts college, from which he graduated in 1986.

After Amherst he moved to Los Angeles, working as a singer, pianist and MOR pop composer; he had a song performed in the Atlanta Olympics ceremonies, but the career failed to materialise. Instead, after a stint studying art history in Seville, Spain, he returned to his old college at Exeter to take up a post teaching English. He quit in 1996, after having his first thriller, *Digital Fortress*, bought for publication by Doubleday. This was followed by *Angels & Demons* (2000), in which Robert Langdon made his first appearance, and *Deception Point* (2001), more on each of which books below. His huge break, of course, was with *The Da Vinci Code*, published in 2003.

Brown continues to live in Exeter, with his wife **Blythe**, an art historian and painter, whom he credits as a collaborator on his research. He comes over in interviews not unlike Robert Langdon: a highly focussed writer who rises at 4am to start work, breaks hourly to do push-ups, hangs upside down using gravity boots 'to get his blood and ideas flowing', and knocks off in the afternoon to play tennis.

Dan Brown's next book – another quest for Robert Langdon – is set in (symbology-rich) Washington DC and New England, and is focussed on the shadowy world of the Masons. It is, as he says, a world he grew up in proximity to, in New England: the 'clandestine clubs of Ivy League universities, the Masonic lodges of our Founding Fathers, and the hidden hallways of early government power.' The novel, entitled **The Solomon Key**, is likely to emerge in 2007.

DIGITAL FORTRESS (1998)

Dan Brown talks of his moment of revelation, knowing he could write a thriller, reading Sydney Sheldon's *Doomsday Conspiracy* on the beach in Tahiti. However, the chief ingredient of a thriller is not classy writing but plot. And it was, as he recounts on his website, the 1995 visit of two US Secret Service to Phillips Exeter campus, where he was then teaching, that gave him the idea for *Digital Fortress*. The Secret Service had arrived to detain one of the students, who had casually sent an email to a friend saying he was 'so mad at the current political situation he was ready to kill President Clinton'. The agents arrived to check out if he was a kid mouthing off, or a potential terrorist threat.

That prompted Brown to look into how the agents got their information, and he began learning about the **National Security Agency (NSA)**, a little-known part of US government, which, as he puts it, 'functions like an enormous vacuum cleaner sucking in intelligence data from around the globe.' It was a gift of a backdrop for a thriller, and Brown neatly grafted on to it some of his knowledge of computers and cryptography. He also introduced his trademark location research – taking the Spanish city of **Seville**, where he had studied, as a major setting – and a cryptographer heroine, **Susan Fletcher** ('a brilliant and beautiful mathematician').

ANGELS & DEMONS (2000)

Digital Fortress was a very clever book of its time, picking up on all kinds of aspects of the privacy debate in a new computer era. But Brown worried that it was too overtly a techno-thriller, and might be perceived as 'a computer book.' With *Angels & Demons*, he shifted terrain firmly towards **conspiracy and art**. The backdrop of this novel is **Rome**, where a series of clues propel the heroes – the 'symbology professor' **Robert Langdon** and a sexy, brilliant woman scientist, **Leonarda Vetra** – through the **Vatican** and around the Renaissance monuments of **Bernini**. (Incidentally, Langdon, who is also the hero of *The Da Vinci Code* and *The Solomon Key*, makes his first appearance in this book. Dan Brown named him after John Langdon, a close friend and typography master who worked with Brown on an ambigram logo for *Angels and Demons*.)

A fair number of readers prefer this book to *The Da Vinci Code*, and in some ways the core of its plot – a clash between religion and science (represented by the Swiss-based scientific research centre, CERN) – has more real depth. The conspirators, too, are hard to resist: that hoary old bunch of anti-Papalists, the **Illuminati**, whose existence, in a nice touch, Langdon suggests are the invention of fantasists... until their dark deeds prove otherwise. **CERN**, of course, is a real establishment, as is anti-matter, their development that falls into dodgy hands.

In his mix of true facts and paranoia, and indeed the whole Illuminati setting, Brown was following on from one of the great cult conspiracy-thrillers of the 1970s, the **Illuminatus!** trilogy by Robert Anton Wilson and Robert Shea. Wilson and Shea's books are (freaky) products of their age – Wilson was a big mate of Timothy Leary – but they remain entertaining reads, packed with esoteric bursts of knowledge on Sufism, futurism, counter culture philosophy and a lot of sex. *Angels & Demons* and *The Da Vinci Code* would appear to owe much to them.

DECEPTION POINT (2001)

Finding a US government agency more secretive even than the NSA must have proved irresistible, and Dan Brown didn't spurn the opportunities with his third thriller, **Deception Point**. The agency is the **National Reconnaissance Office (NRO)**, which despite a $10bn budget and more than 10,000 employees is unknown to most of the American taxpayers who underwrite it. The resulting novel is rather more traditional thriller fare, with real-life boys toy technology (the Aurora 'secret' aircraft, stealth ships undetectable by radar) setting the pace. Locations, this time, include **Washington** and the **Arctic**. Robert Langdon wouldn't have been the man for this job, and takes time out, as Intelligence analyst (and President's daughter) **Rachel Sexton** gets down to action.

THE DA VINCI CODE (2003)

> My hope in writing this novel was that the story would serve as a catalyst and a springboard for people to discuss the important topics of faith, religion, and history.
>
> **DAN BROWN, INTERVIEW**

The Da Vinci Code was Dan Brown's breakthrough book, taking his sales and status from modest to phenomenal. With fifty million copies in print worldwide in forty-four languages, and still rising, it is the best selling novel of all time. And the movie, released in 2006, directed by Ron Howard and starring Tom Hanks and Audrey Tautou, looks set to break all box office records.

Just why the book has been so big is hard to pin down. As far as publishing goes, Random House in the US did an amazing job of setting the initial hype, sending out an unprecedented 10,000 review copies. But it needs more than hype to create any kind of bestseller, and the appeal of *The Da Vinci Code* – which purely as a piece of thriller writing is little different from Dan Brown's three earlier books – has everything to do with its particular backdrop of art and religion, of fantasy and very deliberately-stated 'fact'.

It is the 'fact', of course, that has created all the controversy: the books of rebuttal from Catholic and other Christian writers, the websites detailing each and every error ... the guides from publishers such as ourselves. On publication, the book had predominantly enthusiastic reviews, but from the get-go, those that found the book objectionable shouted the message from the rooftops, with Christian scholars even dubbing the novel 'hate literature'.

Of course, a thriller that takes as its big theme the idea that the established **Church is based upon a lie**, and has distorted the true

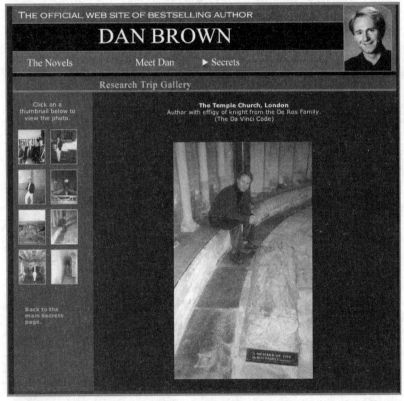

Dan Brown's official website, danbrown.com, is well worth a visit – to view galleries of sites featured in his novels, and to take the Da Vinci challenge...

message and history of Christianity, was never going to appeal to the conventionally religious. (Dan Brown on his website defines himself loosely as a Christian and 'a student of many religions'). But the offence that the novel has created is not just about religion, but **truth**. One of the most critical and influential comments on the book came in a *New York Times* article by Laura Miller, entitled 'The Da Vinci Con', in which she laid into its 'frisson of authenticity', and in particular its drawing upon *Holy Blood, Holy Grail* (see p.206), 'one of the all-time great works of pop pseudohistory' with its ludicrous claims for the Priory of Sion. This article now appears all over the Internet, as indeed it should – for, despite the claims of its frontispiece (and some Dan Brown interviews), *The Da Vinci Code* is no more true than anything by Tom Clancy or Terry Pratchett, or JK Rowling and the world of Hogwarts, come to that. And as Miller writes of *Holy Blood, Holy Grail*, its real bits are 'fact-ish' rather than 'factual'.

But what interesting territory those fact-ish ideas occupy: the early Christian church, the editing of the Bible, the loss of the goddess and the sacred feminine, the iconography of Leonardo da Vinci, the hidden language of codes. You could write a whole *Rough Guide* on that kind of thing.

THE SOLOMON KEY (2007?)

Dan Brown has recently admitted that he placed clues about his next novel, which already has the title of **The Solomon Key**, on the dust jacket of the American version of *The Da Vinci Code*. The author, who says he grew up in New England surrounded 'by the Masonic lodges of our Founding Fathers', confirmed that his next novel is 'set deep within the oldest fraternity in history, the enigmatic brotherhood of the Masons'. Having explored Paris, London and Rome in previous Robert Langdon novels, Brown says that his Harvard symbologist hero's next adventures will centre on **Washington, DC**, where many architectural features, including the gigantic obelisk known as the Washington Monument, built to commemorate the first president of the United States, are loaded with **Masonic symbolism and allusions**. At least eight signers of the Declaration of Independence were Masons, as were 13 U.S. presidents, including George Washington.

Even before Brown finished the manuscript of his new novel, enthusiasts were decoding his clues in order to figure out its subject matter and to string together tentative plotlines. They claim that *The Solomon Key* will not only link Freemasons to the founding of America but also to the Mormon Church, and that the action will involve a search for buried treasure across the United States.

A **grid reference** written faintly and in reverse on *The Da Vinci Code* dust jacket gives a location in latitude and longitude. If the co-ordinates are moved one degree north they pinpoint a sculpture called **Kryptos** in the courtyard of the Central Intelligence Agency's headquarters in Langley, Virginia. The sculpture, intended as a challenge to members of the CIA, contains a dense matrix of 1800 or so letters, some in similar style to the German wartime Enigma code deciphered at the Bletchley Park spy centre in Buckinghamshire. One passage is taken from the account of Howard Carter, the British archaeologist, of the opening of Tutankhamun's tomb in 1922.

Another clue on the jacket of *The Da Vinci Code* reads '**Is there no help for the widow's son**'. The codebreakers have linked these words to **Joseph Smith**, the founder of the Church of Jesus Christ of Latter-day Saints, also known as the **Mormons**. Smith uttered the phrase as he fell from an upper storey window after he was shot and fatally wounded by a mob who stormed his prison in Carthage, Illinois, in 1844. The Mormons believe that Smith had a vision in which gold plates containing the mysteries of God were buried in a New York hillside. Some believe that these were similar to the treasures found by the masons building King Solomon's temple at Mount Moriah in Jerusalem. Brown, whose wife Blythe is reported to have been raised a Mormon, seems well disposed towards thinking of Freemasons as an important historical underground movement, pushing the world towards democracy and enlightenment.

Others trying to unravel the plot of Brown's next novel believe the answer is linked to the **pyramid** and all-seeing eye on the back of every **dollar bill**. Officially the unfinished pyramid is meant to show that America is still growing and the eye reflects the importance of God to all Americans. But some say it shows that a secret order of Masons helped create the United States and is now running the world.

Several books have already been published, imaginatively forecasting and explaining the contents of the unpublished *The Solomon Key*. Among these are:

Da Vinci in America **Greg Taylor** 2004 *Daily Grail Publishing, Brisbane 2004.* Website: www.dailygrail.com

Secrets of the Widow's Son **David A Shugarts** 2005 *Weidenfeld and Nicolson, London, and Sterling Publishing, New York.*

Further Reading

Here is our selection of the best books on the subjects raised in *The Da Vinci Code*. Books that Dan Brown cites as having used in his research are reviewed in the article beginning on p.205.

Da Vinci Code

Secrets of the Code **Edited by Dan Burstein** *2004. CDS Books (US), Weidenfeld and Nicolson (UK).* This is a veritable *Da Vinci Code* encyclopedia – a lively combination of interviews, commentaries and extracts from Dan Brown's sources which will give you a taste of the issues which have been thrown into the debate.

Breaking the Da Vinci Code **Darrell L. Bock** *2004. Thomas Nelson (US).* Written by a theologian, this book engages the reader with some of the serious theological issues raised by *The Da Vinci Code*, and offers a well-informed and highly readable critique.

The Da Vinci Code Special Illustrated Edition **Dan Brown** *2004. Random House.* Yes, the original novel – but lavishly packaged with 126 photos of key sites and references. A fun browse.

The Da Vinci Code Illustrated Screenplay **Akiva Goldsman** *2006. Doubleday.* And here's the film script, again nicely illustrated, with scenes from the movie.

Early Christianity

The Golden Legend: Readings on the Saints **Jacobus de Voragine, trans. William Granger** *1993. Princeton University Press (US). Originally c.1250.* For serious saint-seekers. This medieval sourcebook recounts the lives of the saints and their cults in Western Europe, among them Mary Magdalene. This was the most printed book in Europe between 1470 and 1530.

Beyond Belief – The Secret Gospel of St. Thomas Elaine Pagels *2003. Macmillan (UK), 2003 Random House (US)*. Elaine Pagels, professor of religion at Princeton University, considers one of the excluded gospels and how its exclusion has helped to shape Christianity. Pagels approaches the issue with a combination of academic expertise and a very readable heartfelt concern for her topic.

The Gnostic Gospels Elaine Pagels *1980. Weidenfeld and Nicolson (UK)*. Pagels is the leading authority on the Nag Hammadi texts, and remains open to their potential significance while resisting the lure of sensationalising them.

The Gnostics Jacques Lacarriere *1977. Peter Owen (UK)*. Brilliant review of the power and poetry of Gnosticism, with an introduction by Lawrence Durrell.

The Early Church Henry Chadwick *1987. Penguin Books (UK)*. A comprehensive overview of the roots of Christianity and its early development. Useful for clarifying some of the generalisations and idiocies you will find in *The Da Vinci Code*.

Lost Christianities Bart D Ehrman *2003 Oxford University Press (US)*. A scholarly, highly readable survey of the diversity of early Christianity, explaining how we came to be left with the New Testament, and ruminating over what has been lost.

History of the Church Eusebius, trans. G.A. Williamson *1989. Penguin (UK)*. Almost as good as being there – the good friend of Constantine the Great and groundbreaking eclesiastical historian Eusebius tells the story of the early Church, its fearful persecution, its schisms and its heresies, all told by an eyewitness on the spot.

Pagans and Christians Robin Lane Fox *1988. Penguin (UK). 1987. Alfred A. Knopf (US)*. Fox, a leading Oxford University ancient historian, lays out an absorbing and detailed portrait of the transition from paganism to Christianity in the ancient world up to the death of Constantine.

The Nag Hammadi Library in English James M. Robinson *1978. Harper Collins (UK/US), rev. edn. 1988* One of Dan Brown's sources – see p.213.

SACRED FEMININE

The Gospel of Mary Magdalene Jean-Yves Leloup *2002 Inner Traditions (US)* A text and commentary of the gospel of Mary Magdalene allows you make up your own mind about the 'lost bride'.

Adam, Eve and the Serpent Elaine Pagels *1998 Weidenfeld and Nicolson (UK)*. An eminent religious historian

examines the Christian paradox of freedom from earthly values and bondage to the spiritual idea of original sin.

The Chalice and the Blade. Our History, Our Future Riane Eisler *1998 Thorsons (UK), 1988 Harper & Row (US)* Another of Dan Brown's sources – see review on p.214.

This Female Man of God: Women and Spiritual Power In the Patristic Age, AD 350-450 **Gillian Cloke** *1995. Routledge (UK)*. A study of how the role of women underwent a change after the first liberating centuries of Christianity.

The Making of the Magdalene: Preaching and Popular Devotion in the Later Middle Ages. **Katherine Ludwig Jansen** *2000. Princeton University Press (US)*. This is a brilliant study of the development of the legends and cult of Mary Magdalene in medieval Europe.

Mary Magdalene: The First Apostle **Ann Graham Brock** *2003. Harvard University Press (US)*. This Harvard academic discusses the issue of apostolic authority. Could Mary Magdalene have had an important role amongst the apostles? Evidence from the Gospels informs the debate which is still relevant today in the midst of the discussions over the ordination of women in the Church.

The Goddess in the Gospels: Reclaiming the Sacred Feminine **Margaret Starbird** *1998 Bear & Company (US)* Another of Dan Brown's sources – see review on p.211.

The Woman with the Alabaster Jar: Mary Magdalene and the Holy Grail. **Margaret Starbird** *1993. Bear and Company (US)*. Another of Dan Brown's sources – see review on p.210.

Mary Magdalen: Myth and Metaphor **Susan Haskins** *1995. Riverhead Books (US)*. Scholarly but readable history of Mary and her place in art, history and literature.

HOLY GRAIL, TEMPLAR AND SECRET SOCIETIES

The Holy Grail, Imagination and Belief **Richard Barber** *2004. Allen Lane/ Penguin (UK)*. The true biography of a medieval myth. Serious and reliable.

The Trial of the Templars **Malcolm Barber** *1996. Cambridge University Press (UK)*. The accusations made against the Templars are reassessed in this intelligent and well-written account of the tortured and immolated knights.

Montaillou **Emanuel Le Roy Ladurie** *1980. Penguin Books (UK)*. The history of a small mediaeval village in the French Pyrenees, the last to actively support the Cathar heresy, told from a thoroughly human perspective.

Arthurian Romances **Chretien de Troyes** *1991. Penguin Books (UK)*. Where the Grail trail began. This twelfth century French writer of courtly romance left his story of the Grail hanging in mid-air and has tantalised people ever since.

OPUS DEI

Opus Dei: Secrets and Power Inside the Catholic Church John L Allen *2005. Allen Lane (UK) Doubleday (US).* Allen reports for CNN, NPR and the BBC on Catholic affairs, in which he is considered the most informed source in the English language. Based on numer-ous interviews with heads of Opus Dei and comparing their attitudes with those of critical Opus Dei members and outsiders, this book claims to uncover closely guarded secrets and to separate fact from fiction, presenting the first comprehensive study of the organisation.

LEONARDO

Leonardo da Vinci, The Flight of the Mind Charles Nicholl *2004. Allen Lane/ Penguin Group (UK).* Absorbing in-depth biography constructs a sensitive portrait of Leonardo as a domestic and affectionate individual as well as genius.

Leonardo Frank Zollner *2000. Taschen (Germany).* An excellent way of getting to know Leonardo's art – this features beautifully reproduced illustrations and paintings as well as some light back-ground information on Leonardo's life.

Leonardo Serge Bramly, Sian Reynolds *1995. Penguin (UK).* Another of Dan Brown's sources – a highly recommend-ed biography of Leonardo. See p.215.

Lives of the Artists Giorgio Vasari *1987. Penguin (UK).* This is one of the earliest, indeed near-contemporary, sources on Leonardo, and used extensively by all subsequent biographers.

The Notebooks of Leonardo da Vinci Leonardo da Vinci *1970. Dover (UK/ US).* Another of Dan Brown's sources – see review on p.215.

CODES AND SYMBOLS

Signs and Symbols in Christian Art George Ferguson *1961. Oxford University Press (UK).* This slim volume offers itself as a straightforward and very clear reference guide to signs and symbols. This will help you to under-stand more about the meaning of flow-ers, numbers and shapes in art.

The Code Book Simon Singh *1999. Fourth Estate (UK).* The story of codes from twelfth-century Islamic cryptana-lytic achievements to twentieth-century linguistic and computer code-cracking, illuminated by fascinating anecdotes.

Codes, Ciphers and Secret Languages Fred B Wrixon *1989. Harrap (UK).* This book explains all manner of tech-nical crypto-phrases like polyalphabetic substitution cipher and so forth which Brown cites. Peppered with engaging anecdotes to break up the technical jargon.

Websites

The Da Vinci Code has prompted enormous discussion online, and of course such subjects as the Holy Grail, Gnosticism and the Sacred Feminine have a major presence on the Web. Here are some of the more interesting sites.

THE DA VINCI CODE AND THE MOVIE

Dan Brown's website
http://www.danbrown.com/
The website provides background material – including an excellent selection of photographs of locales – on *The Da Vinci Code* as well as Dan Brown's other novels. And there are interviews, photographs, puzzles and competitions. That said, Brown reveals next to nothing about himself.

Da Vinci's Code
http://witcombe.sbc.edu/davincicode/contents-schedule.html
Professor Whitcombe of Sweet Briar College, Virginia, has built an entire art history course around *The Da Vinci Code*, and posted it online. This is an attractive and fascinating site with plenty of resources and links allowing you to study Renaissance painting, geometry, codes, the cult of Mary Magdalene, and much more.

The Da Vinci Code Research Guide
http://altreligion.about.com/library/bl_davincicode.htm
Full of resources and links covering such subjects as Jesus, the Early Church, Sacred Spaces, Secrets and Lies, the Gnostic Magdalene, etc..

CENSUR: Center for Studies on New Religions
http://www.cesnur.org/
Examines everyone from Bin Laden through Rev. Moon to Dan Brown.

The Da Vinci Code Official Film Site
www.sonypictures.com/movies/thedavincicode
Sony Pictures' official site.

Cryptophyle
www.SeekTheCodes.com
A playful website set up by Sony to offer puzzles, codes, clues to do with *The Da Vinci Code* film and its successors.

Da Vinci Code Blog
http://whatisthedavincicode.blogspot.com/
A bloggers constantly updated file on news and information about the book and film. A varied and useful resource, with a huge amount of material.

CHRISTIANITY

King's College, London
http://www.kcl.ac.uk/
King's College is mentioned in *The Da Vinci Code* specifically for its excellence in religious studies. It is strong also in ancient studies. Try searching for 'Jesus' or 'goddess', and you will be given reams of course outlines, reading lists, etc.

Beliefnet
http://www.beliefnet.com/
Beliefnet is a multi-faith e-community designed to help people meet their religious and spiritual needs – which it does by hosting interviews, discussions, topical articles and masses of other information on all religions, not just Christianity. It is independent and not affiliated with any religion or spiritual movement.

From Jesus to Christ
http://www.pbs.org/wgbh/pages/frontline/shows/religion/
This website of America's Public Broadcasting Service traces the development of Christianity during its first few centuries.

The One that Got Away
http://jesus.com.au/html/page/jesus_in_india
If it is true that Jesus was not crucified, then where did he go? This Australian website has the answer. There is more of the same at http://www.tombofjesus.com

Christianity Today
www.christianitytoday.com/history/special/davincicode.html
The Da Vinci Code's assertions about the Church are examined by this online Christian Evangelical organisation. It is strong on history; among other things, it looks at the Council of Nicaea and what happened to the lost Gospels.

Leadership U
http://www.leaderu.com/focus/davincicode.html
In the words of the Texas-based Leadership U, this is 'a one-stop shopping superstore in the marketplace of ideas'. Run by Christian Leadership Ministries ('Telling the truth at the speed of life'), it is an informal online university that does not provide degrees but, as 'an internet crossroads' with links to external sites, does make available a huge amount of useful material.

Catholic Enquiry Office
http://www.life4seekers.co.uk/TheDaVinciCode-resources.htm
This agency of the Catholic Bishops' Conference of England and Wales, has set up its own website on Mary Magdalene, to provide resources for those interested in *The Da Vinci Code*.

GNOSTICISM

The Gnostic Society
www.gnosis.org
Website of the Los Angeles-based Gnostic Society, with endless information on Gnosticism including translations and photographs of the Nag Hammadi codices.

Sacred Feminine

Religious Tolerance website
http://www.religioustolerance.org/
cfe_bibl.htm
Handy overview of Jesus's teachings
regarding women, from a liberal website
aiming to break down fundamentalism
based on a lack of information.

Mary Magdalene
http://www.magdalene.org
Devoted to Mary Magdalene, this
website takes something of a Gnostic
line. It has links to the Gospel of Mary
Magdalene and other Nag Hammadi
gospels.

Ancient History

The Perseus Digital Library
http://www.perseus.tufts.edu/

One of the great online resources for the
ancient world, papyri, etc.

Holy Grail, Templar and Secret Societies

The Camelot Project
www.lib.rochester.edu/camelot/grlmenu.htm
This educational website features the history of the Grail legend as told through
art and literature. It is part of a project
which looks at the Arthurian legend.

Priory of Sion Website
www.priory-of-sion.com
This regularly updated site contains
reports, reviews and commentaries on
the intriguing story of the Priory of
Sion. It is not a Priory site, but rather an
observer on the phenomenon – often
amusing and cynical, always interesting,
it aims to tell you the truth behind the
conspiracy.

**Knights Templar 'Official'
International Website**
www.ordotempli.org/priory_of_sion.htm
Reams of unfiltered pseudo-fact on the
Priory of Sion from one of the many
groups that like to make out they are the
modern-day Knights Templar.

Opus Dei

Opus Dei, US headquarters
http://www.opusdei.org/
Apart from the Manhattan HQ, which
looks like an above-ground bombshelter,
Opus Dei and its members come across as
teddy bears. Here you can find out about
its founder, Josemariá Escrivá, 'the man
who loved God' and was made a saint
in record quick time. The site contains
Opus Dei's rebuttle to Dan Brown, which
states: 'We want to point out that *The Da
Vinci Code*'s bizarre depiction of Opus
Dei is inaccurate, both in the overall
impression and in many details...'

Opus Dei Awareness Network
http://www.odan.org/
ODAN exists, it claims, to help those who have been harmed by Opus Dei. Many are former Opus Dei members and have inside information. Want to know about aggressive recruiting, alienation from families, and corporal mortification? This is the place.

LEONARDO

The Last Supper
http://ccat.sas.upenn.edu/~lbianco/project/home.html
This wonderful site is devoted entirely to the Last Supper. It is presented by the people who have most recently restored it, and so it is highly informed.

Drawings of Leonardo da Vinci
www.visi.com/~reuteler/leonardo.html
This site offers 39 drawings of Leonardo's for downloading plus very useful links to sites where you can learn more about Leonardo's life and works.

Leonardo Museum
www.leonardo.net
An easy-to-navigate site which will take you on a gallery tour round Leonardo's paintings.

The Web Museum
http://gallery.euroweb.hu/html/l/leonardo/
A good selection of Leonardo's works, with helpful links to themes and other artists.

CODES

Symbols
www.symbols.com
Around 2,500 symbols have been compiled on this website. Very useful for learning more about familiar symbols or discovering all sorts of symbols you never knew existed.

Fibonacci Numbers and the Golden Section
www.mcs.surrey.ac.uk/Personal/R.Knott/Fibonacci/fibnat.html
If you want to find out more on the interelated areas of the Divine Proportion, Phi, the Golden Ratio and the Fibonacci sequence take a look at this comprehensive site. The extensive use of illustrations will help put the mathematical jargon into context.

Royal Holloway College
http://www.rhul.ac.uk/Index.html
Royal Holloway, a college of the University of London and located out by Windsor, offers degrees in all sorts of things to do with computers, security and codes. Sophie Neveu studied here, and you can too. Search under their postgraduate programmes for MSc degrees in Information Security, which involves cryptography.

The Da Vinci Code Movie

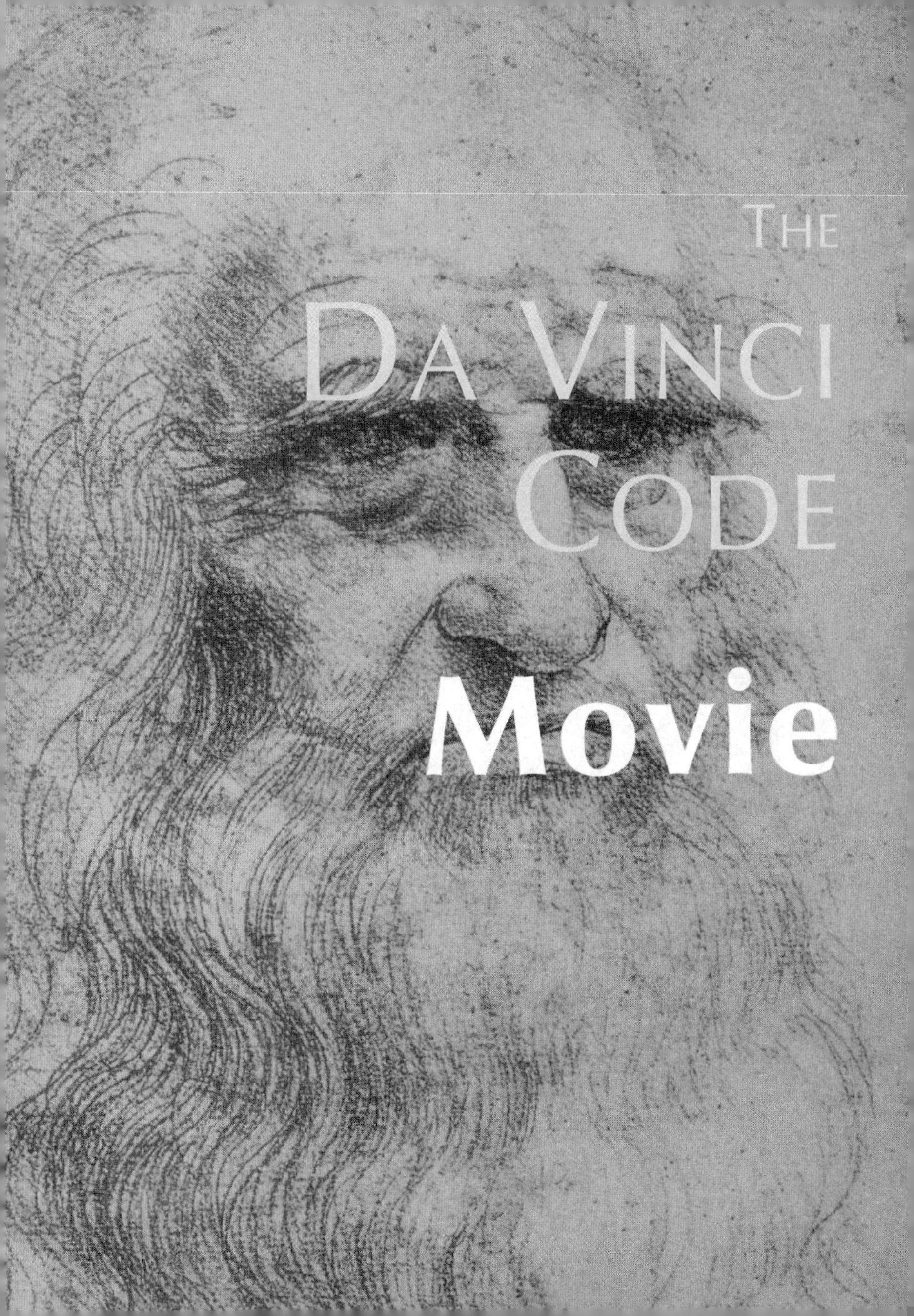

From Book to Movie

DA VINCI GOES TO HOLLYWOOD

The number of copies of *The Da Vinci Code* that have been sold rises by another million every time somebody checks the figures. In America the novel has been at the top of the bestseller lists since it was published in April 2003, a yet more remarkable achievement for a book available only in hardback until a paperback edition appeared in time for the opening of the film on May 19 2006 – five million paperbacks, to be exact, the largest paperback print-run ever undertaken in one go.

But however many millions have already read the novel, hundreds of millions more will see the film of *The Da Vinci Code*, and the controversy it has ignited is likely to be fanned. The Vatican, Opus Dei and an array of American evangelical Christians have protested against the film, have demanded changes, and in some cases have consigned its makers, along with its cast, to the lowest depths of hell for the mortal sin of blasphemy.

Here we look at the filming of the book, including the stories behind its casting, its production, its negotiations with places like Westminster Abbey and the Louvre... and the various pressures and condemnations that the film makers, Sony Pictures and director Ron Howard, have faced.

The Deal

When Dan Brown's *The Da Vinci Code* was first published in April 2003 it caught the attention of Joel Surnow, the creator of the American television drama '24' – a series in which each episode covers an hour of real time, and the entire story, broadcast over a season, takes place in a single day. As the action in *The Da Vinci Code* is crammed into a hectic twenty hours, the novel seemed ideal for the series concept, and so Surnow suggested to his boss, producer Brian Grazer, that they acquire the rights to the book. But Dan Brown was aiming higher than television and rejected their bid. He was right. Within two months the novel was turning into an international sensation and bidding got serious.

The winners turned out to be Sony Pictures, whose then President and CEO, **John Calley**, had established a good working relationship on previous ventures with **Michael Ruddell**, Dan Brown's lawyer. Everybody in Hollywood wanted the film, but the Calley–Ruddell relationship gave Sony the advantage: 'I think Ruddell thought I was an okay guy and that I wasn't crazy', said Calley, 'which in this business is as good as it gets'. One phone call did the trick, and for what very soon looked a bargain price – **$6 million** – Sony not only got the rights to *The Da Vinci Code* but also the future movie rights to the Robert Langdon character, meaning that film versions of **Angels & Demons** as well as Dan Brown's projected *Da Vinci* sequel, **The Solomon Key**, are likely to follow.

That was just the beginning of a complex series of deals, contracts, arrangements and negotiations that led to the successful filming of the book. Sony Pictures is part of Japan's gigantic **Sony Group**, the 123rd largest company in the world, which includes electronics, games, motion pictures, music, banking and insurance. Its aim, says the Sony Group, is 'to emotionally touch and excite our customers'. Within the group, Sony Pictures handles motion picture production and distribution, as well as television programming and syndication, in sixty-seven countries. *The Da Vinci Code* was assigned to **Columbia Pictures**, founded in Hollywood in 1924 and bought by Sony Pictures in 1989, and John Calley, though no longer president and CEO, was made overseer of Sony's interests under the title of producer.

THE TALENT

But Columbia did not make the film alone; instead it was partnered by **Imagine Entertainment**, an independent production company established in 1986 by former child-star (*The Music Man*; *American Graffiti*) turned director **Ron Howard** and producer **Brian Grazer** – yes, the same Brian Grazer who was Joel Surnow's boss on the TV series '24', which in fact is made by Imagine Entertainment. Sony had the rights to *The Da Vinci Code*, and they had the facilities of Columbia Pictures, but they needed the talent to make the film, which is why they turned to Howard and Grazer.

Through Imagine Entertainment, Ron Howard and Brian Grazer have made numerous award-winning television programmes and motion pictures, not least the 2001 film *A Beautiful Mind* which won four Academy Awards. The Oscar for Best Picture went to Howard as director and Grazer as producer; the Oscar for Best Director went to Howard; and the Oscar for Best Writing went to **Akiva Goldsman**, who was later hired by Howard and Grazer to write the filmscript for *The Da Vinci Code*.

THE LOCAL HELP

Location negotiations and other practical details for *The Da Vinci Code* in Britain and France were handled by **Rose Line Productions Limited**, a company invented for the purpose of throwing fans and protesters off the scent. Everything to do with the shooting of the film was booked under the Rose Line name. Rose Line Production's registered office is at Sony Pictures' London address, but it seems to have been one of those off-the-shelf companies which has gone through several incarnations since created in 1996. Its earlier names were Dancelane Limited, BB Film Productions Limited, Life of the Party Limited and Dance Movie Limited, until the makers of *The Da Vinci Code* took it over towards the end of 2004 and gave it the name Rose Line, after the solar meridian mentioned in the novel.

Director Ron Howard on location in Britain, filming *The Da Vinci Code*.

PRINCIPAL PRODUCTION CREDITS

Director Ron Howard
Novel Dan Brown
Screenplay Akiva Goldsman
Executive Producer Dan Brown
Producer Brian Grazer
Original Music Hans Zimmer
   Also, under *Art Department,* the credits show:
Painter Leonardo Da Vinci

Casting the *Code*

Once the producer, director and scriptwriter are in place, the most important task facing the makers of a $125 million big-budget Hollywood movie like *The Da Vinci Code* is choosing the male lead. Why? Because it is the big-time male actors who draw the audiences. The money tells the story: even the most famous female stars like Julia Roberts and Cameron Diaz can expect to earn only half as much as actors like Tom Cruise or Russell Crowe. The deal in the case of *The Da Vinci Code* was that the producer, the director and the actor playing Robert Langdon would, in addition to their normal fees, share anywhere between 25 and 40 percent of box-office receipts. Dan Brown takes an undisclosed share on top of that.

CASTING ROBERT LANGDON: YOU CAN'T FAKE INTELLIGENCE

Director Ron Howard and producer Brian Grazer looked at many actors for the lead role of Robert Langdon, among them Ralph Fiennes, Russell Crowe, Hugh Jackman, George Clooney and Tom Hanks. For a long time **Russell Crowe** was the favourite; he had starred for them in *A Beautiful Mind*, but that was more a critical

Hanks on location in Paris – a suitably cerebral actor for the lead part of
symbologist hero Robert Langdon

than a financial success. In November 2004 they decided on **Tom Hanks**, who is one of Hollywood's most bankable stars, with his presence in a movie almost guaranteeing box-office success.

The Da Vinci Code is Tom Hanks's third collaboration with Grazer and Howard, who helped to make him a star with their 1984 comedy *Splash*, and hired him again eleven years later for *Apollo 13*, which earned the filmmakers their first best-picture Academy Award nomination. Hanks himself won two best-actor Academy Awards for his leading roles in *Philadelphia* (1993) and *Forrest Gump* (1994) – the first actor to pull off back-to-back Oscar wins since Spencer Tracy in the 1930s.

But according to Howard, neither money nor friendship explain why he and Glazer chose Hanks for the role of Robert Langdon. For all the chasing around in *The Da Vinci Code*, much of the action is cerebral and involves cracking codes, solving riddles and even a tense Boolean keyword search at a library in King's College in London. 'Tom is an exciting actor to watch thinking', said Howard. 'He gives Langdon instant legitimacy.' Scriptwriter Akiva Goldsman agreed: 'Tom is wildly intelligent, and you can't fake intelligence. A good actor can act anything – except the sense that he is thinking deeply if he really isn't.'

CASTING SOPHIE NEVEU

As *The Da Vinci Code* is an international thriller, Grazer and Howard decided that rather than fill all the parts with American actors they would hire foreign actors to play the book's foreign roles. Three Oscar-winning Hollywood actresses apparently lobbied hard to play Sophie Neveu, but the producer and director thought that the audience would be disappointed if Sophie was not actually French. That also ruled out English actress Kate Beckinsale, who in American terms was foreign enough to be considered for the part.

Howard and Glazer were in Paris in December 2004 conducting auditions for the role of Sophie Neveu when they were summoned by French president **Jacques Chirac** to the Elysée Palace. They assumed it would be a five-minute courtesy call, but instead the meeting went on for an hour, during which Chirac pressured them to give the part of Sophie to the best friend of his daughter Claude, who works at the Elysée as her father's communications manager. The filmmakers have discreetly not mentioned the name of the woman Chirac had in mind for the casting couch. As many as thirty French actresses are known to have auditioned for the part, among them Sophie Marceau, Virginie Ledoyen, Judith Godrèche, Elsa Zylberstein, Linda Hardy and Audrey Tautou. The rumour in French film circles is that Chirac's choice was Sophie Marceau, with whom he is besotted and who indeed is a close friend of his daughter.

The moment was fraught for Howard and Glazer, as they were also still negotiating with the Louvre to shoot on location in the Grand Galerie, and during the same meeting Chirac told his guests to alert him if their request to film at the Louvre ran into any problems. You scratch my back, I'll scratch yours, is the way the filmmakers could have taken Chirac's suggestion for the lead female role.

Nevertheless, and to the surprise of many, including herself, in January 2005 the part of Sophie Neveu went to **Audrey Tautou**. Precisely because she had charmed audiences all over the world as the star of the romantic comedy *Amélie*, she had been seen as too cute for the role. But she has acted in a variety of French films, some of them fairly gritty, and has shown herself capable of developing and adapting her style. After Howard was shown a tape of her playing Charlie Rose in the French war film *Un long dimanche de fiançailles* (*A Very Long Engagement*), he saw her in a new light, and he flew her to Los Angeles to run through some scenes with Hanks. The two worked together like a dream.

The dream team? French star Audrey Tautou with Hanks, in pursuit of the Holy Grail.

Audrey Tautou has a withdrawn and haunted beauty, which is perfect for her part in *The Da Vinci Code*. Sophie is the emotional focus of the story, but she is more than that, for as the plot unfolds all the pieces of the jigsaw, potent and disturbing, point back to her. As Audrey Tautou has said, speaking English with a heavy French accent, 'Sophie is very serious, like a little soldier. She wants to keep her eyes closed – to her past, to everything that's happening to her. And during the movie, she opens them slowly, slowly'. For all the audience pulling-power of Tom Hanks, much of the artistic success of the movie is likely to depend on the slight figure of Audrey Tautou.

CASTING BEZU FACHE

As well as trying to promote the actress of his choice, Jacques Chirac also tried to haggle a higher fee for **Jean Reno** – the film-makers' choice for Bezu Fache – at his Elysée meeting. 'That was hilarious', said Howard, with the grimace of a man straightening out his twisted arm, but 'fortunately the deal was already closed.' For his antics, Chirac was mercilessly pilloried in the French press, the satirical weekly *Le Canard Enchaîné* crowing that the president had been rebuffed by the American filmmakers: 'Chirac Veni, Vidi, Da Vinci', went its headline. Reno, who was signed up in December 2004, was an early choice for the role of the bullish Gallic police inspector. Born in Morocco to Spanish parents, his family settled in France where he studied drama and has made a career as a character actor in theatre, television and film.

CASTING SIR LEIGH TEABING

Despite not being fat, **Sir Ian McKellen** was given the role of Sir Leigh Teabing, but that had less to do with any principle that an Englishman should play an Englishman and a knight should play a knight, than with his incomparable mastery of the English stage. McKellen, raised near Manchester in the coal mining town of Wigan, became stagestruck at the age of eleven when his school's summer camp near Stratford on Avon allowed him to see the greats like Sir Laurence Olivier perform. McKellen himself has since become the outstanding Shakespearean actor of his generation, and he was knighted in 1991 for his services to the arts. He is perhaps most widely known, however, for his role as Gandalf in all three films of *The Lord of the Rings*.

Howard offered McKellen the role in April 2005 after only half an hour's chat at London's Dorchester Hotel, an important factor being his experience of the stage where words need to be translated

Ian McKellen tries a few tombs for size, on location at Lincoln Cathedral, August 2005.

economically into action. As McKellen has himself observed, 'There is an awful lot of conversation in the novel which wouldn't easily make for a good film. I am very impressed with Akiva Goldsman's cunning adaptation of Dan Brown's book, which allows the history of the Grail to be presented cinematically. The actors have been rehearsing it round a table with Messrs Howard and Goldsman'.

CASTING BISHOP ARINGAROSA

Although every inch an Englishman, London-born **Alfred Molina** can play characters of almost any background thanks to the mixed heritage bequeathed to him by his Spanish father and Italian mother. A veteran of the Royal National Theatre, he has also appeared on Broadway where he has twice been nominated for a Tony award as Best Actor, once for *Art* and again for *Fiddler on the Roof*. His recent films have included *Chocolat* and *Spider Man 2*. Molina was signed up at the same time as McKellen, in April 2005. As Bishop Aringarosa he plays a deluded Spanish prelate who is the patron of Silas, the murderous monk.

CASTING SILAS

In his novel Dan Brown describes Silas as a crazed albino monk and a member of Opus Dei. Given the intention of Howard and Grazer that foreign roles should go to foreign actors, Silas should have gone to an albino Spaniard; and indeed they did audition several albino

Another foreign star – the Smart Car – in which Tautou takes Hanks for a spin.

actors, but none was convincingly self-flagellating, murderous and creepy. The next best thing to an albino, they cheerfully decided, was to hire an Englishman. And so in May 2005 the part went to fair-haired **Paul Bettany**, born into a London acting family, who until the release of *The Da Vinci Code* was better known as Mr Jennifer Connelly, after his Oscar-winning wife with whom he appeared in *A Beautiful Mind*. But now he is out there on his own: according to Grazer, it is the weird performance turned in by Bettany that 'drives the eeriness of the movie'.

THE CAST LIST

Tom Hanks	*Robert Langdon*
Audrey Tautou	*Sophie Neveu*
Jean Reno	*Bezu Fache*
Ian McKellen	*Sir Leigh Teabing*
Alfred Molina	*Bishop Aringarosa*
Paul Bettany	*Silas*
Marie-Françoise Audollent	*Sister Sandrine*
Jean-Yves Berteloot	*Remy*
Clive Carter	*Police Captain at Biggin Hill*
Etienne Chicot	*Lt Collet*
Daisy Doidge-Hill	*Sophie as a child*
Christopher Fosh	*PC Edwards*
Seth Gabel	*Cleric*
Joe Grossi	*Church Official*
Dhaffer L'Abidine	*PTS Agent*
Jean-Pierre Marielle	*Jacques Saunière*
Michael Norton	*French Detective*
Peter Pedrero	*Young Silas's father*
Jürgen Prochnow	*André Vernet*
Harry Taylor	*British Police Captain*

Sister Mary Michael – formerly a Carmelite – makes her one-nun protest against the filming of *The Da Vinci Code* at Lincoln Cathedral.

Protests and Pressures

Extraordinary secrecy surrounded the filming of *The Da Vinci Code*. Location negotiations and bookings were handled by the mysterious Rose Line Productions. Outsiders were banned from the set. The names of the actors were disguised on the shooting scripts. Everyone associated with the film had to sign confidentiality agreements. And Sony released only the barest details about the film and where and when they were shooting.

'It is easier for everybody to just go make the movie', said one Sony executive, explaining why everybody was keeping schtum. But this is not normally the language of studios with a blockbuster movie in the making, when the publicity machine and the razzmatazz are working overtime. Of course when a film is based on the biggest-selling novel of all time, its makers may feel that any promotional effort on their part would be superfluous – but that was not the reason either. Instead it was the very nature of the book itself, with its potentially incendiary assertion that the Roman Catholic Church has been lying about Jesus for two thousand years. The silence underlined a genuine fear that the filmmakers would be faced by angry and damaging public protests.

SONY SOUND OUT CHRISTIAN SENSIBILITIES

Sony hired Jonathan Bock, a marketing expert, to approach Catholic and other Christian experts for their views on how the plot might be altered to avoid offending the devout. The answers that came back boiled down to three demands: [1] make ambiguous the central contentions of the book, that Jesus's message promoted the sacred feminine, that he and Mary Magdalene had a child, and that their bloodline exists to this day; [2] remove all mention of Opus Dei; and [3] amend the book's errors over coded religious meanings in works of art. But the proposals, of course, attack the very core of the book; if they were all adopted, the film would have no point.

Columbia Pictures producer John Calley has said that critics of the story should look upon it in a positive light. 'The amazing thing about this book is it's provocative. As a history book it's extraordinary. As an exploration of the evolution of a particular religion, it's extraordinary.' *The Da Vinci Code* is anti-Catholic, he admitted, but not destructively so. The film could be used as a tool for discussing the origins of religion and challenging its basic assumptions, which he thought was a good thing. 'In our society, most societies, we grow up with our religion given to us by our parents. We are never truly oriented into the history of it, the subtlety of it.'

Yet Calley was careful to stress that Sony were not introducing ideas of their own, emphasizing that Howard was an easygoing film-maker – 'Ron is not a polariser' – and that 'We all knew the book was quite controversial, and we were ready for that. But we didn't want to add to it'.

CATHOLIC PROTESTS AND 'LEMON INTO LEMONADE'

Amazingly, the **Vatican** seems genuinely rattled by the continuing worldwide success of Dan Brown's thriller, and in spring 2005 it appointed **Cardinal Tarcisio Bertone**, a close confidant of Pope Benedict XVI, to rebut what it dismisses as the lies, distortions and errors in *The Da Vinci Code*.

At around the same time the producers Brian Glazer and John Calley and the director Ron Howard received letters from the **Catholic League** in the United States, and from **Opus Dei** and other groups. The Catholic League asked for the film to begin with a statement that it is a work of fiction, not of fact. William Donohue, president of the Catholic League, said he wrote to Sony before shooting began, demanding a disclaimer. 'As long as you say it's purely fictional, you can say Christ had three heads. I don't give a damn. But you can't play both sides of the street.' Sony, he said, sent him a polite but noncommital reply.

Opus Dei, concerned that it was defamed and misrepresented in the book, asked that its name not be mentioned in the film at all. 'Nobody likes to see themselves caricatured on the big screen', said Brian Finnerty, a spokesman for Opus Dei in the United States. 'I hope that Sony will play by the same rules of fairness in portraying the Catholic Church as you would expect for the portrayal of any other religious or ethnic group.'

But though the Roman Catholic hierarchy is concerned about the film, they also see it as an opportunity to put across their own message. In Rome, Marc Carroggio, who oversees Opus Dei's relationship with the international media, said that interest about the book and the film 'is turning out to be a sort of indirect publicity for us'. *The Da Vinci Code*, he explained, 'is essentially parasitical: the author makes a name for himself by attacking a major cultural figure, and he presents it as art. If the plot did not centre on Jesus Christ, the book would lose its appeal. I suspect that in the coming year, many people will be moved to read the Gospels or a book about the life of Jesus Christ. They will be drawn to consider the great themes of faith, which give light to the most difficult questions of human existence. For me, these are all ways of turning the lemon into lemonade'.

BURNING AT THE STAKE

Sony is walking a tight-rope, on the one hand trying not to alienate the core audience for the film, that is those who have read *The Da Vinci Code* and expect nothing less than its faithful reproduction on the big screen, while on the other not wanting to alienate the great mass of cinema-goers who bring in the bucks and want a 'popcorn movie'. In fact Sony is hoping to cash in on what is known in the trade as the 'Passion dollar', meaning attracting those religious moviegoers who ensured the success of recent Christian-themed films such as *The Chronicles of Narnia* and *The Passion of the Christ*.

In fact it is probably not Catholics that Sony has to worry about, but Protestant evangelical Christians who hold simplistically literal views of the Bible, which they claim to be the absolute word of God. They are legion across the US, and they definitely like popcorn with their movies. Judging from phone-in radio programmes, *The Da Vinci Code* for them is not some wayward piece of fiction, or even a heretical departure from dogma, but a blasphemy which invites burning at the stake.

But right from the start Ron Howard said he was against diluting the message of *The Da Vinci Code*. 'It would be ludicrous to take on this subject and then try to take the edges off. We're doing this movie because we like the book.' But he did make one concession, saying he would not open the film with Dan Brown's notorious foreword which claims 'All descriptions of artwork, architecture, documents and secret rituals in this novel are accurate'.

And so the filming went stealthily forward.

Shooting the Film

Shooting *The Da Vinci Code* lasted from the end of June to the beginning of November 2005, which was a fairly long haul, but there were a lot of locations, and it is a relatively lengthy film. The first location shot was in Paris on June 30 and the last was at Rosslyn in September. Filming was also done at Shepperton Studios in Surrey, outside London, during the course of the summer and right up to November.

In preparing to film *The Da Vinci Code*, director Ron Howard looked at classic thrillers with spiritual elements, such as *Rosemary's Baby* and *The Exorcist*, as well as films in which the drama lies in the conversation, like *All the President's Men*. His aim was to dupli-cate the experience of reading the book, which meant reducing the wordiness of the novel, which unfolds in real time over the course of twenty hours, while the film had to tell the story in less than three.

Knights Templar and Abbey Rumours

Under the rubric of Rose Line Productions, Howard and Glazer also had to negotiate **location filming rights** at such iconic places as London's Westminster Abbey and the Louvre in Paris, which form the backdrop to the most frantic action in the novel. There were additional locations, too, for shooting surprise scenes which do not appear in the novel – as the scriptwriter, Akiva Goldsman, had come up with various flashbacks as a way of quickly and visually filling in the historical background.

One of these meant shooting scenes involving the **Knights Templar** at **Winchester Cathedral**. The Dean of Winchester, the Very Reverend Michael Till, welcomed the filmmakers, saying, 'A novel that sells so many copies can afford to laugh at its critics. The Holy Grail, an oppressive Church, the Templars – first lorded, then sup-pressed – a sexual scenario about Jesus and Mary Magdalene and the secret descent through the Merovingian Line makes a rich soup to be devoured greedily chapter by chapter'. Filming was in the north transept and earned the church a handsome though undisclosed fee – very welcome, as Winchester is falling to pieces and faces very high bills for even the most basic maintenance.

Meanwhile negotiations were apparently going on smoothly with both **Westminster Abbey** and the **Louvre** when Howard and Grazer received a shock. Westminster Abbey abruptly broke off talks, issu-ing the statement: 'We cannot commend or endorse the contentious and wayward religious and historic suggestions made in the book – nor its views of Christianity and the New Testament. It would therefore be inappropriate to film scenes from the book here'.

There was something fishy about the Abbey's behaviour, though, as the Dean and Chapter had known the nature of Dan Brown's book through several months of negotiations. Ian McKellen has reported dark rumours: 'Might not The Royal Family, who have special jurisdiction over the Abbey, might not They Themselves, have complained right royally? What if there were to be a royal demise and Hollywood interfered with a state funeral in the Abbey and vice-versa? The growing rapprochement between the Catholic hierarchy and the Anglican communion who worship in the Abbey might equally have been crucial. With a new Pope to get on with, could even an ex-Catholic foundation comfortably house a project which not only questions Christ's divinity but challenges the source of the Vatican's power? More mundanely, perhaps the proposed financial arrangements were deemed insufficient by the Abbey's Chapter.'

FILMING IN FRANCE

Talks with the French Culture Ministry went better, particularly after Howard's and Grazer's now infamous meeting with president Jacques Chirac and their agreement to hand over one million euros (about $1.25 million or £700,000) for shooting rights in the **Louvre**, and thousands more for street scenes in Paris. **St-Sulpice**, however, refused permission to shoot inside.

In the early hours of June 30 2005 filming began on *The Da Vinci Code* in the Place Vendome, just outside the Ritz Hotel, the place where Dan Brown first introduces Robert Langdon to the readers of the novel. Nearly twenty-four hours later, when darkness had again fallen, the crew and cast began shooting inside the Louvre as Jacques Saunier was done to death in the Grand Gallery.

On July 12 and 13 the team were at the **Château de Villette** at Condecourt outside Paris, identified in the novel as the home of Sir Leigh Teabing. In fact most of the interior scenes were filmed later in the controlled conditions of Shepperton Studios, but the staircase and the downstairs stone-clad rooms that you see in the film are authentic. It was odd, Ian McKellen observed, to walk into one of these vast rooms stuffed with papers, books, charts, models and works of art, all evidence of Teabing's obsession with the Holy Grail, and 'see my photo on the circular table, standing with an unknown woman – ah, of course, the late "Lady Teabing", an invention of the rehearsals that Ron Howard held in London and Paris a couple of weeks before shooting began'.

SHEPPERTON AND LINCOLN

Two weeks later the cast were at **Shepperton Studios**, filming in a long wood-panelled hall where a gas fire burns in the massive fake- stone fireplace late at night when Langdon and Sophie come knocking at Teabing's gate. McKellen hobbles around glass display cases, mahogany desks and chairs and piles of Grail literature on two sticks, not crutches as in the novel, but which are visually effective in 'translating the page-turning excitement of the book into a thriller of a movie', he observed. 'At two in the morning, cinematographer Salvatore Totino's low lighting is sinister and full of that sense that "something-is-about-to-happen".' McKellen noticed Dan Brown and his wife Blythe watching the scene on monitors from beyond the set: 'He is full of enthusiasm for the filming, a new experience he will soon be used to now his series of Langdon novels is set to be transferred to the big screen'.

By mid-August, the action had moved to **Lincoln**, whose Cathedral had been adopted in place of Westminster Abbey. Looking tired and wary, Tom Hanks was driven the short distance from the White Hart Hotel to the Cathedral. This was six weeks since shooting began in the dead of night in the Place Vendôme, but in story terms the following day. As Robert Langdon, he is a hunted man, but he also senses that he is on the trail of some momentous revelation – for the scene at 'Westminster Abbey' is a climax of the film. Possibly Hanks was already acting the part as he stepped out of his chauffeur-driven car. Or maybe as he did so, he saw the crowds gathered at the cathedral gates, and at their head an Irish nun who was condemning the enterprise to eternal damnation: 'To a believer, to any believer, what is happening is blasphemous'. As Tom Hanks, he may have thought that he was about to become toast, the first sacrificial victim of an anti-*Code* crusade. But the truth was that the crowd of around two hundred people were curious and friendly and had gathered, as McKellen said, 'hoping for a glimpse of Amélie, Gandalf and Forrest Gump'. As for the nun, she was more a figment of the Holy Order of Newspaper Hype than anything else. It turned out she was a kind of freelance nun, having been asked to leave the Carmelite order.

Protests notwithstanding, **Lincoln Cathedral** was a fine choice to replace the forbidden precincts of Westminster Abbey. Completed in 1072, this gigantic church, once the tallest building in the world, is contemporaneous with the Abbey and built in the same Gothic style. If Westminster's hope was to avoid any association with the heretical plot of the book and film, it has failed: using meticulously moulded plaster casts of monuments within the Abbey, including Isaac Newton's, and careful camera angles, Lincoln's interiors appear on screen to be Westminster's, and when married to genuine exterior shots of the Abbey the identification is complete.

The **Dean of Lincoln**, the Very Reverend Alec Knight, does not share the views of his fellow Anglicans at Westminster Abbey about how to deal with *The Da Vinci Code*. 'The book is not offensive to the Christian faith, merely speculative and far-fetched', he said. 'It is not blasphemous in that it does not denigrate God in any way. Some of what is said in the book about the church and its teaching is heretical and is based on ideas that have been around for centuries, surfacing every now and again only to be refuted each time. *The*

Da Vinci Code stimulates debate and the search for truth and we are glad to be part of this process. The book claims that the church has suppressed important facts about Jesus. The way to counter this accusation is to be open about the facts as we understand them and welcome vigorous debate'.

London Climaxes

On August 25, the *Da Vinci Code* caravan arrived at **Temple Church** off Fleet Street in central London. The Reverend Robin Griffith-Jones, Master of the Temple Church, had been waiting for this moment for some time. 'Until recently the church has been one of London's best kept secrets', he said soon after *The Da Vinci Code* was published – since when he had been eagerly looking forward to it being filmed. 'They would have to film on location', he said cheerfully. 'For huge fees.' Clearly the money-making instinct of the Templars is not dead.

In the novel, the trail leads from the Temple Church to Westminster Abbey with a murder along the way. The film crew followed suit, arriving outside the Abbey two days later, on Saturday, August 27, to take exterior shots of the church, and shoot scenes along Victoria Street, which the police helpfully closed off for the occasion.

Rosslyn Revelation

The last location shoot for *The Da Vinci Code* was during the week of September 26 2005 at the famed fifteenth-century **Rosslyn Chapel**, outside Edinburgh, where in the story the secret of the code is finally revealed. Using the chapel would 'enhance the value of the film', said a spokesman for Rose Line Productions – who paid a paltry £7000 a day, according to reports. Graeme Munro, vice-chairman of the Rosslyn Chapel Trust, which faces a £3million bill for its current restoration project, defended the decision to allow the film-makers access, but at the same time asserted, 'Many of the stories surrounding Rosslyn are highly speculative. The trust would not subscribe to the legends presented by *The Da Vinci Code*'.

THE END

The filming of *The Da Vinci Code* was completed at Shepperton Studios outside London in October and November 2005. During all the location work from June to September, there were no more than a handful of protests directed at cast or crew. The real judgement lies in the reaction of cinema audiences to the film.

Audrey Tautou dons the tartan as *The Da Vinci Code* cast reach Rosslyn.

THE
DA VINCI
CODE

Glossary
& Index

THE DA VINCI CODE Glossary

Words in **bold type** refer to further entries in this glossary.

A

Adonai The Hebrew word for 'Lord' as used in the Old Testament in place of the tetragrammaton *YHWH* – the name of God that must not be spoken. The Jews invented a pronounceable name for God by combining the vowels of Adonai with the consonants of YHWH, thus creating the name *Yahveh*. In medieval England, this was rendered as *Jehovah* – many centuries too late and half a continent too far north for the Dan Brown idea that it is 'derived from Jehovah, an androgynous physical union between the masculine Jah and the pre-Hebraic name for Eve, Havah' to be credible.

Adoration of the Magi **Leonardo da Vinci** painting originally commissoned by the monks of San Donato a Scopeto, near Florence, though the artist abandoned it, unfinished, in 1481 when he moved to Milan. It now hangs in Florence's Uffizi gallery, and attracted controversy in 2002 when the engineer-critic Maurizio Seracini declared that scans showed that only the preparatory underdrawing was by Leonardo, the painting having been added later by another hand. *The Da Vinci Code* draws on this controversy to suggest that this unknown artist who tried to change a Leonardo sketch into a Leonardo painting was also trying to change the message it conveyed.

Albigensian Crusade In 1209 Pope Innocent III called for a crusade against the heretical **Cathars** of Languedoc, in southern France. His appeal was taken up eagerly by northern French nobles, including king Louis VIII. The attacks quickly developed into a kind of civil war between those aligned with and those opposing the papal cause, and culminated in a number of infamous massacres, none more so than that at Béziers, where the papal legate instructed Simon de Montfort's besieging forces to spare none of the townspeople, neither Cathar nor Catholic. 'Kill them all', he said. 'God will know His own'. The town of Albi, a Cathar stronghold, lent its name to the crusade.

Amon Otherwise known as Amun, or 'the hidden one', Amon was one of the chief Egyptian divinities, primarily associated with creation and the protection of the poor, as well as justice (and fertility, as cited by Dan Brown). He is usually shown bearded, wearing a headpiece with two tall, feathery plumes, though he sometimes appears with a ram's head or as a ram. Originally the chief god of the Thebans, when their city became ascendant under the powerful New Kingdom, from around 1570 BC, he was adopted as the supreme god of all Egypt and the father of the pharaohs, taking the second part of his new name *Amun-Ra* (or Amun-Re) from the sun god, Ra.

Androgyny Literally 'man-woman', from the Classical Greek words *andros* (man) and *gynaika* (woman), androgyny refers to one person having both male and female gender traits. The term is usually reserved for someone physically or sexually both male and female.

Ankh The ancient Egyptian hieroglyph for 'life' was a cross with a ring at the shorter, top end. It is still used in place of the 'standard' cross symbol by the Coptic Church, and known to other Christians as the *crux ansata*.

Apostles Usually used to refer to the disciples, though this meaning is not found in the early gospels, and Paul claims the title for himself. The original meaning of the word is betrayed in its Greek root *apostello*, meaning to send out or dispatch. The apostles were thus those sent by Jesus to spread his teachings.

Apostolic Succession The idea that the authority of the Church is derived from a lineage running back to the apostles and thus to Jesus himself. Appointed as the 'rock' or founder of the church by Jesus, St Peter is seen as the first bishop in a line extending down through the popes to the present. The papal seat in Rome is similarly traced back to Peter's martyrdom in the city, the saint's tomb lying directly underneath the main altar of the church named after him, in the very heart of the Vatican.

al-Aqsa Mosque First built in around 715 by the Caliph al-Walid, the al-Aqsa Mosque occupies some of Jerusalem's most historic ground, on the **Temple Mount**, next to Solomon's Stables. It was constructed over the remains of the Jerusalem base of the Crusader **Godfroi de Bouillon**, a complex originally known as the Templum after its location. Bouillon's headquarters in turn lent its name to the military order based there: thus the **Knights Templar**.

Aramaic Semitic language, spoken by Jesus and still alive today, mostly in Syria and Kurdish areas. Matthew's Gospel renders Jesus's last words – *eli eli lama sabachthani*, or 'My God, my God, why hast thou forsaken me?' – in the original Aramaic.

Arius Lent his name to the Arian heresy condemned at the **Council of Nicaea**. Arianism argued that Christ and the Father were not 'of the same substance', which the proto-orthodox church believed risked leading believers into claiming that Christ was inferior to the Father, or that he was not divine at all.

Atbash cipher One of the most basic of the ciphers used by Hebrew scribes, in which each letter of the Hebrew alphabet is substituted for another counted an equal distance from the opposite end. The English equivalent would be Z for A, Y for B, X for C and so on.

The word is more properly written as ATBSH or ATBaSH, as it is made up from the words for the first and last two letters in the Hebrew alphabet, in their order of substitution: *aleph–taw*, and *beth–shin*.

B

Baphomet When the Knights Templar were brought down by Philip IV of France and the Inquisition, they were accused of having worshipped an idol called Baphomet (possibly a corruption of Mohammed), which had a goat's head and an ass's body.

Bernard of Clairvaux Bernard (1090–1153) was one of the leading spiritual figures of the medieval era, famous principally for the establishment of the austere Cistercian monastic order, for condemning the Scholastic theologian Abelard as a heretic, and for preaching the Second Crusade to Louis VII and his wife, Eleanor of Aquitaine. At the Synod of Troyes, in 1128, he argued for the foundation of the new militaristic order of **Knights Templar**, and may have drawn up its regulations.

Black Madonnas Found predominantly in France, but also in Spain, Italy and eastern Europe, most Black Madonnas are paintings of Mary as the Madonna (ie the mother of Jesus) that show her with a dark-coloured face. In some cases the blackness is owed to candlesmoke or a church fire, but in others the darkness appears to be inherent. Though there is a popular theory that Black Madonnas come from Egypt, in fact they originate in Asia Minor.

Blasphemy Any word, sign or action that has the deliberate intention of demonstrating contempt for God. Jesus himself was accused of blasphemy (Mark 2:7) for claiming to forgive sins. In Europe until the Enlightenment blasphemy was punishable by death, and even today in many Christian countries, including Britain, blasphemy is still technically a crime, though the law is rarely enforced. The Muslim definition of blasphemy is wider as it includes mockery of Mohammed, the Koran and the angels, and it can also include holding heretical beliefs; in those countries where Sharia law applies the punishment is death.

Boaz and Jachin According to *I Kings 7:15-22*, these were the twin pillars that stood at the gates of Solomon's Temple. They were giant-sized (23 cubits high, says *I Kings*, and a Biblical cubit was slightly longer than a foot) and capped by enormous bronze capitals decorated with pomegranates and lilies. 'Copies' are found in Masonic temples, some interpreting the lily motif as the fleur-de-lis. Dan Brown, following some modern Rosslyn enthusiasts, interprets the elaborately sculpted columns at Rosslyn Chapel as versions of the originals at the Temple.

Bois de Boulogne Giant park on the western fringe of Paris incorporating racecourses, lakes, playgrounds, forested areas and, as Dan Brown describes, the odd bit of transvestite prostitution.

Botticelli Florentine painter (c.1445–1510) listed as one of the Grand Masters of the **Priory of Sion** in the dodgy **Dossiers Secrets**. Botticelli's listing is presumably made on the basis of his famous, large-scale mythological paintings, as found in Florence's Uffizi gallery, where the *Birth of Venus* and *Primavera* draw on Neoplatonist symbolism. They depict a powerful, erotic and quintessentially feminine spirituality. The works of his last period, however, in which he turned towards the radical orthodoxy of Savonarola, could hardly be further in spirit from the ideals attributed to the Priory of Sion.

C

Caravaggio Proper name Michelangelo da Merisi, Caravaggio (1571–1610) was the great painter of the Italian Baroque. His works are characterized by dramatic *chiaroscuro* – the juxtaposition of darkness and light – and virtuoso foreshortening effects. As he struggles to escape his assassin at the opening of *The Da Vinci Code*, Jacques Saunière tears a Caravaggio painting down from the wall of the Grande Galerie. It could be any of a number of canvases by the master that hang there, though the *Death of the Virgin* would seem to be the most appropriate candidate.

Castel Gandolfo One of thirteen small towns nestling in the Collia Albani, just south of Rome, Castel Gandolfo is the summer retreat of the pope. It was also the former location of the Vatican Observatory, before light pollution forced the star-gazing prelates to seek a new location in the Arizonan desert. The Astronomy Library is the location for Aringarosa's rendezvous with the mysterious cardinals who tell him they are going to disassociate the Vatican from Opus Dei.

Cathars The people of Languedoc in the eleventh and twelfth centuries who followed the Albigensian heresy. The Cathars themselves saw the mainstream Church as heretical, calling themselves *katharos*, after the Greek for 'pure ones'. Their most contentious belief was the essentially Gnostic idea that the world was evil – created by a deity known as the Demiurge, aka Satan – and that all its manifestations should be rejected. Luxury and pleasure, in particular, were condemned, as was marriage and procreation, women were held to be equal (as all flesh is evil, it doesn't matter what kind of flesh you have), and Jesus was held to be only a kind of holy ghost, untainted by bodily form. The Cathars were suppressed in the **Albigensian Crusade**.

Catholic Church Catholic means universal, as the original Church was universal before the eleventh century, when it formally divided into the Orthodox Church in the East and the

Roman Catholic Church in the West. But the term today tends to refer to the Roman Catholic Church, which is how Dan Brown invariably uses it while at the same time identifying it with the Vatican. This creates historical absurdities, as when he refers to the machinations of the Roman Catholic Church and the Vatican at the **Council of Nicaea** – there was no separate Roman Church in 325, and the Vatican would not be built for over a hundred years yet.

Château Villette Real French château, just southwest of Paris, and fictional home of Leigh Teabing.

Christology Theological term for the study of the nature of Christ, focusing particularly on his humanity and/or divinity, his status as Messiah, king, prophet, rabbi and Son of Man/Son of God.

Cilice Properly, a hair shirt, used by the devout wearer to 'mortify' the flesh in memory of the sufferings of Jesus, to do penance for sin, or to suppress bodily appetites to better free the soul from its mortal chains. Distinctly out of fashion these days, although some Carthusian and Carmelite monks still wear it. According to the Opus Dei Awareness Network, some members of **Opus Dei** do indeed, like Silas in *The Da Vinci Code*, wear spiky wire bands round their thighs for two hours a day, and they call these cilices.

Clement V Pope from 1305 to 1314 and a toady of Philippe IV, the king of France, who obliged him to leave Rome for Avignon, the better to control him. He was at first opposed to Philippe's suppression of the Knights Templar in 1307, but later upheld the order's dissolution, handing over such of its resources as lay beyond the reach of Philippe to the Hospitallers.

Cocteau, Jean French poet, artist, novelist, filmmaker and opium addict (1898–1963), listed as the last of the Priory of Sion's Grand Masters in the so-called *Dossiers Secrets*.

Codex A book with pages, as invented in the first century AD and used by early Christians. The Gnostic gospels were codices (plural of codex), while the Dead Sea scrolls were, uh, scrolls. Dan Brown does not seem to know the difference.

Codex Leicester One of Leonardo da Vinci's surviving notebooks, named after its third owner, the Earl of Leicester, who bought it in 1717. It was briefly renamed the Codex Hammer by a later owner, but when Bill Gates purchased it in 1994 – for $30.8 million – he restored the earlier name. Its 72 pages of scientific notes and observations, with sketched illustrations, are all in Leonardo's characteristic right-to-left handwriting, which is more likely a product of Leonardo's left-handedness than any desire for secrecy. In fact it is not much of a code, notwithstanding Langdon's apparent trouble deciphering the script.

Constantine I, The Great Reigning from 308 until his death in 337, Constantine is regarded as the first Christian Roman Emperor. In 313 he promulgated his Edict of Toleration, permitting all religions to be practised without hindrance, and he himself was baptised on his deathbed. He convened the Council of Nicaea and made Constantinople (present-day Istanbul) the capital of the Roman Empire.

Cryptex 'Cryptex' is a Brownism, a portmanteau word presumably created out of cryptology, the science of encoding messages, and codex. Before Brown got to it, the word had more to do with computer gaming and encryption programs than with Leonardo da Vinci. Still, post-Brown you can now actually buy the things online at *www.cryptex.org*, and elsewhere. Technically, Brown's cryptex is not really a form of 'public key encryption' – otherwise known as *Diffie-Hellman encryption* after its 1970s inventors – as it lacks the requisite pair of keys: a 'public key' used to encrypt the message individually for the recipient, and a 'private key', known only to the receiver, that is used to unlock it.

D

Dagobert II Catholic saint and Merovingian dynasty king. For much of his short life, the palace mayors had de facto power and he lived in exile to Ireland, out of trouble, before reclaiming the throne in 676.

As Sophie Neveu remembers, he was murdered by Pepin the Fat in 679, though the idea of there being a Vatican-Carolingian conspiracy to do away with this tail-ender of the **Merovingian dynasty** is pure legend, as is the story that he or his descendants moved down south to **Rennes-le-Château**. Incidentally it is difficult to think of a worse advertisement for Jesus and his bloodline than these incompetent Merovingian nincompoops.

DCPJ Or *Direction Centrale de la Police Judiciaire*. The headquarters of the *Police Judiciaire* (*PJ*), or justice police, a force attached directly to the French judiciary. Its main roles are internal security, collecting proof and witnesses to crimes, and identifying criminals; various sub-directorates deal with high-profile crimes such as terrorism and art theft. Captain Bezu Fache belongs to this elite group, which Brown rightly compares to the FBI in the US.

Dead Sea Scrolls Discovered by Bedouin shepherds in a cave near the Dead Sea in 1947 (not in the 1950s, as Teabing has it), the Dead Sea Scrolls are some of the earliest Jewish texts ever discovered: carbon-14 dating has placed them around the second century BC. Their origins are hotly disputed, but most scholars agree they are the part of the library of an ascetic Jewish sect, the Essenes, which had a community at nearby Qumran. Whatever, they are not Christian texts, as Teabing claims. Some are Biblical, others relate to the beliefs of the Qumran community – which reveal some fascinating parallels with early Christianity. Academic disputes and rivalries, and the lack of speedy publication, led to decades of conspiracy theorising that someone, probably 'the Vatican', was trying to suppress the truths they would one day reveal. However, the scrolls are all openly published today.

Dossiers secrets A collection of documents and privately printed texts 'discovered' in the Bibliothèque Nationale de France, the French national library, where they had been deposited as a file in 1967. In fact the Dossiers Secrets are the work of a French surrealist writer who had no interest or belief in any such thing as the Priory of Sion but found it suitably surreal, and enormously amusing, to plant his bogus material in the Bibliotheque. In this he was cheerfully in league with **Pierre Plantard** (1920–2000), a self-publicist with an extreme right-wing French nationalist background who styled himself the latest Grand Master of the **Priory of Sion**. Baigent, Leigh and Lincoln tracked down Plantard for their best-selling **Holy Blood, Holy Grail**, and discovered a man who seemed to be the prime source for most of the Rennes-le-Château material, and who claimed to be the inheritor of the most ancient Templar traditions and a descendant of the Merovingian dynasty, for whatever

that was worth. In any case the last claim was disproved, and Plantard publicly dissociated himself from the idea that the Holy Grail was the 'holy blood' of the descendants of Jesus and Mary Magdalene.

E

Escrivá, Father Josemaría The facts about Josemaría Escrivá de Balaguer are almost exactly as they are given in *The Da Vinci Code*. He was born in Spain in 1902 and founded **Opus Dei** in 1928 as a way of bringing holiness into the everyday life of laypeople, particularly the young. He died in Rome in June 1975, and was made a saint in October 2002 by Pope John Paul II, who declared that 'St. Josemaría untiringly preached the universal call to holiness' and could be called 'the saint of the ordinary'. Detractors claim that he established a reactionary, secretive network that operated in the darker corners of the Catholic community, and was personally overfond of discipline, including self-flagellation. His chief work is published as *The Way*.

Essenes One of many Jewish sects that flourished in Palestine at around the time of Jesus, along with the better-known Pharisees and Sadducees. They were ascetically minded, rigorously maintaining the Sabbath, eschewing Temple sacrifice, and practicing purifying rituals. It is widely believed that the community behind the Dead Sea Scrolls was Essene, and many scholars believe that John the Baptist may have been an Essene; some go further, and claim that the Jesus himself had Essene connections.

F

Fibonacci sequence Fibonacci, which probably means 'son of Bonaccio', was a twelfth-century mathematician from Pisa, whose real name was Leonardo. He gave his nickname to a series of numbers that can be created by starting with 0 and 1 and continually adding the last two numbers together to create the next in the sequence. So: 0, 1, 1, 2, 3, 5, 8, 13 etc. It is frequently observed in nature, as Langdon explains to his Harvard audience, though it isn't quite such a universal rule as he makes out. See also **Phi**.

Fleur-de-lis The three-pointed flower symbol has nothing whatsoever to do with 'Lisa' as in *Mona Lisa*, whatever Dan Brown likes to make out, but was the heraldic symbol of the French monarchy from the time when Philippe-Auguste first used it (golden, on a blue field) on his royal seal in the late twelfth century to the end of the Bourbon dynasty. Its origins are much older – similar symbols have been found on Assyrian bas-reliefs – and somewhat uncertain: no one even knows whether it represents a lily or an iris. As a symbol, it has been used to represent sovereignty and sanctity and has been linked with the Trinity and the cult of the Virgin Mary.

G

Gnomon Pronounced *no-mon*, in its most general sense a gnomon is the object that casts a shadow on a sundial: the direction of the shadow gives the hour. More specifically, a gnomon is used to calculate the declination of the sun's rays, and thus the time of year, by marking the angle of the sun's rays as they cross the gnomon: the angle is highest at the summer equinox, lowest at the winter solstice. Gnomons are ancient instruments, invented by the astronomers of Babylon and well known in Classical Greece – the Greek *gnwmwn* (gnomon) meaning he who knows, or judge. St-Sulpice is one of many European churches with a gnomon, due to the association of the date of Easter with the vernal equinox (though in fact Easter's exact date is established using a fixed ecclesiastical calendar rather than an actual astronomical one).

Gnosis Like gnomon, gnosis is another Greek word pronounced without the initial 'g'. In a religious sense, gnosis means knowing God or having personal experience of or insight into the spiritual dimension of the world.

Gnostic gospels A collection of early Greek texts, including a number of 'alternative' gospels, found at Nag Hammadi, in Egypt, in 1945. Until this date, awareness of Gnostic teachings was limited to the scornful reports of early orthodox opponents, such as Irenaeus, and a few partial manuscript fragments. One of the key Gnostic gospels mentioned in *The Da Vinci Code* is the *Gospel of Philip*, from which Teabing highlights the controversial phrase in which Jesus is described as having kissed Mary 'on the the m...' (at this point in the text there's a tantalizing missing fragment). Another is the *Gospel of Mary*, which describes Mary as having a unique and important position among the apostles, though Teabing, as ever, exaggerates and misrepresents the significance of this text. Teabing's most culpable piece of historical sleight of hand is to fail to mention that most of the Nag Hammadi texts are almost certainly much later in date than the New Testament gospels. In fact, the Council of Nicaea's main criterion for inclusion or exclusion seems to have been remarkably reasonable: was a gospel directly drawn from an apostolic or eye-witness account or not?

Gnosticism The words comes from the Greek *gnostikos*, or 'good at knowing', and means the belief that personal wisdom and insight can lead to religious truth. Gnostic ideas are often taught as a series of secret or hidden teachings through which the initiate progresses towards a fuller or 'higher' understanding.

Godefroi de Bouillon Godefroi (or Godefroy), lord of Bouillon (c.1060–1100), was one of the leaders of the successful First Crusade. After the capture of Jerusalem, he was elected as ruler, though he wasn't titled king, as Langdon imagines, assuming only the modest title of 'Advocate of the Holy Sepulchre'. His later fame as the perfect Christian knight stems from tales about him in the medieval French *chansons de gestes*, or romances. This legendary status, and his connection with the Temple Mount – his headquarters were built here, on a site later used by the Knights Templar – have given birth to an alternative, spurious biography which turns him into the original Knight Templar, the guardian of the secret of Solomon's Temple and the founder of the Priory of Sion.

Golden Section (and Golden Mean, Ratio, Rectangle etc) See **Phi**.

Grail The cup or chalice legendarily supposed to have been used at the Last Supper, and/or to catch the blood of Jesus during the crucifixion. The earliest mention of the grail is found in the fictional *Conte du Graal*, by the twelfth-century French poet Chrétien de Troyes, and it seems likely that he simply made it up. It caught on, and became one of the great stories of the Middle Ages, the stuff of endless questing romances written all over Europe in the twelfth and thirteenth centuries. As Umberto Eco snorted in a television interview, 'the historical reality of the Holy Grail is the same as the reality of Pinocchio and Little Red Riding Hood.' Which hasn't stopped generations of writers attempting to explain what or where the Grail is; more serious scholars have tried to trace the presumed origins of Chrétien's idea in Celtic or Eastern traditions. The theory that the Holy Grail is in fact a code word referring to the bloodline of Mary Magdalene was concocted by the authors of *Holy Blood, Holy Grail* in the 1980s and has no basis in reality.

H

Heresy To deny or doubt a doctrine of the Church. **Arianism** was declared a heresy at the **Council of Nicaea** in 325 and Arius himself was excommunicated. Heresies had been identified long before Nicaea, but as that was the first ecumenical council held by the Church the decisions made then had universal validity. In a sense orthodoxy developed and defined itself by reacting against heresy; it expressed the need for some sort of standard rather than 'do your own thing', though it is unlikely that any universal standard could have been imposed until Christianity itself was tolerated within the Roman Empire by Constantine in 313.

Hieros Gamos The sexual-mystical union between god and goddess that produces the fertility of the earth. Used by Homer in the Iliad (XIV.152–353) to describe the sexual intercourse between Zeus and his wife Hera, the goddess of marriage and birth, an act that produces fresh grass out of the barren earth. Ritual prostitution, to give it another name, was sometimes practised by the priestesses of pagan cults, such as that

of Aphrodite at Byblos, and also of Cybele, though when practised by Cybele herself, she sometimes took the opportunity to rip her lovers' balls off.

Holy Blood, Holy Grail This 1982 book by the British authors Michael Baigent, Richard Leigh and Henry Lincoln was a key source for *The Da Vinci Code* – and is discussed by Leigh Teabing (whose name is an anagram-combination of its authors) in the novel. Brown adopted their supposedly non-fictional claims of Jesus's marriage to Mary Magdalene, and the Grail as bloodline, along withir acceptance of the **Priory of Sion** as a real body.

Holy Grail See **Grail**.

Horus One of a triad of Egyptian gods, Isis being his mother, **Osiris** his father. Between them they enact the cycle of death and rebirth.

I

Innocent III Pope from 1130 to 1143, he helped launch the Fourth Crusade which wound up sacking Christian Constantinople. He also promoted crusades against the **Cathars**.

Isis At the advent of Christianity, the Egyptian goddess Isis was the major deity in the Mediterranean world, with temples in Greece and Rome, but none in Roman *Lutetia* (Paris), as Dan Brown claimes, either on the present site of St-Sulpice or anywhere else. As the wife of the slain **Osiris** and the mother of the infant **Horus**, she was the central figure in the cycle of death and rebirth. The familiar image of her suckling Horus became the model for Mary and the infant Jesus. It was probably in response to the popularity of Isis that the new Christian religion formally gave the Virgin Mary the title 'Mother of God'; indeed the campaign was led by one of the early fathers of the Church, an Egyptian called Origen, whose own name was connected with Horus.

J

Joan, Pope The old legend of a 'female pope' is wheeled out by Langdon in reference to the tarot card of the same name – which does indeed exist. Pope Joan, however, turns out to be pure myth, although she was universally believed to have existed in the fifteenth and sixteenth centuries. The original tall tale, as told by the Dominican chronicler Jean de Mailly in the thirteenth century, makes out that an English Pope in the ninth century, John or Johannes of Mainz, was revealed to be a woman – hence 'Johanna' or 'Joan' – when s/he gave birth to a child during a procession from St Peter's to the Lateran church. She was apparently stoned to death by the righteously shocked crowd. A slightly later version of the tale, probably adapted by one Martinus Polonus, places the incident in around 1100 and describes a clever, scheming woman dressing as a man and working her way up through the Church

hierarchy before, once again, her pregnancy gives her away.

K

Knights Hospitaller The Hospitallers of St John of Jerusalem began by running a pilgrim hospice and infirmary next to the Church of the Holy Sepulchre, but gradually the order expanded and adapted to include knights who shared with the **Knights Templars** the task of defending the Crusader states. In 1309, after the loss of the Holy Land, they withdrew to Rhodes, and after that island fell they were granted the island of Malta until it was ceded to Napoleon in 1798. A spuriously-linked order exists today, primarily as a charitable ambulance service and humanitarian aid organisation (*www.orderofmalta.org*).

Knights Templar Separating the history of the Knights Templar from the legends and conspiracy theories that surround the order is not as hard as Robert Langdon imagines when he relates their history to Sophie Neveu while they drive through the Bois de Boulogne. Langdon's version of the 'standard academic sketch' is accurate in parts, such as the Knights' 1118 vow to King Baldwin II to defend the Holy Land, and the story of their suppression under Philippe IV 'The Fair' in 1307. But his notion that a '**Priory of Sion**' was the eminence grise lurking behind the facade of the Templars comes from a twentieth-century hoax, and far from agreeing that in Jerusalem 'the Knights discovered something down in the ruins', 'all academics' would dismiss the story as nonsense. One thing is certain: this once-powerful religious military order has not existed in any meaningful sense since Pope **Clement V** dissolved it in a Papal Bull of March 22, 1312, though endless groups have since tried to make claims on its name, traditions and iconography.

L

Last Supper, The As described in the *Gospels of Matthew, Mark and Luke*, the Last Supper is the final meal shared by Jesus and his disciples in Jerusalem on the eve of his betrayal by Judas at which he asks his companions to eat bread and drink wine in memory of him. But **Leonardo da Vinci**'s painting *The Last Supper* is based on the *Gospel of John* where the supper is over, the table has been cleared, and Jesus dramatically announces that one among them will betray him. There is no reason why there should be a cup or chalice evident in this scene.

Leonardo da Vinci To everyone but Dan Brown he is Leonardo (1452-1519), not Da Vinci, which is not a surname, rather the town that he came from. The early part of Leonardo's career was spent in Florence, but in 1483 he moved to Milan to enter the service of Duke Ludovico 'Il Moro'. Here, he did his greatest work, including *The Last Supper* and the *Virgin of the Rocks*, but after the collapse of Ludovico's regime in 1499, Leonardo

spent a number of years travelling from job to job in northern Italy. During this 'nomadic period' he painted the **Mona Lisa**. In 1516 he accepted semi-retirement at the court of François I in Amboise, France.

Louvre The name of both the royal palace at the heart of Paris, and the public museum and art gallery that now occupies it, displaying one of the oldest, largest and most important art collections in the world.

M

Madonna of the Rocks Dan Brown's term for the **Virgin of the Rocks**, a painting by Leonardo da Vinci, where Sophie Neveu finds the key to a safe deposit box. Using the word 'madonna'-allows him to create the anagram 'so dark the con of man'.

Malleus Maleficarum The persecution of 'witches' – a title that could be applied to anyone from heretics, devil-worshippers and practictioners of 'magic' to prostitutes and superstitious old women – received a new impetus in 1486 when the Papal Inquisition, an institution dedicated to the suppression of heresy, published the *Malleus Maleficarum*, or 'Hammer of Witches'. The book was written by two experienced, enthusiastic Dominican witch-hunters, Jacob Sprenger and Heinrich Kraemer. Its descriptions of witchcraft, citing scriptural authority, were nothing new – the Spanish Inquisition thought it crude and naive – but it did establish the procedural rules for witchcraft trials and quickly became notorious. To that extent, Langdon's version of this 'dark con of man' is correct, but most witch trials in fact took place in the seventeenth century, under secular courts, and in Protestant countries as much as Catholic ones. As for Langdon's statement that 'five million women' were burnt at the stake over three hundred years, this must be a muddle of the 'nine million dead' claimed by the American feminist Matilda Joslyn Gage in 1893, a figure much repeated ever since, and the numbers killed in the Holocaust. Current academic estimates are that witch killings – few were burnings – amounted to 50,000 dead. An appalling figure, but a hundredth of the number quoted by Robert Langdon.

Mary Magdalene One of Jesus's followers, Mary Magdalene witnessed the crucifixion and Jesus's resurrection and carried the news to the male disciples who had gone into hiding, making her the apostle to the apostles. In the sixth century, Mary's profile changed after Pope Gregory declared that three women mentioned in the Bible – Mary Magdalene, Mary of Bethany and an unnamed sinner forgiven by Jesus just before Mary Magdalene first enters on the scene – were one and the same. Mary Magdalene was thus described as a repentant prostitute, and as such became the great symbol of Christian penitence during the medieval era. A French legend holds that in later life Mary travelled to Marseilles or to Les Saintes-Maries-de-la-Mer, along with Lazarus and various other companions, thus establishing Christianity in France. But the Greek Orthodox church maintains that she retired to Ephesus along with the Virgin Mary, and was buried at Constantinople.

Matriarchy There are some who imagine that societies were once matriarchal, that is, they were ruled by women during an era that coincided with the worship of a mother goddess. In fact there has never been a matriarchy anywhere, at any time. But there have been matrilineal societies, where descent is traced through the woman's family, so that a newborn child becomes the responsibility not of its natural father but of its mother's brother, and it is from this uncle that the child inherits. It is a system that leaves fathers with less responsibility and allows mothers somewhat more independence. It is followed in some parts of India today, while on the Greek island of Leros all property is inherited through the female line.

Merovingians When Clovis, the king of the Franks, defeated the last representative of Roman power in Gaul in around 481, he established a new Merovingian dynasty – named after his grandfather Merovech. Like most European royal families, this one claimed descent from a number of historical and legendary figures, including a sea monster called a 'Quinotaur' that, according to a seventh-century chronicle, supposedly sired Merovech. (The family never claimed to have been descended from Jesus and Mary Magdalene.) Under the influence of his wife, Clotilde, Clovis converted to Christianity in the 490s. For the next two hundred years, Clovis's descendants ruled chaotically and violently over the kingdoms of Neustria, Austasia and Burgundy, which covered much of present-day France, until they were gradually supplanted by their palace mayors in the late seventh century. The last official Merovingian king was Childeric III, who was deposed by Pepin III 'the short' in 751. Pepin was thus the founder of the new Carolingian dynasty, though it was named after his all-conquering son, Carloman, aka Carolus Magnus, aka Charlemagne.

Mithras A sun god popular among Roman soldiers; but as initiation involved standing in a pit and having a bull slaughtered over your head, Mithraism never really caught on with women, who plumped for that nice Mr Jesus instead. Would-be debunkers of Christianity, such as Sir Leigh Teabing, have long pointed out similarities between Mithras and Jesus, notably that both were born of a virgin and had shepherds present at their birth, both were said to have saved the world (Mithras by sacrificing a bull), and the followers of both performed a ritual memorial banquet.

Mona Lisa This portrait was probably brought by **Leonardo** to France towards the end of his life, when he entered the service of François I. It now hangs in Paris's Louvre museum. It is far and away the most famous painting in the world, thanks to a combination of gushing nineteenth-century art critics, a notorious theft in 1911 and endless modern reproductions. *Mona Lisa* is an English term, a corruption of how Leonardo's contemporary Giorgio Vasari politely referred to the painting – as a portrait of Monna (an abbreviation of madonna, or my lady) Lisa. The Italians dub it *La Gioconda*, after Lisa's husband, Francesco del Giocondo, and no one knows what Leonardo called it. Even *Mona Lisa*'s famous smile was first commented on in the nineteenth century, and is usually described as 'knowing'-in the erotic rather than gnostic sense.

N

National Gallery The famous London gallery houses Leonardo's second version of the *Virgin of the Rocks*.

New Testament That part of the Bible that concerns the life and the teachings of Jesus and his disciples, including the *four Gospels*, the *Acts of the Apostles*, the *Epistles* and the *Revelation of Saint John*.

Newton, Sir Isaac An English scientist and mathematician, Newton (1642–1727) studied and researched at Trinity College, Cambridge. The closure of the university, due to the outbreak of the Great Plague in 1664, forced him to go home to Lincolnshire for the next few years. It was in this period that his contemplation of the fall of an apple led to his formulation of the theory of gravitation which is expounded in his work *De Motu Corporum* (1684). His greatest work, *Philosophiae Naturalis Principia Mathematica* (1687), describes the theory in more detail. The apple that inspired Newton is therefore the missing orb mentioned in the riddle Langdon finds in the rosewood box. Newton is buried in Westminster Abbey, where you will also find his monument.

Nicaea, Council of The first ecumenical council, held in Nicaea in present day Turkey in 325 AD, was convened and presided over by **Constantine the Great**. Among other things it decided the date of Easter and anathaematised Arianism.

Nicene Creed The confession of faith adopted at the first **Council of Nicaea** in 325 AD, it proclaimed that Jesus and God were of the same substance, one not less than the other.

O

O'Keeffe, Georgia (1887–1986) A pioneer of abstract art in the United States, O'Keeffe later worked in a more figurative style, with flowers and architecture her chief subjects. *The*

Da Vinci Code interpretation of her roses as symbolising female genitalia is not too far fetched, but it is just one way of viewing the artist's sensual style.

Old Testament The Christian name for the Holy Scriptures of Judaism and the first of the two divisions of the Christian Bible.

Opus Dei The name means 'God's work' in Latin. This international organisation aims to spread the call to holiness among ordinary people through sanctification of their work and their social and family activities. Founded in Spain in 1928 by **Father Josemaría Escrivá**, the organisation became the first Personal Prelature of the Vatican in 1982, having first received official approval from the Vatican by the Bishop of Madrid in 1941. Opus Dei is not therefore a sect, as *The Da Vinci Code* describes it, and is keen to point this out, as 'sect' implies a more distant relationship to the Vatican. There are five different classes of membership, in addition to non-members who donate funds, who are known as *Co-operators*. The *Numerary* class live at an Opus Dei house where according to **ODAN** they use the **cilice**, and their personal letters are read by Opus Dei directors. Opus Dei acknowledges the use of the cilice by figures in the Church's history but appears neither to emphatically assert or deny more painful methods of self-mortification. Mortification is part of their practice, though this they say more usually takes the form of small sacrifices like abstinence from meat.

Opus Dei Awareness Network (ODAN) Since 1991 this network has devoted itself to bringing attention to the practices of **Opus Dei** which it considers harmful. In particular they are concerned with corporal mortification, the use of aggressive recruitment methods that bear resemblance to those used by cults, a lack of informed consent, and the alienation of members from their families. The network aims to gather accurate information on Opus Dei by communicating with everyone from families to the press to religious awareness groups who have had experience of the organisation. In addition the network provides support for those who have been adversely affected by their association with Opus Dei.

Original Sin In Christian theology this is the idea that mankind is inherently flawed with a tendency toward sin as a result of Adam's rebelliousness in the Garden of Eden.

Orthodox Church See **Catholic Church**.

Osiris Lord of the Underworld and originally a god of vegetation and fertility. The worship of Osiris became popular in the Middle Kingdom period (2040–1648 BC) of Egypt's pharaonic period as, according to this cult's practice, anyone who lived a pious life could achieve immortality. Legend has it that Osiris was a king who was dismembered by his jealous brother Seth. Osiris's wife, the goddess **Isis**, gathered together the pieces so making him whole and alive once more. He then reigned as judge and king of the Underworld.

P

Parousia Meaning 'presence' in Greek, in pagan converse it described the aura possessed by a person – usually a powerful person like an emperor. Among Christians the *parousia* meant the Second Coming of Jesus, which in the early years of the new faith was an event that was expected imminently.

Pentacle A five-pointed star, which according to *The Da Vinci Code* symbolises the sacred feminine.

Pentagram Any shape having five lines. Used by Pythagoreans and by others as protection aginst sorcery as well as representing the five wounds of Christ for Christians.

Peter, Saint He was a fisherman in Galilee when Jesus called on him to be an apostle. Peter is in Jesus's words the rock on which he will build his church (*Matthew 16:15ff*).

Phi The awestruck tone of the many alternative names for this geometrical principle – Divine Proportion, Golden Mean, Golden Section – stems from a long-recognised kind of mathematical beauty. As the sixteenth-century astronomer Johannes Kepler put it, 'Geometry has two great treasures: one is the theorem of Pythagoras; the other, the division of a line into extreme and mean ratio. The first we may compare to a measure of gold; the second we may name a precious jewel'. Here's the theory: if you divide a straight line into two unequal sections using the 'divine proportion' (1.6180339887...), the ratio of the larger section to the smaller is exactly the same as that of the whole line to the larger section. It mirrors itself. You can continue the process of extending the line as long as you like, thereby creating the Fibonacci sequence. Langdon is right that Phi is often observable in nature; it is the most efficient way of forming a spiral, for example, hence the ratio's presence in shells and sunflower heads. It isn't found in the numbers of male and female bees in a hive, however; this is a misunderstanding of the real story, which is as follows: given that female bees have two female parents (they are born when the queen's eggs are fertilized by a male) and that male bees have one parent (the queen's egg is unfertilized), the ratio between the number of ancestors of male and female follows Phi. In the Renaissance, architects used Phi as a way of establishing the proper (or most pleasing) ratios of the length and height of buildings, thus creating what is called 'the Golden Rectangle'. Pentagons can also be drawn to illustrate Phi: for a five-sided shape with equal angles and equal sides, a line drawn between any two of the angles, ie across the pentagon, is 1.618 (etc) times longer than

the length of any of the pentagon's sides.

Philae An island in the Nile near Aswan in Upper Egypt on which stands the Temple of Isis. The temple was the centre of Isis worship up until the sixth century, when the Christian Emperor Justinian closed the place down.

Plantard, Pierre (1920–2000) Born in Paris, Plantard is the impostor who founded the **Priory of Sion**. He claimed to be directly descended from the Merovingian King **Dagobert** II but later changed his story, saying he was related to Otto von Hapsburg, who was the actual direct descendant of Dagobert II. In fact Plantard was descended from a sixteenth-century walnut-picker and his father was a butler.

Priory of Sion Founded in 1956 by **Pierre Plantard**, the so-called Priory was named after a hill called Mont Sion near where he was living in Arnesses, Hautes-de-Savoies. Originally the organisation served the purpose of protecting low-cost housing, but this Priory of Sion terminated in the same year, after Plantard was convicted for corrupting minors. He then revived the Priory in the 1960s, this time claiming that he was descended from the **Merovingians**. Plantard forged documents to support his claim and came up with stories about Berenger Saunière, the one time priest in the village of **Rennes-**

Le-Chiateau. In 1984 Plantard gave up the Priory of Sion after facts about his past were dug up and published. But in 1989, the tireless forger set up a third Priory of Sion and produced a second version of the Grand Masters List. This time Plantard took back his claim that the Priory of Sion was connected to the Templars and **Godefroy de Bouillon**. Finally he admitted under oath that he had made the whole lot up, but of course if you are a true conspiracy theorist you will know what that means! Bizarrely, Dan Brown, still asserts that the Priory of Sion is historical fact. See also **Dossiers secrets**.

Pyramide The modernist pyramid standing in front of the classically inspired **Louvre Museum** in Paris was designed by I.M. Pei and commissioned by President François Mitterrand. Because of the clash of styles between the old and the new, the structure generated a wave of controversy when it was completed in 1989.

Pyramide Inversée This smaller and inverted pyramid has been described as a 'monumental chandelier' owing to spotlights and mirrors that give it such an effect at dusk. Its architectural function is at least in part to bring light into the **Louvre**'s recently added underground complex.

Q

Q document The hypothetical source which, along with the Gospel of Mark, the authors of Matthew and Luke drew. Q stands for *quelle*, German for 'source'.

R

Rennes-le-Chateau The village featured in the book **Holy Blood, Holy Grail**, where the priest Berenger Saunière is said to have found certain secret papers relating to the **Priory of Sion**. See also **Dossiers Secrets**.

Resurrection The belief that Jesus died and rose again is the central doctrine of the Christian faith.

Roman Catholic Church See **Catholic Church**

Rose Line The mystical term for a solar meridian, which is not the same thing as the scientifically determined prime meridian which in *The Da Vinci Code* is said to fall across St Sulpice, in Paris. The prime meridian does not in fact pass through St Sulpice.

Rosslyn Chapel An Episcopalian chapel six miles south of central Edinburgh, Scotland, Rosslyn is also known as St. Matthew's Collegiate Church. Founded in 1446 by Sir William St. Clair and noted for its varied and eccentric architectural design. A vault underneath it houses the bones of the St. Clair family. In *The Da Vinci Code* the chapel is supposed to be riddled with pagan symbolism and to have once housed the relics of **Mary Magdalene**.

S

Sacred feminine The female aspect of the spiritual which when united with its male counterpart results in perfect harmony.

Sacred Geometry Using geometry, it is said to be possible to pass knowledge in symbol form between initiates.

Sainte-Baume According to Provençal legend, **Mary Magdalene** lived out her days here.

Saint-Maximin Abbey In her old age, goes the story, **Mary Magdalene** came down into the plain, received the sacraments and died. She is buried at the abbey here and her bones are protected by Dominicans.

Saint-Sulpice Dating from c 1700 and located in the St Germain area of Paris, this is where the hopeful Silas reaches a dead end in his search for the secret to the **Holy Grail**.

Saintes-Maries-de-la-Mer The fishing village in the Camargue where **Mary Magdalene** and her companions are meant to have landed in their little boat after sailing from Palestine.

Sangreal, Sangraal The Middle English word for **Holy Grail** derives from the Middle French *Saint Graal*. There is no truth in the alternative meaning of 'royal blood', which it is given in *The Da Vinci Code*. The word grail does not have to refer to a cup or a chalice; a grail is also a plate or platter.

Saunière, Jacques This is the curator of the Louvre in *The Da Vinci Code*, and he is also Sophie's grand-père. His name is a reference to Berenger Sauniere, the priest of **Rennes-le-Chateau**.

Scroll A rolled up piece of paper, parchment or papyrus as opposed to a **codex**.

Silas The unfortunate albino monk is given this name by Aringarosa because he miraculously escapes from his prison cell by the intervention of an earthquake, just like biblical Silas in *Acts 23:26*.

Sophie The name derives from the Ancient Greek meaning not just 'wisdom' or 'knowledge' but also 'philosophy, cleverness, skill, prudence' and 'craft'. Many of these might apply to Sophie Neveu.

Symbology Loosely, the study of symbols, though usually taken to mean theological and mystical symbols. Dan Brown is inventing a new word when he describes Robert Langdon as a symbologist; the correct word for a person who studies symbols is a symbolist. Harvard, where Langdon is said to lecture, offers no academic discipline called symbology.

Synoptic Gospels The Gospels of Matthew, Mark and Luke. Synoptic means 'seen in parallel' and refers to the way that the stories in these gospels run in close parallel to one another.

T

Tarot The origins of these cards have been variously traced to the ancient Egyptians, to China, to Italy and to gypsies who are said to have brought the cards to Europe. The earliest known deck, the Visconti di Modrone deck, also known as the Cary/Yale deck, appeared in Italy around 1440. In Northern Italy and Eastern France the cards became popular for use in the 'Game of Triumphs', a game a little like Bridge. There are 78 cards in a deck, 22 of which are the *Major Arcana*, said to represent the road of life starting with the Fool and ending with the World. The *Minor Arcana* make up the rest of the pack. When used for the purpose of personal readings, the suit of penatacles, one of the Minor Arcana suits associated with the earth element, is read in terms of the material realm.

Teabing, Sir Leigh The authoritative 'British Royal Historian' who is desperately seeking the grail in *The Da Vinci Code*. His surname is an anagram of 'Baigent', one of the authors of the book **Holy Blood, Holy Grail** from which Dan Brown has drawn heavily.

Templars See **Knights Templar**

Temple Church London chapel built in 1185 by the **Knights Templar** who had their base here until 1312. The original round church was modelled on the Church of the Holy Sepulchre in Jerusalem.

Temple Mount The eminence on which Solomon's Temple once stood and where two mosques, **al-Aqsa** and the Dome of the Rock, still do. An exposed foundation wall of the temple is the famous Wailing Wall, to which Jews come from all over the world to make their prayers. The **Knights Templar** take their name from this quarter, where they had been based since the conquest of the city.

Trinity In the Christian tradition, the Trinity refers to the three aspects of the godhead, the Father, the Son and the Holy Spirit.

V

Valentinus **Gnostic** teacher who flourished in Alexandria and Rome around 140AD. He called the world an abortion.

Vitruvian Man More properly known as 'The Proportions of the Human Figure', this work was executed in pen, ink and watercolour by **Leonardo** in 1490 with the intention of arriving at a truer human figure than those of the ancient Roman architect Vitruvius.

Y

Yahweh The name of God in the **Old Testament**.

THE DA VINCI CODE
Index

PHOTOGRAPHIC CREDITS